On Jean-Luc Nancy

'There is something like a general loss of sense. Sense, that's the word that matters to me today. A general flight of sense, whether it occurs in political or aesthetic or religious or whatever other form. Sense matters to me since, philosophy deals with nothing else but sense. Absolutely nothing else'.

Jean-Luc Nancy

The work of Jean-Luc Nancy has introduced and reinvigorated a startling new 'political' edge in continental philosophy at a time when our very notions of what it means to 'do' philosophy are under attack. His notions of *sense*, of the *birth to presence* and of the *inoperative community* have been acknowledged by key figures such as Jacques Derrida as having powerfully influenced their own work.

On Jean-Luc Nancy draws together a number of outstanding commentators to provide an invaluable companion to Nancy's own work. In addition to contributions by Howard Caygill, Rodolphe Gasché and Alphonso Lingis, there is a text by Nancy's renowned long-time co-author, Philippe Lacoue-Labarthe. These essays approach the main themes in Nancy's work. From Nancy as a philosopher of the contemporary and of the disorientation in thinking today to Nancy and the significance of anger and sacrifice in philosophy, the recurrent themes of community, freedom, being and the divine in his work are brought out.

This collection provides a fascinating picture of what, today, Nancy's contemporaries seek to negotiate with in his thought, and it demands to be read by those interested in philosophy, political theory and French studies.

Contributors: Georges Van Den Abbeele, Miguel de Beistegui, Howard Caygill, Fred Dallmayr, Francis Fischer, Rodolphe Gasché, Werner Hamacher, Philippe Lacoue-Labarthe, Jeffrey S. Librett, Alphonso Lingis, Michael B. Naas and Wilhelm S. Wurzer.

Edited by: Darren Sheppard, Simon Sparks and Colin Thomas.

Warwick Studies in European Philosophy

Edited by Andrew Benjamin
Professor in Philosophy, University of Warwick

This series presents the best and most original work being done within the European philosophical tradition. The books included in the series seek not merely to reflect what is taking place within European philosophy, rather they will contribute to the growth and development of that plural tradition. Work written in the English language as well as translations into English are to be included, engaging the tradition at all levels – whether by introductions that show the contemporary philosophical force of certain works, or in collections that explore an important thinker or topic, as well as in significant contributions that call for their own critical evaluation.

On Jean-Luc Nancy

The sense of philosophy

*Edited by Darren Sheppard, Simon Sparks
and Colin Thomas*

London and New York

First published 1997
by Routledge
11 New Fetter Lane, London EC4P 4EE

Simultaneously published in the USA and Canada
by Routledge
29 West 35th Street, New York, NY10001

Selection and editorial matter © 1997 Darren Sheppard, Simon Sparks and Colin
Thomas; individual chapters © 1997 the contributors

Typeset in Perpetua by J&L Composition Ltd, Filey, North Yorkshire

Printed and bound in Great Britain by
T J International

British Library Cataloguing in Publication Data
A catalogue record for this book is available from the British Library

Library of Congress Cataloguing in Publication Data
A catalogue record for this book has been requested

ISBN 0–415–14793–X (hbk)
ISBN 0–415–14794–8 (pbk)

Contents

Contents

List of contributors

Georges Van Den Abbeele is Professor of French and Italian at the University of California, Davies. His publications include *Travel as Metaphor: From Montaigne to Rousseau*. He is the translator of, among other things, Jean-François Lyotard's *The Differend: Phrases in Dispute*.

Miguel de Beistegui is Lecturer in Philosophy at the University of Warwick. He has published essays on both Hegel and Heidegger and is the author of a forthcoming book on Heidegger and the political.

Howard Caygill is Professor at the Department of Historical and Cultural Studies, Goldsmiths College, London. His principal publications include *Art of Judgement* and the *Kant Dictionary*. He has also published numerous articles on modern Continental philosophy.

Fred Dallmayr is the Dee Professor of Government at the University of Notre Dame. His principle publications include *Twilight of Subjectivity*; *Polis and Praxis*; *Language and Politics*; *Margins of Political Discourse*; and *Life-World, Modernity and Critique*.

Francis Fischer teaches philosophy and drama, and leads a philosophical seminar on 'everyday life' at the Université de Strasbourg. He has published several papers on Heidegger, Nietzsche and Derrida, and is the author. of *Heidegger and the Question of Man* (forthcoming).

Rodolphe Gasché is Professor of Comparative Literature at the State University of New York, Buffalo. His books include *The Tain of the Mirror* and *Inventions of Difference*. His forthcoming book is entitled *The Wild Card of*

Reading. He is currently writing another book-length study on the concept of Europe.

Werner Hamacher is Professor in the Department of German at the Johns Hopkins University. He has published extensively in the areas of philosophy and modern German studies.

Philippe Lacoue-Labarthe is Professor of Philosophy at the Université des Sciences Humaines de Strasbourg. His most recent works include *Musica ficta (figures de Wager)* and *Passolini, une improvisation (d'une sainteté)*. His publications in English include *The Title of the Letter* and *The Literary Absolute* (both co-authored with Jean-Luc Nancy); *Typography*; *Heidegger, Art and Politics*; and *The Subject of Philosophy.*

Jeffrey S. Librett is Professor of Modern Languages and Literature at Loyola University, Chicago. He has published widely on German philosophy and is currently completing a book entitled *The Rhetoric of Cultural Dialogue: Jews and Germans in the Epoch of Emancipation.* He is also the translator of *Of the Sublime: Presence in Question* and Jean-Luc Nancy's *The Sense of the World.*

Alphonso Lingis is the author of *Excesses*; *Eros and Culture*; *Phenomenological Explanations*; *Deathbound Subjectivity*; *The Community of Those Who Have Nothing in Common*; *Abuses*; and *Foreign Bodies.* He is currently preparing two books for publication: *Imperatives* and *Passions.*

Michael B. Naas is Associate Professor of Philosophy at De Paul University, Chicago. He is co-translator of Jacques Derrida's *The Other Heading* and *Memoires of the Blind.*

Wilhelm S. Wurzer is Professor of Philosophy at Duquesne University. His publications include *Filming and Judgement: Between Heidegger and Adorno* and 'The Critical Difference' in *The Textual Sublime: Deconstruction and its Differences.*

Darren Sheppard, **Simon Sparks** and **Colin Thomas** are doctoral students in the Department of Philosophy at the University of Warwick.

Acknowledgements

The editors would like to thank the following: David Wood for initially introducing us to Jean-Luc Nancy while at Warwick and for inspiring this project; Andrew Benjamin for commissioning and encouraging the volume throughout its prolonged gestation; Emma Davies, our (patient) editor at Routledge; and Marian Hobson for allowing us to print Werner Hamacher's paper.

We also thank Leslie Hill, Richard Stamp and Ian Magadera for their translation work, and would like to express our gratitude to Stephen Flood, without whom this volume would not have been possible.

Lastly, but most importantly, we would like to thank Jean-Luc Nancy for his unqualified help and support over the last two years. This book is dedicated to him, as a token of our respect and gratitude.

Introduction: the sense of philosophy

Darren Sheppard, Simon Sparks and Colin Thomas

> I know Jean-Luc Nancy to be always ready for everything, resolved to change
> everything, even sense, and more than anyone else, he still, always, talks of
> sense all the senses of the word sense . . .
>
> Jacques Derrida, *Le toucher*[1]

To say of Jean-Luc Nancy that he is a 'contemporary philosopher' is to state the
obvious: a prolific author, Nancy has continually taught in the faculté de
philosophie at the Université des Sciences Humaines de Strasbourg in France
since 1967 and he has consistently sought to situate his work in an explicitly
contemporary context – the collapse of communism, the Gulf War, the conflict
in the former Yugoslavia. However, such an appellation has a much deeper
resonance with regard to Nancy, for there is an important sense in which he is
also a philosopher *of* the contemporary. That is to say, of what it means for us,
today, to think and write 'today', *of* today, and *for* today.

In answering the question, 'What does the work or the activity of the
philosopher mean today?', Nancy responds with the formulation, 'There is
something like a general loss of *sens*. *Sens*, that is what matters to me today'.[2]
Sens: sense, meaning, direction, this is what matters to Nancy (and to us) today.
Two hundred years after Kant, Nancy's work might best be regarded as tracing
the contours and possibilities of a general *disorientation* in thinking. But this
disorientation is not an occasion for nostalgia or mourning because 'far from
considering the general flight of *sens* as a catastrophe and loss, I want to think of
it as the event of *sens* in our time, for our time'.[3] Rather, then, a recognition
that this event provides the condition for thinking in and of the present.

This indicates one of the many Heideggerian resonances in Nancy's work,
namely that thinking is a matter of *Destruktion*. Which, following Heidegger,

does not mean that tradition can simply be overcome, disavowed or abstractly negated. If the breakdown of tradition, the general loss of *sens*, abandons us to thinking freedom, *sens*, art and community anew, this abandonment does not thereby entail the freedom to abandon tradition. Such aporias situate and condition the work of Nancy, and this work enters into the tradition of thinkers who have exposed and limned the nature of the aporia – paradigmatically, Hegel, Marx, Nietzsche, Heidegger, Bataille, and Derrida, with all of whom Nancy's thought incessantly engages – then this is to say nothing other than that Nancy, in his own way, exemplifies the thrust of this particular philosophical tradition, by seeking to break with tradition *once again*.

Not a work in the sense of *une oeuvre*, 'the philosophy of Jean-Luc Nancy' can be described as a work only in the sense of *un travail* – a working. In English, one might say that this is, essentially, a work-in-progress, on the condition that one understands by this not the present incompletion of a project which one day will be realized (such a closure would be anathema to a thinker like Nancy), but, rather, the labour of a thinking which is pursued at the very limit of exhaustion. Nancy's is a thinking which refuses to settle down. One cannot say that his is *a* thought *of sens*, *of* literature, *of* the political, *of* plurality, not even *of* philosophy. Provided we hear the doubling of the genitive, it is all of these. But if Nancy is a thinker of any *one* thing, then this can only be the thinking of the obscure imperative to think – what, in *L'impératif catégorique*, he will call the 'secret summons' of thinking.[4] Accordingly, his continual and persistent return to themes whose very givenness or ossification within the philosophical tradition would seem to preclude their being thought anew – community, freedom, being, the divine – is itself no guarantor of a defining preoccupation. Nancy's thinking responds to no imperative save that of the necessity to think this ossification.

The following collection of essays seeks to impose no constraint on the terms of, and grounds for, negotiation with Nancy's work. Certain aspects of his thought are not engaged with here – for example, his work on psychoanalysis, German Romanticism and painting – while other aspects occur with regularity – for instance community, the political, and his relation to Heidegger. It has not been our intention, as editors, to prescribe what is central and what is peripheral to Nancy's work. Rather, this collection can be taken as a 'snapshot' of what, today, Nancy's contemporaries seek to negotiate with in his thought.[5] Such negotiations inevitably involve situating that thought within heterogeneous contexts, the multiplicity of which attests to the power of his work to rework the very context(s) of contemporary philosophy. The essays brought together here might best be regarded as *deviations* from Nancy's work. As Nancy himself continues to think and to write, as his work becomes ever more available in translation, it is hoped that these essays will provide a spur for further engagement with Nancy's work.

Notes

1 'Le toucher', trans. Peggy Kamuf, in *Paragraph* 16, 2 (July 1993), p. 124.
2 Jean-Luc Nancy, 'You ask me what it means today . . . ', ibid., p. 108.
3 Ibid., p. 109.
4 Jean-Luc Nancy, *L'impératif catégorique* (Paris: Flammarion, 1983), p. 10.
5 A number of the essays collected here are translations from the original French or German. The use of square brackets in such essays denotes the author's original phrasing, reproduced here for clarity or emphasis.

1

Phrase VII

Philippe Lacoue-Labarthe

Pour Jean-Luc
'Muss es sein? — Es muss sein'

I

Si ma mémoire est exacte, mais à vrai dire
je n'en sais rien, c'était à l'angle de Sutter
et Mason, ou Taylor, peut-être, il faudrait vérifier.
Mais je ne reviendrai plus là-bas, c'est certain,
et je vois bien qu'il faut que je me fasse au contraire à
l'idée que ce fut pour la dernière fois. (Qu'indiquait
donc, avant ce pont d'enfer, le dernier panneau?
Embarcadero, je crois, *Main street*, mais peut-être aussi
Last exit to SF, je ne sais même plus.
Ce n'est pas faute, pourtant, de l'avoir franchi, ce pont.)
Le vent était immense, il emportait papiers
et poussière jusqu'au plus haut des bâtiments,

dans leur ombre tranchée: *Men and bits of paper*
whirled by the cold wind. Cela, je pouvais le comprendre,
comme je comprenais, dans cette langue que je ne saurai
jamais, que c'était là, il dit: *a place*
of disaffection. (Ensuite il parle, me semble-t-il,
ou bien est-ce un peu avant, de l'obscurité
propre à purifier l'âme, *cleansing affection*
from the temporal, et de nous il énonce que nous
sommes *empty of meaning*.) Cependant, 'gare à la
suffisante pensée qui se croit la pensée'.
Toujours est-il que de là, je me souviens, on
pouvait la voir, telle une plaque de métal,

une tôle, éblouissante, la baie. Et plus
loin, les collines sèches. *Internal darkness, deep lane, the*
unprayable prayer: je l'ai lu et relu,
de même que le début de 'The Dry Salvages':
I do not know much about gods; but I think that the river

Is a strong brown god. J'imaginais possible
d'y arrimer Ovide, Hölderlin — Baudelaire
surtout, parce que, me conduisant (moi, la mort dans l'âme),

For Jean-Luc
'*Muss es sein? — Es muss sein*'

I

If my memory serves, but to be honest
I really can't be sure, it was on the corner of Sutter
and Mason, or Taylor, perhaps, I'd have to check.
But I won't be going back there again, that's for sure,
and I can see I'll have to get used to the idea
that that was the last time. (But what did
the last street sign say, before that bridge over hell?
Embarcadero, I think, *Main Street*, but perhaps also
Last Exit to SF, I really can't remember,
though it's hardly for want of crossing over, the bridge, that is.)
The wind was tremendous, and was blowing litter
and dust to the very tops of the buildings,

in their sharply defined shadow: *Men and bits of paper*
whirled by the cold wind. That I could understand,
just as I understood, in this language I will never
know, that this was what he calls *a place*
of disaffection. (Afterwards he refers, I think,
or else perhaps just before, to a darkness
fit to purify the soul, *cleansing affection*
from the temporal, and as far as we're concerned he says that we
are *empty of meaning*.) However, 'beware the
self-important thinking that believes itself to be thought'.
The fact remains that from there, I remember, it was
possible to see, like a sheet of metal or

corrugated iron flashing in the sun, the bay. And in
the distance, the dry hills. *Internal darkness, deep lane, the*
unprayable prayer. I read it over and over,
like the beginning to 'The Dry Salvages':
I do not know much about gods; but I think that the river

Is a strong brown god. I imagined it possible
to make the connection with Ovid, Hölderlin, especially Baudelaire,
because, driving me in her car (and me feeling sick at heart)

à la veille de ce départ, elle avait dit
que toujours c'est à ce vers qu'elle avait pensé:
'Andromaque, des bras d'un grand époux tombé'.
Quelle âpreté, quelle envie déraisonnable de mettre un terme . . .

J'étais devant la rue comme au bord d'un fleuve qui gronde,
en crue (le bruit de moteurs, là-bas, des foules, est tout
    différent),
et j'étais aveuglé, dans l'ombre bleue, par trop
    d'éclat.
Il me semblait que ce fracas, pareil à la clameur,
était celui que fait l'immémorial anéantissement
de nous-mêmes en tant que, générations après générations,
sans répit nous sombrons, sans cesse. Et j'attendais
dans la crainte que le signal m'enjoignît de tenter
la traversée: *Walk*!, est-il écrit soudain; et il faut
bien passer, quelque répugnance on ait à se soumettre,
impuissant de colère, à la plus scandaleuse
des injustices, à la trahison même, la pire – la pure.

II

A cet angle donc (*round the corner*), elle, de l'autre
côté du carrefour, lisait, j'imagine, une lettre.
Elle pleurait aussi, elle manifestait sa peine
par ces sortes de gestes ostentatoires qu'ils ont, eux,
là-bas, souvent, cette manière de dramatiser
comme s'ils récitaient du Shakespeare et comme si, d'abord,
ils n'éprouvaient rien mais voulaient à toute force
éprouver ce dont ils savent précisément
comment par d'autres ce fut éprouvé, tant d'autres
qu'ils supposent être à leur origine – mais ce n'est pas
vrai. Je la regardais lire et pleurer, et quand
elle redressait la tête en murmurant quelque chose

comme: Oh non! Oh non!, on aurait dit qu'elle invectivait
le ciel et demandait à une foudre de s'abattre.

the day before my departure, she had said
this was the line she had always thought of:
'Andromaque, des bras d'un grand époux tombé'.
What fierce determination, what insane desire to put an end . . .

I was on the sidewalk, as by the edge of a roaring river overflowing
its banks (the noise of engines, in that part of the world, and of
    crowds is entirely different),
and I was blinded, in the blue-coloured shade, by too much
    brightness.
It seemed to me that the din, like a clamour,
was what you get from the immemorial annihilation
of ourselves insofar as, generation upon generation,
without respite we founder, and without cease. And I waited
fearful that the sign might enjoin me to attempt
the crossing: *Walk!*, the word was suddenly written; and one has
to pass on, however loath one may be to subject oneself,
impotent with rage, to the most scandalous
injustice of all, betrayal itself, the very worst, the purest form.

II

So at the intersection (*round the corner*), she, on the other
side of the crossing, was reading, I imagine, a letter.
She was crying, too, displaying her distress
with the kind of demonstrative gestures that they often go in for
in that part of the world, this way they have of dramatizing
everything as if they were reciting Shakespeare and as if, at first,
they could feel nothing, but wanted at all cost
to feel that of which they know precisely
how by others it was felt, so many others
they take to be their ancestors – but it isn't
true. I watched her reading and weeping, and when
she lifted her head to murmur something

like: Oh no! Oh no!, it was as if she was addressing her invective
to the heavens and demanding that a thunderbolt come crashing
    down.

5

J'ai traversé, au signal. Lorsque nos regards
se sont rencontrés, normalement, elle a cessé de pleurer.
J'ai entendu la plainte: 'On m'a dit que pareille
au désert elle est devenue' (le blasphème, dit-il).
Partial horror. J'ai su qu'il m'était arrivé
de savoir que j'étais mort. Deux fois. La première,
je ne peux rien en dire. De la seconde je pense
qu'il ne m'est pas interdit de parler: ce n'était donc
que ce franchissement sans peine d'une vie
pas si profonde ni très large, un va-et-vient
à peine entre deux rives dont l'une est sans fin
inabordable, de fait. Mais dans ce regard paru
il y avait, oui, 'le sentiment de ma légère existence'.

C'est une grande chose que d'avoir ce droit
d'aller, simplement, d'aller – au plus près, pas loin.

(Plus tard, une fois encore, j'ai relu: '*I raised my head. The
offing was barred by a black bank of clouds, and the tranquil
waterway leading to the uttermost ends of the earth flowed sombre
under an overcast sky – seemed to lead into the heart of an immense
darkness.*')

III

En marge, ainsi que vers la fin il en avait
pris l'étrange habitude, il a donc écrit, dans
sa langue (comme s'il récusait l'usage qui
    voulait
qu'on prescrivît les temps en italien: *molto
adagio*, ici, par example, puisqu'il a
tout de même maintenu la mention): *in der
lydischen Tonart*: en mode lydien. On dit
que c'est le mode ancien du chant d'Eglise, et sans
doute y a-t-il pensé lorsqu'il a tenu à traduire

en allemand l'indication: *canzone di
ringraziamento*, au début, par cette sorte de
paraphrase où de fait une déité est nommée:

6

I crossed, at the signal. When our eyes
met, in the normal way, she stopped crying.
I heard the lament: 'On m'a dit que pareille
au désert elle est devenue' (blasphemy, he calls it).
Partial horror. I knew that it had happened to me before
to know that I had died. Twice over. About the first time
there is nothing I can say. As for the second I think
it is not something of which I am prevented from talking; it was
just the easy crossing over from a life
not very deep nor very broad, a coming and going
at best between two shores of which one is in fact endlessly
out of reach. But in the look that appeared
there was, yes, 'le sentiment de ma légère existence'.

It is a great thing to have the right
to go, simply, to go – as near as possible, not far.

(Later on, once again, I reread the words: '*I raised my head. The
offing was barred by a black bank of clouds, and the tranquil
waterway leading to the uttermost ends of the earth flowed sombre
under an overcast sky – seemed to lead into the heart of an immense
darkness.*')

III

In the margin, as towards the end he had adopted
the strange habit of doing, he had therefore written, in
his own language (as though to protest against the convention
  requiring
tempi to be marked in Italian: *molto
adagio*, in this case, for instance, since in
spite of all he kept the terms): *in der
lydischen Tonart*: in the Lydian mode. It is said
that this is the ancient mode of ecclesiastical chant, and no
doubt he was aware of this when he insisted on translating

into German the indication: *canzone di
ringraziamento*, at the beginning, by a sort of
paraphrase in which in fact a deity is named:

7

Heiliger Dankgesang eines Genesenen
an die Gottheit (et du reste, c'est bien à elle
qu'il s'adresse, plus loin, *neue Kraft fühlend*,
en action de grâce: *Doch du gabst mir wieder*
Kräfte mich des Abends zu finden — on dirait le texte
d'un choral ou l'annonce énigmatique d'un salut
malgré la fin du jour et la nuit proche, immense,
où nous nous en allons, nous nous perdons). Pourtant,
depuis au moins Platon, d'après ce que je sais,
la lydienne, mixte ou soutenue, accompagne
des chants de déploration, élégies ou thrènes, c'est un mode
de l'expression réprouvable de la douleur. Du deuil,

puisque tel est maintenant le mot qui convient
lorsque je pense à ce jour de septembre mille
neuf cent quatre-vingt trois où il s'élevait de nouveau,
le chant, celui-là, toujours, qui semble trépasser, s'il
est permis de parler ainsi, toute mémoire.
Cela fait à peu près trente ans que je écoute,
dans la même version, toujours, où la respiration
difficile de l'un des interprètes, presque
exténuée, fait que je retiens mon souffle moi-même lorsque
revient, élevé d'une octave, le motif
initial, là où précisément il a de nouveau
noté en marge: *Mit innigster Empfindung*,

avec ces mots qu'on croirait qu'il a lus dans Hölderlin.

Parfois le ciel aussi est ce qui nous émeut,
d'être à ce point nul et d'une telle intense lumière,
serait-ce en effet le soir, qu'à l'abandon, oui, la fièvre
nous délaisse et que des larmes ne sont d'aucun recours.
Mais c'est non qu'il faut dire, non à cet inadmissible

apaisement, à ce vertige, car cette lenteur
d'avant le franchissement, expirante, il est certain
qu'il en a calculé le suspens, juste au seuil
de l'ultime déclaration qui revient de très loin

Heiliger Dankgesang eines Genesenen
an die Gottheit (and, as it happens, she is indeed the one
he addresses, shortly after, *neue Kraft fühlend,*
by way of thanksgiving: *Doch du gabst mir wieder*
Kräfte mich des Abends zu finden — the words are like those
of a chorale or an enigmatic prophecy of salvation
despite the end of the day and the approach of boundless night,
the night into which we go and are extinguished). And yet,
since Plato at least, as far as I am aware,
the Lydian mode, whether Mixolydian or Hypolydian, accompanies
songs of lamentation, elegies or threnodies, it's a mode
for the reprovable expression of grief. Of mourning,

since this is now the appropriate word
when I think of that day in September in nineteen
hundred and eighty-three when I heard it again,
the song, always the same, which seems to pass on, if
one can use the word this way, beyond all memory.
I've been listening to it now for about thirty years,
always in the same version, in which the difficult
breathing of one of the performers, almost
at breaking point, causes me to hold my breath myself when,
an octave higher, the initial motif returns
at the precise point when he noted once
more in the margin: *Mit innigster Empfindung,*

using words you'd think he took from Hölderlin.

At times the sky too is what moves us,
by being so blank, and lit with such intensity,
especially in the evening, that in our abandonment, yes,
the fever leaves us and tears are no help at all.
But no is the word, no to the unacceptable

calm, no to the dizziness, for this slowness
before the crossing, as it dies away, there's no doubt
the suspense is finely calculated, just on the threshold
of the ultimate declaration that returns from afar

comme une tourmente ou une tempête que rien n'annonçait,
si ce n'est ce silence, tu sais, justement ce silence.

IV

Le difficile, dans une journée qui s'achève, est
de consentir à son inachèvement; nul
héroïsme n'y suffit, c'est évident; mais on peut (*suddenly last*
    summer), sinon revenir à
soi (c'est impossible ou ce serait vain), du moins
reprendre les chose où on les avait abandonnées.

Est-ce la même année, ou plus tard, que je revenais,
sous les avions grondant, de l'office arménien
au cimetière de San Jose, sur la colline?
On l'avait brûlé. C'est lui qui m'avait offert
le fac-similé du manuscrit de *The Waste*
Land (I: 'The Burial of the Dead' . . .) et je me souvenais
que nous en avions parlé en écoutant Gundula
Janowitz — *o welch'ein Glück* — entre Santa Monica
et Irvine. Mais la prosodie, c'est à Oakland qu'il
fallait l'apprendre de celui qui a le sang dans son nom. Au cent
    quinze Central, nous disions,
par jeu: *Mehr Licht!*, et je m'obstinais à traduire:
trop de lumière, même lorsque la terre a tremblé.
Le temps s'est donc ainsi sourdement dissocié
dans ce fond dont nul jamais ne voit le fond, tu
es le premier à le savoir, et cette fin
qui n'en finit pas, il faut la perpétuer

encore un peu, très peu, juste comme il nous est licite.

1993–3 Mars 1996

like an unexpected squall or storm, unexpected, that is,
were it not for the silence, you know, that silence.

IV

The hard thing, about a day that reaches its end, is
to accept that it doesn't end; no
heroism is up to this, obviously; but one can (*suddenly last summer*)
    if not return to
oneself (which is impossible if not pointless), at least
pick things up from where they were left off.

Was it the same year, or later, that I was returning
beneath the roar of aircraft, from the Armenian service
at San Jose cemetery, on the hill?
His body was burned. He was the one who made me a present
of the facsimile edition of the manuscript of *The Waste
Land* (I: 'The Burial of the Dead' . . .) and I could remember
we had talked about it while listening to Gundula
Janowitz — *o welch'ein Glück* — between Santa Monica and
Irvine. But prosody had to be learnt in
Oakland from the man with blood in his name. At One Hundred
    and Fifteen Central, we said,
jokingly, to each other: *Mehr Licht!*, and I insisted on translating:
too much light, even when the ground shook.
So time, in its underhand way, fell apart
into this abyss into which nobody can ever see to the bottom, as
you are the first to know, and this end
which never ends, and which it is necessary to perpetuate

still a little, very little, just as is allowed to us to do.

1993–3 March 1996

Translated by Leslie Hill

11

2

Lost horizons and uncommon grounds: for a poetics of finitude in the work of Jean-Luc Nancy

Georges Van Den Abbeele

Somewhere, somehow, a horizon has been lost, the comfort of a limit dissolved, the meaning of a concept irretrievably 'spilled out of itself, like a simple ink stain on a word, on the word "meaning"'.[1] Such could be said to be the ever strange yet strangely familiar *incipit* to many a text signed 'Jean-Luc Nancy'. Yet there is nothing particularly 'Nancean' about such assertions, which are indeed the staple of a certain post-Rousseauian romanticism, whether of the nostalgic or the 'ironic' kind (and about which Nancy, it is well known, also has much to say of course). Rather, such proclamations of finitude or de-finitude, that is, the dislocation of stabilizing bounds, the utter *débordement* of which leaves us all exposed together on the limit, as liminality of being, being on the limit and on the limit of being, such proclamations appear in Nancy as the pretext to something much more peculiar and strange. They serve as the pretext for a reversal of possibilities of thought, if not as the very condition and urgency of thinking anew. The loss of the horizon itself would seem to be the horizon of philosophy. Such is a characteristically Nancean moment, and such perhaps is his appeal today *after* modernism, communism, structuralism, and even after Foucault, Lyotard and Derrida.

In his 'epigraph' to the recent special issue of *Paragraph* dedicated precisely to his work, Nancy writes, after listing a number of the better known 'trouble spots' that have uncannily surfaced as the so-called New World Order from Bosnia to Somalia to Central Asia:

> We'll not come to the end of the list of places and marks of uncertainty, of helplessness, of anguish. There is something like a general loss of sense. Sense, that's the word that matters to me today. A general flight of sense, whether it occurs in a political or esthetic or religious or whatever other

12

form. Sense matters to me since, 'philosophy' deals with nothing else but sense. Absolutely nothing else. If sense is screwed to hell everywhere . . . this is obviously a philosophical concern, and also because philosophy is screwed to hell everywhere.[2]

The 'end of philosophy' (that notion all too readily scorned by traditional philosophers) is, Nancy adds, 'what we have at present, very concretely before our eyes' as the 'sense of words like "nation", "people", "sovereignty" . . . "community" . . . and so many others . . . are leaking out of so many cracked vessels'.[3] Adorno-like is his evocation of the demise of philosophy in the context of a world that has lost all sense, Nancy nonetheless here as elsewhere springs his characteristic move, the only possible move left for whatever might still responsibly be called 'philosophy': 'here is what matters to me: far from considering this general flight of sense as a catastrophe and a loss, I want to think of it as the event of sense in our time, for our time. It is a question of thinking sense in the absencing of sense. . . . It is a question of thinking what "sense" can be when one has come to the end of sense understood in that fashion'.[4] Philosophy can no longer be, as it once was, the very 'giver of sense', nor can it even continue to be (as it has been since Kant) 'the philosophy that does not want to give sense but to analyze the conditions for delivering a coherent sense'.[5]

But if philosophy today can no longer be the giver of sense nor the explication/deconstruction of the conditions for there to be any sense, what can it be? Quoting Nietzsche's injunction 'To introduce a new sense – it being understood that this task itself has no sense', Nancy closes this short text with what seem to be at least two answers, whose compatibility or incompatibility remains to be scripted or ascribed, and whose sense thus remains in suspense. On the one hand, the Nietzschean response to the end of sense 'is revolution itself: the destitution of the authority of sense or of sense as authority, and the entry into the unheard-of. For the unheard-of, one has to get one's ears ready.[6] In its anarchistic zeal and postmodern esthetics of the unpresented, this statement sounds like Nancy playing Lyotard. The other answer, in its enunciation of a constitutive absence that maintains a certain senseless sense, might then sound like Nancy playing Derrida: 'But today this is where there is some sense: in saying sense is absent, in saying that this absence is what we are exposed to, and that this exposition constitutes what I will call not only our present history but with Rimbaud, our refound eternity'.[7] Perhaps this is Nancy's way of doubly tracing a certain line or limit of contemporary philosophical discourse caught between the poetic evocation of a necessarily inchoate outside of philosophy and the philosophically eloquent pronouncement of the end of philosophy. The tracing of this line between these alternatives (if that is even what they are) is perhaps the practice of a certain *exscription* in Nancy's work: a writing that is not so much on the limit between a supposed inside and outside of philosophy, but one that *exposes* philosophical thought to its unheard-of outside *in* the very act of speaking the end of philosophical thought as the internal limit to its sense. The contemporary event of sense that is the absencing of sense is the unheard-of that philosophy tries to let speak within it as what speaks the end of philosophy, an unheard-of that speaks perhaps in the voice of Rimbaud (a possibility to which I will return later).

I think we can see, though, that such a practice of exscription does not simply define a new horizon of philosophy. The line Nancy's texts trace in *and* out of philosophy does not open up some new vista or territory for philosophical exploitation, but exposes philosophy to the contemporary absencing of sense, that is, to the threshold of its being. The trope of finitude, as it appears in Nancy's texts, is thus not a simple one of enablement whose dialectical reversal/sublation would renew the possibility of philosophy, thus allowing it to remain self-same in the face of meaning's vicissitudes. Nancean finitude is not a negativity to be overcome, but an event to dwell in and upon, the very advent of a thought which can never do more than exscribe its compearance. The lost horizon of sense becomes the liminal space from which the absence of sense can be thought, but only to the extent that the horizon is indeed 'lost'.

A similar reversal occurs near the beginning of *The Inoperative Community* when Nancy quotes (or actually misquotes) Sartre's declaration that 'communism is the insuperable horizon of our time',[8] a quotation placed with no small irony within the book's opening evocation of the disappearance of community (and *a fortiori* the ideal of communism) as that to which our time bears witness. Again, though, the issue is not to mourn the loss of community – or of communism – nor even to celebrate that loss, but to lose the very concept of horizon:

> *communism* can no longer be the insuperable horizon of our time. And if in fact it no longer is such a horizon, this is not because we have passed beyond any horizon. Rather, everything is inflected by resignation, as if the new insuperable horizon took form around the disappearance, the impossibility or the condemnation of communism. Such reversals are customary; they have never altered anything. It is the *horizons* themselves that must be

14

challenged. That ultimate limit of community, or the limit that is formed by community, as such, traces an entirely different line. This is why, even as we establish that communism is no longer our insuperable horizon, we must also establish, just as forcefully, that a communist exigency or demand communicates with the gesture by means of which we must go farther than all possible horizons.[9]

The loss of community is an absence sublatable by any immanentism bemoaning that loss and trumpeting a so-called return to communal values, but what Nancy seizes upon is a kind of communism or communality that would be, not itself a horizon but the undoing of all horizons, namely a community founded upon the compearance of singular beings in the commonality of their *difference*.

What Nancy thus deftly disconnects, although he never says so explicitly, is the assumed immanence of communal identities to demarcated geographical spaces in the form of towns, lands or nations. In its most vulgar formation, this relation appears of course as the nationalist ideology of blood and soil. But the equation between land and ethnicity demands the installation of the literalized horizon that is the border, the institutionalized inscription of a cartographical divide that *defines* all those within as ethnically, culturally and linguistically identical and all those without as different, barbarous, savage and inimical. This inscription of cultural identity on to the topography, however, can only ever protect the differential undoing of that identity by the reinforcement of the inscription that is violence. The current greatest fear among nation-states is that of 'losing control' of their borders, a cry echoed today with the most ominous of reverberations from Eastern Europe to southern California. What is this seemingly omnipresent fear all about? What is so different after all about Tijuana and east Los Angeles, for example, and what is the fear – beyond all the hypocritical talk about administrative and economic complications – except that the supposed difference is *not* a difference, and that difference occurs both on this side and that side of the border, and in wanton disregard of the border? Perhaps the fear is that no 'reinforcement' of border patrols, no institution of crossing fees, no control of identity papers, no linguistic legislation, no inter-rogations or agreements can stem this becoming unbordered of the border, its insuperable *débordement*. And indeed that fear is justified (the border is out of control because no border can ever be successfully controlled), but its con-sequences are not as bad as all that, and certainly not as bad as the bloody and brutal efforts to redefine and 'maintain' borders.

What the loss of borders exposes is the contingency of the nation's existence

15

upon a certain *areality* – a word Nancy uses in *Corpus* but which begs to be applied to the immanence of nationhood with its long-standing use of corporeal metaphors (and notably that of the 'body politic') in its legitimating discourses. '*Aréalité*', Nancy writes, 'is an archaic French word, meaning the nature or the property of an *aire* or *area*. By accident, the word also lends itself to suggesting a lack of reality, or else a tiny, light or suspended reality'.[10] The areality of the nation is what suspends or interrupts the myth of the land as a nation's substratum or *subjectum*, that which literally lies or is thrown below the feet of a certain community understood as a sort of vegetative immanence: what sprouts or springs from the soil as its natural outgrowth, the indigenous cultivation of a 'culture' that sees itself as 'natural' possessor of the land from which it comes. The nation as subject, the common ground as the founding locus of a 'common sense': the dangers of this myth are well known, and I hope do not need to be repeated here.

The arealization of the nation leaves it in place but suspended, unbordered in its expanse, exposed on the limit between spatial, ethnic and linguistic differences. Perhaps it is such a becoming areal of the nation that provokes dismay today, the disappearance of its sense as the event *of* its sense. But Jean-Luc Nancy would, I believe, be the first to point out that geographical identity is not the only, or even the most insidious, form of communal immanence. Indeed, the apparently worldwide implosion of borders experienced as post-communist crisis bears eloquent witness to the obsolescence of the old nation-state snugly confined within its borders amid the postmodern plethora of telecommunicational networks and unprecedently vast diasporas and collective migrations that would seem to shatter any last illusions about the identity of place and community. Yet the metaphysics of presence and the ideology of cultural separatism have perhaps never been more manifest than in the contemporary situation where collectivities of all sorts can be convoked in the near instantaneity of media representation.

And here perhaps is where the becoming senseless of the nation can occasion a Nietzschean new sense, or at least a philosophical point of entry into the unheard-of. Becoming irrelevant in its areality, the nation remains the uncommon ground of difference. And by 'ground of difference', I refer to the vertigo of difference within its supposed confines as well, of course, as the difference it marks or demarcates from other nations. *As areal*, the nation is exscribed: not just uncommon ground but ungrounded community. How can we philosophize then in this space without a horizon, or perhaps which is nothing but horizons?

How can we get our ears 'ready' for the unheard-of? How can we think the utopics of difference that is postnational space?

For Jean-Luc Nancy, there seems to be a name for such a thought, and that name is 'poetry', which he says in a short text published a decade ago in *Po&sie* and recently translated and reprinted in *The Birth to Presence*. He specifies there significantly enough that 'poetry is a cadastre, or else a geography'.[11] 'The poet can be recognized', he writes, 'by a certain surveyor's step, by a certain way of covering a territory of words, not in order to find something, or to plant a crop, or to build an edifice, but simply to measure it'.[12] But if the poet is a geographer of words, could there not be a geography that is poetic, an experience of spatial and communal differences that *qua poetry*, to quote again from Nancy, 'takes the form of an effacement: a gesture which itself is, after all, commonplace, which indicates your place, mine, yet another's, and which withdraws'?[13] Such an indication of place is also the event of a kind of *mitsein*, of being in common as different, of being together as apart, of a finitude that is the unheard-of condition of community. Poetry, as described here, is precisely in what semioticians would call its pragmatics, the compearing of singular beings at loose ends that Nancy calls the 'inoperative community', the *communauté désoeuvrée*, not the opus of its own immanence but the undoing of itself as itself. But then the poetry in question cannot be one that issues forth in a work, but one whose gesture must also be irretrievably singular, finite. Poetry too cannot be a new kind of insuperable horizon. Indeed, while the metonym of the nation-state as people grounded in a land demands the horizontality of topographical and discursive borders, of frontiers and myths, poetry since at least Rimbaud (and perhaps that is part of his significance for Nancy) is what speaks the unheard-of verticality or vertigo of sense, what gives new direction or *sens* to sense, a direction that is none other than the other of direction. Is the coming to presence of the unforeseen and the unheard-of not only in language but also in our difference from each other, and from our history, and from the spaces we inhabit. Such a *poein* is a making that is simultaneously an unmaking, a compearing of community that is also its withdrawal, an advent of sense in which sense is eclipsed, a speaking of what cannot be heard. This is not to say that Jean-Luc Nancy is a poet rather than a philosopher, or that he is a philosopher rather than a poet, or even that there is something especially 'poetic' about his philosophical prose, but that philosophy as it is written by him is a *poein* of thought exposed upon its limit, with no comforting horizon in sight, only the endless exscription of sense in retreat.

17

Notes

1 Jean-Luc Nancy, 'Exscription', in *The Birth to Presence*, trans. Brian Holmes *et al.* (Stanford: Stanford University Press, 1993), p. 319.

2 Jean-Luc Nancy, 'You ask me what it means today . . . ', *Paragraph* 16, 2 (July 1993) (special issue on the work of Jean-Luc Nancy, ed. Peggy Kamuf), p. 108.

3 Ibid., pp. 108–9.

4 Ibid., p. 109.

5 Ibid.

6 Ibid.

7 Ibid., p. 110.

8 Nancy, *The Inoperative Community*, trans. Peter Connor, Lisa Garbus, Micheal Holland and Simona Sawhney (Minneapolis: University of Minnesota Press, 1991), p. 1; translation modified. On Nancy's 'misquoting' of Sartre, see Richard Terdiman, 'On the dialects of postdialectical thinking' (p. 118) and my 'Communism, the proper name' (p. 41), both in *Community at Loose Ends*, ed. Miami Theory Collective (Minneapolis: University of Minnesota Press, 1991).

9 Ibid., pp. 8–9; translation modified.

10 Nancy, *Corpus* (Paris: Métailié, 1992), p. 39.

11 Nancy, 'We need . . . ', in *The Birth to Presence*, p. 308.

12 Ibid.; translation modified.

13 Ibid., pp. 308–9.

3

The shared world – philosophy, violence, freedom

Howard Caygill

At an early age, I found myself facing the incomprehensible, the unthinkable, death. Ever since, I have known nothing on this earth can be shared because we own nothing.

Edmond Jabès, *The Book of Shares*

At the beginning of *The Book of Shares* (1987) Jabès evokes in a few bleak words the difficult community which had haunted his work since the publication of *The Book of Questions* in 1963. The writing of this community came from within a culture which was 'violently cracking up' and which, in the graffito MORT AUX JUIFS, had signalled that the Jew could no longer belong to it. Jabès describes his writing as following the dictation of an 'anterior memory' which questioned itself to the point 'where it has no longer any belonging or place or resemblance, where therefore it escapes all categories and traditions'.[1] The experience of the *Shoah* shatters not only the memory of community – the sense of belonging to a land, a people, to oneself – but also the sense of belonging to a shared world.

The path of questioning such a community begins in difficulty, 'the difficulty of being and writing', and ends in difficulty: '"Difficulty is self-contained," said Reb Akad. "It cannot be resolved, except by another difficulty we have to face"'.[2] Jabès insists that this difficult questioning cannot pass through, resemble, or belong to any existing tradition, especially that tradition of questioning known as philosophy. His austere non-philosophical writing of a derelict community in which nothing can be shared because nothing is owned puts a question mark in the margin of the philosophical questioning of politics and the community. It indirectly asks whether it is possible to speak of community after the *Shoah* from within philosophy and does so by doubting the ability of the

19

philosophical tradition to tolerate difficulty and irresolution, as well as its ability to respect the unthought and ultimately to welcome the other.

The self-consciously democratic and anti-racist character of Jabès' writing of the community also brings into relief the political profile of philosophical reflection on the community. His refusal of the philosophical tradition of questioning encourages vigilance *vis-à-vis* the ruses of the philosophical unconscious which has, since its foundation, been beset, happily or unhappily, by the desire to rule the community. It asks whether philosophy can qualify itself to speak of the 'we' that shares nothing except its incapacity to share. Such a speech would require philosophy to abandon the desire to legislate, and to open itself to the experience of dereliction, to being lost and incapable of finding itself, to being silenced and unable to recover its voice.

From its beginnings, philosophy has been adept at feigning dereliction and ignorance as a means both to legislate and to speak with knowledge. Jabès' writing, however, avoids the dialectical ruse of loss and recovery which haunts philosophy. In the *Book of Shares* the 'I' learns that nothing can be shared because before death 'we' 'own nothing'; yet this experience immediately yields the exception of a community of dereliction. We share a 'word of solitude' and 'of refusal', which is also one of 'absolute commitment', forging 'bonds of silence in the unfathomable silence of the bond'. The form of the chiasmas here is not philosophical, since the silence and the solitude of the bond are less a quasi-transcendental condition of the bonds of silence than a force of attrition and ruination.

The law of the community to which it offers an opening is for Jabès sacrificial, but not as the recuperative sacrifice which gives in order to receive back more, whether through dialectical investment or through completed mourning. Such sacrifice requires owners with something to invest or to lose – even if this is only grief – whereas for Jabès we share the participation in the act of sacrifice of these things, and then only precariously. The dialectical ruse, which would hear in silence a sacrifice of voice, is resisted by a silence which ruins any attempt to set it within an economy.

The implications for philosophy posed by Jabès' writing were first explored by Derrida in his review of *The Book of Questions* and later in the 'Ellipsis' that closes *Writing and Difference*. Derrida found in Jabès the chance for a philosophical writing beyond the closure of 'the book' or tradition of philosophy which would 'make and unmake' both book and community. The reading of Jabès in *Writing and Difference* cleared a space for Derrida to inaugurate the 'making and unmaking' of philosophy and community under the title, among

20

others, of 'deconstruction'. The questions put by Jabès to the book and the community following the dereliction of the *Shoah* became questions put to philosophy and its own writing of community. The 'making and unmaking' of philosophy increasingly entailed the deconstruction of the writing of community until, in the work of Jean-Luc Nancy, the making and unmaking of philosophy ventured in *La communauté désoeuvrée* (1986), *L'expérience de la liberté* (1988) and *Le sens du monde* (1993) required precisely the opening of philosophy to the dereliction of community.

The specificity of Nancy's questioning of community has a particular pathos, since his inquiry is framed in terms of the Heideggerian 'distinction' between *Mitsein* and *Dasein*. The questions to philosophy posed by Jabès' writing of community from out of the non-belonging of the Jew following the *Shoah* assumes a critical urgency when addressed to the Heideggerian tradition. Can this tradition, haunted by the memory of national socialism, yield another thinking of community beyond that of the *Volksgemeinschaft*? This yields the further questions of whether there can be a thought of *Mitsein* and a *Dasein* able to tolerate difficulty and the unthought and so welcome the other, and whether this can be conducted in terms of the protocols bequeathed by philosophy. Nancy's work has been guided by such matters, informing all of which is the fundamental question of whether philosophy is transforming itself before the experience of the dereliction of community.

For Jabès, the community of those who, before death, can own nothing is simultaneously established and disestablished around the precarious *share*. The share is the movement of inauguration and dissolution of community, not as a dialectical movement of loss and recovery, but as the folding of both into each other. In the share, the individual is neither master nor slave, neither owner nor owned, but is both divided from and joined with others. The share violently sunders and brings together community, not in terms of a sacrificial liturgy in which violence is followed by redemption, but as a simultaneous and inseparable experience of founding and destructive violence. In this thought of the share, violence does not assail the community from without, but is ever implicated within it.

Jabès' understanding of the share is quite distinct from the shared world of Heidegger's *Mitsein*. The latter, discussed in section 26 of *Being and Time* remains within an extremely subtle dialectic, in which the being of *Dasein* is *Mitsein*, is 'original comprehension', but also an elaboration of a similarity between Self and Other. The share which joins and divides in Jabès is here a property which is shared, whether in the indifference of everyday life or the

21

enthusiasm of authentic decision. The shared property of being together is endangered by alterity, but this danger can always be contained liturgically, through care, sacrifice and decision. It is here that a *rapprochement* between Heidegger and Bataille becomes conceivable, since both render community dynamic, making it into an act. The experience of community explored in *Being and Time* section 26 and *The Accursed Share* is in both cases sacrificial: it is lost in order to be found; it exceeds in order to reinaugurate. Desolation remains an episode in a larger narrative of loss and redemption.

The development of the implications of Heidegger's abbreviated discussion of *Mitsein* in the light of Bataille has characterized not only Nancy's recent work. Writers as diverse as Agamben, Blanchot, Dastur and Lingis have engaged in a rethinking of *Mitsein*, exploring the implications of regarding 'Being with' as more primordial than 'being' and the consequent priority of the question of community to that of being. The emphasis upon *Mitsein* signals a move from a thinking of being as substance to one which thinks being as act. The act is motivated by the excessive character of the relation of the I to the Other, with the excess generating a movement or a dynamic sharing of the world between us. In this understanding, community is not a substance that is shared, but a dynamic movement of sharing. The shift from a substantial to a dynamic conception of community appears to offer a philosophical questioning of being and community which escapes the strictures of a substantivist metaphysics; but is this more than another philosophical ruse to remain the master of the community.

Nancy's elaboration of *Mitsein* which culminated in *The Experience of Freedom* prepares for the retrieval of the concept of being-in-the-world which is evident in more recent work such as *Le sens du monde*. This path of thought has been cast by Nancy in terms of a reconsideration of Part 1 of *Being and Time*, without the heroic transcendence of Part 2. This requires a fresh alignment of community and the political under the sign of a finite transcendence, one which entailed the reconfiguration of being, love and the Other, and which issued in reconsiderations of the topology of the political and the concept of democracy. For Nancy, finite transcendence, following Bataille, designates the excessive moment of the Other, and informs his understanding of the dynamic character of community.

Central to Nancy's dynamic concept of community – one which brings together *Dasein* and *Mitsein* – is the notion of the share. For Nancy, the share is not thought in substantivist terms of something that is owned and shared by already constituted owners and sharers, but as an act of finite being. In Nancy's own words: 'If being is sharing, *our* sharing, then "to be" is to share'.[3]

Following this direction of questioning, Nancy is able to discern within *Dasein* a dynamic *Mitsein* driven by freedom, one which is manifest in movements and vectors rather than in states or substance. This conception of the share of being thus appears to provide radical reconceptions of freedom, ethics and the political.

In the pivotal chapter of *The Experience of Freedom* entitled 'Sharing freedom', Nancy develops the notion of the share in the context of the 'contemporaneity' of *Dasein* and *Mitsein*. The chapter rigorously deletes any remnant of substantive metaphysics from the concept of community by developing the theme of the 'sharing of singularity' (p. 68). The share forms the locus for freedom and relation and, with the claim that *'freedom withdraws being and gives relation'* (p. 68), it becomes clear that freedom is the dissolution of being as substance, the substitution of relation for identity. Freedom, Nancy continues in a character- istic chiasmas, is relation and relation is freedom. In the first case freedom is 'the mode of the discrete and insistent insistence of others in my existence as originary for my existence', that is freedom lies in the relation to the Other, while in the second case 'relation happens only in the withdrawal of what would unite or necessarily communicate me to others and to myself' (p. 69). Relation is consequently a movement of withdrawal from any substance, a movement which in vanquishing the necessity of substance is free. Yet is this freedom itself free, or is it substance in another, dynamic guise?

The outcome of the freedom withdrawing being and giving relation is a renunciation of the two opposed metaphysical conceptions of community. In the first, the community is a substance or common being; in the second, the individual is substantial and contrives relations with others. Accordingly, rela- tion/freedom undermines 'being's immanence to itself' whether this is of the community or the individual. What takes the place of this metaphysics of community is a modal conception of *Mitsein* in which 'being is not common to us except in the mode of *being shared*'. This sharing is not the distribution of a 'common and general substance' between the sharers, nor is it the act of owners who, in Heidegger's terms, already primordially recognize each other in the shared world of *Mitsein*. For Nancy the *act* of sharing itself effects the spacing which sunders and joins those who share:

> Consequently, on the one hand, there is no being between existents – the space of existences is their spacing and is not a tissue or support belonging to everyone and no one and which would therefore belong to itself – and on the other hand, the being of each existence, that which it shares of being

23

and by which it *is*, is nothing other – which is not a 'thing' – than this very sharing.

(p. 69)

The act of sharing itself makes the community; it is not a substance prior to the sharers, nor do they share a common being prior to the act of sharing. Freedom, Nancy continues, 'can in no way take the form of a property' whether of a community or of individuals, and calls for a thinking that 'must be substituted for every dialectic' by virtue of its excess and its refusal to 'return or to belong to itself'. This excess of freedom, however, is not simply destructive, but is precisely what is shared: 'The community shares freedom's excess' (p. 72).

It is here that Nancy appears most close to Jabès, in so far as *we* share our inability to own or possess. Yet the very choice of freedom as the issue distinguishes the philosopher from the writer, since for Jabès the share is not implicated in freedom. For Nancy, on the contrary freedom is at the heart of the share, and as such permits the restoration of metaphysics and the dialectic at the very moment of protest against them. Although freedom is excessive and itself riven, it nevertheless assumes a metaphysical dynamic which both exceeds and reinstates law and economy. By naming the dynamic of sharing 'freedom' and by discovering community in the experience of freedom, philosophy, through the work of Nancy, seems to reinaugurate itself as metaphysics, but this time in terms of a dynamic contradiction rather than in terms of a substantial identity. Accordingly, in sentences such as 'Freedom is therefore singular/common before being in any way individual or collective' (p. 74) there is the destruction of a substantivist metaphysics of community based upon individual and collective being as well as the inauguration of dynamic metaphysics in which freedom none the less 'possesses' being – it *is* before being.

At this point in his argument, where philosophy seems to turn back to metaphysics, Nancy specifies the act of freedom as sharing through a critique of Hannah Arendt. He questions her conception of public space and the idea, allegedly hers, that public is anterior to private freedom. He argues against the view that 'external' public space cannot be treated as a condition for freedom, just as little as 'internal' private freedom, since both emerge from an originary spacing. This is described as 'a sharing and partitioning of origin in which singularities space apart and space their being-in-common (points and vectors of the "at every moment," shocks and encounters, an entire link without link, and entire link of unlinking, a fabric without weave or weaver, contrary to

Plato's conception)' (p. 75). Freedom again is cast as a dynamic force, which '*is* the beginning and endlessly remains the beginning' (p. 77), it is a principle prior to principles, yet nevertheless remains within a metaphysics of the inaugural act.

With the final stage in the analysis of freedom, Nancy turns to the revolutionary tradition and the question of political freedom. Freedom is inaugural and revolutionary, it opens space: freedom permits 'the reopening of the framework and the liberation from every establishment, or its overflowing, by freedom in its *each time* irreducible (re)beginning: this is the task of politics as the liberation of freedom, as the (re)opening of the space of its inaugural sharing' (p. 79). Citing St Just on the need for a just and courageous public to support revolutionary France's armies and judges, Nancy closes this chapter with the call for permanent revolution, for a thought of freedom's unfinished 'arising' and 'breaking open'. The metaphysics of freedom informing this chapter clearly emerges in its final pages where *Mitsein* is aligned not with the German but with the French national revolution.

In spite of all its qualifications, the experience of freedom described here in terms of action and relation is analogous in many ways to a substantial, metaphysical concept. To a large extent it is more terrible, because the violence of its breaking open and its overflowing can neither be recognized nor mourned. It is also in close proximity to the Jacobin concept of the free, republican nation, whose freedom consists in their armed vigilance and preparedness freely to defend the nation through a peoples' war. Nancy anticipates such an alignment of his concept of freedom with 'Jacobinism' in the *fragments* that end *The Experience of Freedom* when he says:

> what I will have tried to say here about a freedom which lays claim to republican and democratic mottoes, but which disengages itself from 'democratic freedoms', will be charged with Jacobinsm, even terrorism, if not outright Fascism (or in another version, nihilism).

> (p. 170)

Yet his reply to these charges addresses only that of Fascism, and the case of Heidegger; the Jacobin heritage of the permanent Revolution of a free people is nowhere disavowed by Nancy, even though, as will be seen, some of its implications are overlooked.

Nancy's Jacobin concept of freedom contrasts strongly with another elaboration of *Mitsein* in terms of the share, that of Hannah Arendt. Arendt's development of *Mitsein* was also shaped by the experience of the *Shoah*, and also arrives at a concept of the share, but one quite different from that of both Jabès

25

and Nancy. For her the concept of the share is inextricably bound with the collateral issues of violence and historical time; it attempts to think political difficulty historically, while avoiding both Jabès' desperate anti-philosophical paradox and the formal equivocations of the concept of freedom explored by Nancy.

The distance between Arendt's philosophical history of *Mitsein* and Nancy's more orthodox philosophical analysis is evident throughout Nancy's critiques of Arendt. However, Nancy consistently underestimates the force of her attempt to redefine the limits of philosophy in the face of the catastrophic experience of modern politics. This is already evident in the joint article written with Philippe Lacoue-Labarthe *'Le "retrait" du politique'* in 1982.[4] In this text the philosophical agenda of Arendt's work almost disappears, it being understood and criticized in terms of political science (her description of totalitarianism) and of history (her description of the *polis* as a site of transcendence – a point restated in *The Experience of Freedom*). Although the authors refer to her work in *The Human Condition* on the theory of labour, work and action and the transformation of public space into that of the social, they regard this as an 'empirical' contribution to political science and history, and not as one of the most sustained elaborations of *Mitsein*. In this way, the challenge to philosophy represented by Arendt's work is dissipated into a flight from philosophy into empirical political science.

By casting Arendt as an empirical analyst of politics, the authors are able to establish their own position as quasi-transcendental analysts of the political. Arendt's elaboration of *Mitsein*, however, is neither empirical nor transcendental, but a genealogy of the conditions of the possibility of totalitarianism. The genealogy rests on a notion of being as sharing, but this sharing is set in the context of a historical struggle for time and space. The being in common of modern *Mitsein* or community is the state of war, of class struggle on a world scale. The struggle for the share is not played out at the level of paradox or equivocation, but through the strategies of imperialism and totalitarianism.

The view of *Mitsein* or community being at war with itself over 'meaning' or the share of space and time is axiomatic for Arendt, but largely absent from the work of Nancy. For him it is enough to show that community is not a substance, but dynamically excessive and relationally mobile. The link between a philosophical dynamics of vectors and relations and modern military strategy is nowhere admitted, nor is the close relationship between this conception of strategy and the Jacobin concept of freedom based on the people's army through which, in Nancy's words, 'France was to free itself for its own being free'.[5] Yet by admitting violence into *Mitsein* Arendt provides the conditions for a politics and philosophy that recognize its violence, and which are able to accept that the battle for the share is not benign and pacific but itself requires violent limitation. Philosophical reflection is in turn implicated in this violence, and for Arendt is not permitted to occupy a space outside the logistics of *Mitsein*.

The challenge posed to philosophy by the battle for the share of the world is explored by Arendt in her 1957 essay 'Karl Jaspers: citizen of the world'. In this essay Arendt reflects on the implications of her genealogy of the modern political in *The Origins of Totalitarianism* for philosophy. She contrasts the philosophical vision of the cosmopolitan 'perpetual peace' of a world state with the bequeathed 'plurality, diversity and mutual limitations' of political concepts. While this distinction may be read, criticized and defended *philosophically* – as one between transcendental and empirical concepts of the political and politics – this requires a violent simplification of Arendt's phenomenology of *Mitsein*. Her own working-through of the Heideggerian heritage involved the elaboration of a political phenomenology of *Mitsein*, one which required a description of the ways in which the world is shared. This phenomenology in its turn has to recognize its own responsibility for the violence of this sharing, especially the violence of its disavowal.

For Arendt, *Mitsein* is above all a question of the historical experience of the laws and violences which 'hedge in, protect, and limit the space in which freedom is not a concept, but a living, political reality'.[6] It is an experience of freedom not easily described within the language of philosophy, which remains confined within a commitment to universal and necessary concepts and ideas, in this case by the commitment to justify freedom. In the essay Arendt alerts her readers to the dangers posed by the experience that 'for the first time in history all peoples on the earth have a common present'[7] produced by the technologies of communication and violence: 'global communication' and the threat of 'global destruction' through nuclear war. For Arendt, this experience may be translated philosophically into the vision of a world government of perpetual peace, one which for her represents a nightmare of 'unchecked and uncontrolled violence' and would literally mark the 'end of world politics'.

Arendt ends the essay with a sympathetic but shrewd reflection on Karl Jaspers' philosophical 'history of mankind' which prescribes a Kantian 'perpetual peace' in the shape of a 'framework of universal mutual agreements, which would eventually lead into a world-wide federated structure' (p. 93). These mutual agreements to share the world lead eventually to the possibility that 'war must be ruled out of the arsenal of political means' – precisely the realization of the philosophical dream of a perpetual peace in a shared world. However, in Arendt's eyes, 'The abolition of war, like the abolition of a plurality of sovereign states, would harbour its own peculiar dangers', namely the regulation of the share through other strategies. These strategies are above all those of the totalitarian police state, in which the share is policed but not contested:

> the various armies with their old traditions and more or less respected codes of honour would be replaced by federated police forces, and our experiences with modern police states and totalitarian governments, where the old power of the army is eclipsed by the rising omnipotence of the police, are not apt to make us overoptimistic about this prospect.
>
> (p. 94)

The violence involved in the war for a share of the world is ineluctable, and Arendt seeks a philosophical recognition of this necessity. If it is ignored in favour of universal abstractions, the result is not a pacific philosophy, but one in which violence has become inconspicuous and unrecognized. This leads to a realization of philosophy which is the end of politics, that is, the thought of an administered violence – a bureaucratic policing of the shared world.

For Arendt *Mitsein* compromises both communication and violence, a combination whose experience can be described but not translated into philosophical abstractions. To do so would be to qualify its specificity and to limit its possible futures. Her fear in 1957 was that the 'new reality of mankind' might become the occasion for philosophies of pacific cosmopolitan citizenship which served only to conceal the battle for the share. This objection had been explored historically in her critique of the Jacobin concept of freedom in *The Origins of Totalitarianism*. There she describes the 'perplexities' at the heart of the 'Jacobin concept of the nation based upon human rights – that republican view of communal life which asserts that (in the words of Clemençeau) by infringing on the rights of one you infringe on the rights of all'.[8] As testified by the Jews' experience of this freedom, universal human rights mean nothing if they are not enforced by a sovereign nation-state, but if they are so defended they lose their universal character. They do not offer a defensible freedom, but can become a universalist rhetoric for defending a particular share of the world. For Arendt, indeed, the national element of the Jacobin concept of freedom eventually compromises the universal and 'in the countenancing of such slogans as "Death to the Jews" or "France for the French" an almost magic formula

28

was discovered for reconciling the masses to the existent state of government and society' (p. 106).

Arendt's critique of the Jacobin concept of freedom and her citation of the same slogan that awoke Jabès to the link of freedom and death returns us to the reflections on 'liberty, equality, fraternity' and *Mitsein* in fragments that end *The Experience of Freedom* and that return to the themes of Chapter 7 on 'Sharing freedom'. The motto – in Nancy's words, the French 'lie of the State' – seems to him 'somewhat ridiculous and difficult to introduce into philosophical discourse', yet he does so by means of the discussion of *Mitsein* in Section 26 of *Being and Time*. Freedom gives rise to an 'unbreachable equality' of being in the world, as well as to a problematic fraternity. The latter is especially difficult to discourse of philosophically, since it appears to be informed by the relation to a murdered father – that is, it remains a 'sharing of hatred'. For Nancy, this fraternity may prove to be a 'communion with an identical substance/essence (in the totemic meal)?' as opposed to the 'sharing of a maternal thing which precisely would not be substance, but sharing – to infinity' (p. 168).[9]

The question of this sharing, if it is not a mourning of violence, is then explored in the fragment on death. Nancy distinguishes between death as 'presence, property, self-identity' and freedom as the 'inappropriable of death' (p. 169). The latter is the shared death of the community that lives with the dead. In this fragment Nancy intimates an experience of death which 'gives birth to me', describing it as a *Mitsein* or 'being-in-common' that opens the

> free space where we come into mutual presence, where we com-pear. The opening of this space – spacing of time, exposure, event, surprise – is all there is of being, inasmuch as it 'is' free. Death does not belong in this space, for it effaces itself in pure time as a figure of effacement and the effacement of all figures. Yet common space, while it is at every moment new, also bears the mark, at this moment ineffaceable, of this effacement.
>
> (p. 169)

The question remains of the character of the mark of effacement: is it, as in Jabès, a difficulty that may be questioned in difficulty; or is it, as for Arendt, the violently established border of the share? For Nancy, it seems as if the birth/death mark serves as the sign of a militant concept of sacrificial freedom: 'the dead person (not abstract "death") never ceases to be present . . . .. His death, whatever its cause, gave him back to an inappropriable freedom'

(p. 169). The return of freedom even in death affirms the life of both the individual and the community.

Nancy places freedom before 'equality, fraternity and justice' and says that fighting 'for' it 'is not simply on the order of a project, but also consists of immediately affirming, *hic et nunc*, free, equal, fraternal, and just existence' (pp. 169–70). However, by placing freedom first, he assumes that it lies at the heart of the share, and that equal, fraternal and just shares are the issue of freedom. For Jabès and for Arendt the shared world is not one that can be 'immediately affirmed' nor is it one in which freedom can be principle and principled. It is one in which injustice and violence ineluctably compromise the share, making it difficult and perhaps inextricable. Precisely the thinking and the writing of the difficult share is not free, for it too is qualified by, implicated in and responsible for, the injustice and the violence of the share.

Notes

1 Edmond Jabès, *From the Desert to the Book*, p. 50.
2 Edmond Jabès, *The Book of Questions*, Vol. 1, p. 107.
3 *The Experience of Freedom*, p. 72.
4 For the English reference, see 'The retreat of the political', in *Retreating the Political*, trans. and ed. Simon Sparks (London: Routledge, 1997).
5 *The Experience of Freedom*, p. 80. The alliance between Jacobin military strategy and an anti-substantivist metaphysics is clearly evident in the work of Clausewicz, and later in Carl Schmitt and Ernst Jünger. See Paul Virilio, *Speed and Politics* (New York: Semiotexte, 1900) and Howard Caygill, 'Violence, civility and the predicaments of philosophy', in D. Campbell and M. Dillon, *The Political Subject of Violence* (Manchester: Manchester University Press, 1993).
6 Hannah Arendt, 'Karl Jaspers: Citizen of the World?', in *Men in Dark Times*, pp. 81–2.
7 Ibid., p. 83.
8 *The Origins of Totalitarianism*, p. 106; see also the extended discussion of 'The perplexities of the Rights of Man' pp. 290–302.
9 Might the 'maternal thing' be Marianne, the evanescent figure of the freedom of the nation, as opposed to the dead father in the guise of the executed King?

Bibliography

Arendt, Hannah, *The Human Condition* (Chicago and London: University of Chicago Press, 1958).
Arendt, Hannah, *Men in Dark Times* (San Diego, New York and London: Harcourt Brace Jovanovich 1968).

Arendt, Hannah, *The Origins of Totalitarianism* (San Diego, New York and London: Harcourt Brace Jovanovich, 1973).

Arendt, Hannah, *Eichmann in Jerusalem – A Report on the Banality of Evil* (Harmondsworth: Penguin, 1984).

Derrida, Jacques, 'Ellipsis', in Writing and Difference, trans. Alan Bass (London: Routledge, 1993), pp. 294–300.

Heidegger, Martin: *Being and Time*, trans. J. Macquarrie and E. Robinson (Oxford: Basil Blackwell, 1962).

Jabés, Edmond, *From the Desert to the Book*, trans. Pierre Joris (Barrytown: Station Hill, 1990).

Jabés, Edmond, *The Book of Questions*, Vol. 1, trans. Rosemary Waldrop (New England: Wesleyan University Press, 1991).

Nancy, Jean-Luc: *The Inoperative Community*, trans. Peter Connor (Minneapolis: University of Minnesota Press, 1991).

Nancy, Jean-Luc, *The Experience of Freedom*, trans. Bridget McDonald (Stanford: Stanford University Press, 1993).

Nancy, Jean-Luc, *The Birth to Presence*, trans. Brian Holmes *et al.* (Stanford: Stanford University Press, 1993).

Nancy, Jean-Luc, *Le sens du monde* (Paris: Galilée, 1993).

4

Jean-Luc Nancy:
the place of a thinking

Francis Fischer

The thinking is singular, silent, yet also difficult and demanding, which beats a path through the commotion of our times. It opens us to what happens and before which we are without measure, destitute, *exposed* to the weight/the thought of existence [*la pesée/la pensée*].

'*Exposé*' – 'an exposition', 'exposed' – is one of his words, a particular hallmark of Jean-Luc Nancy's writing just like 'existence' and many others; consequently, *exposé* is even a style, a comportment, a posture through which he introduces himself.

> When you introduce yourself and give your name, it does not mean anything . . . . It does not take place because it is first of all the presentation of a place: that of your presence and of your naming. This is a very simple and even very humble truth . . . which doubtless, for the moment, does not mean a great deal – one which, as our epoch attests, we have to think.[1]

This quotation is taken from *L'oubli de la philosophie*, a small book published in 1986 which seems to me to open the way for thinking to come; a text which, more than any other, notes the dereliction and the end of an epoch (our *fin de siècle*) in order to engage positively and joyously in what, for us, is now possible as a chance.

It is generally futile to want to grasp the emergence or the turning-point of a work. The very most I could say is that I have felt myself to be touched by this voice. And it spoke to me first of all of the question of sense [*sens*] which has become not simply the question but the ordeal [*l'épreuve*] of Jean-Luc Nancy's text. Once undergone, this question also concerns the senses and more specifically the sense of touch.[2] Recent history has not spared us from any manifestation of the insane [*l'insensé*] and we are always in pursuit of meaning [*sens*].

In place of the epoch of losing meaning [*sens*], dedicated to absence and to the nothing, falling short of any return to 'ideas', to values, to projects, Nancy speaks of the entirety of the West at its ends. The manner of thinking that belongs to the West (and it is still unable to imagine any other) has not ceased to produce itself and project itself on the basis of the retrospective illusion of a loss; the lack of sense will have been the motor of the desire for meaning (of desire *tout court*) which runs throughout philosophy, or rather what Nancy, following Nietzsche and Heidegger, will call metaphysics 'essentially dedicated to the misfortune of desire, and that is to say, to the distancing of the projection and to the permanent return of the project'.[3]

For 'metaphysics' does not exhaust the sense of philosophy, whose responsibility it is to open and to think another history of sense (which began with Heidegger, Wittgenstein, Benjamin) and equally to welcome another sense of thinking, outside the unfortunate circle of desire: a thinking which is neither fortunate nor unfortunate, one which will, much later, claim to draw its inspiration from love, from joy or from taking pleasure. But we are going too quickly, even if the refusal to submit to the appropriating logic of desire (albeit negative) remains permanent.

Against all the calls for returns, all 'visionary' discourses, meaningful projections or meaning itself as project, one must affirm the exhaustion of sense, its *arrival at the limit*; which assuredly means the 'closure of the possibilities of meaning for the West'. The death of God or of History or of Man would be the mark of this arrival. And in so far as this is neither the rule of distress nor its absence, the nihilism which fed on the infinite vista of sense, on disappointment and nostalgia, on loss and distance, is overcome.

But sense arrives at the limit, and one should add that the strongest injunction of Nancy's texts will have been not to give up on the thought of the limit, the limit of meaning on the basis of which sense arrives. Equally, Nancy will not have given up on the thought of the limit of philosophy where, from the beginning, this thought exceeds every meaning or vision of the world in order to lay itself open to the nudity of existence or to its infinitely finite opening. The limit carries us into this place: to be touched there by every sense would be the ordeal of a thinking proper to our times.

L'oubli de la philosophie begins with a citation from Benjamin which clears the way: 'Truth is the death of intention'.

Our exposure to sense is beyond all meaning (intention), even before every ideality or finality of truth, and sense does not 'result from' this, but comes about through this shared exposure and opens itself to meaning or to the insane [*l'insensé*] or to insignificance. There is no sense of or before this exposure, rather being exposed is the whole of sense; this is the simple truth: a presentation which makes sense only by happening to sense as our sharing [*partage*]. 'We are the community of sense and this community has no meaning . . . it is community *of* having no meaning.'[4]

Thus one must not merely rethink politics or ethics or the erotic on the basis of this common exposure; rather, the greatest test today is to sketch out a genuine ontology of appearing-together [*comparaître*]. Such an ontology is the ontology of being abandoned to the finite singularity of an existence, an existence itself open and breached in abandonment to the world and to the in-common – not an 'individuality', but punctuations, encounters, crossings.

[For] there are cruel abandons and gracious abandons, there are gentle, ruthless, voluptuous, frenetic, happy, disastrous and serene abandons. Abandonment's only law, like that of love, is to be without return and without recourse.[5]

This is Aristotle's *pollakôs*: the multiplicity of abandoned being as the meaning [*sens*] of being, and that is to say at each moment as existence. One could, taking into account the constant debate with Heidegger, say the following: the meaning [*sens*] of being is existence, on the condition that one stands firm on the *without essence* of existing.[6] One must (and this is the ethical demand) give existence back to itself, but only in so far as it neither precedes nor proceeds from essence, only in so far as it maintains itself at the limit, at the point of its simple exposure.

There is no sense given to existence, nor any to be produced; this was, up until the present day, the project of existentialisms, their struggle, their freedom. Rather, existence *is exposed to* sense because it is given back to itself, not (as with Sartre) charged with self-signification but given back *to* itself in the infinite separation [*l'écart*] which prescribes its finitude; and that is to say, as free existence.

'Freedom is the very fact of existence as open upon existing itself, and this fact is sense.'[7] This is precisely why there is no completed, closed sense. In its ideal presentation this sense would be only the crushing of existence, its infinite negation, insanity itself [*l'insensé même*], which our epoch will have experienced to the point of nausea. Access to sense is lies in its inaccessibility. One should say, then, that sense is open in proportion to the opening of existence. Sense always happens to exposed existence and it happens as event, dispersion, brilliance or shard, punctuation: in short, *writing* – providing it rids us of that metaphysics of the written which haunted theoretical reflection in the 1970s. For writing reveals nothing.

> Nothing precedes, nothing is given – and nothing will be given in order to finish. It is a matter of holding oneself very precisely upon the very thin line where sense is proposed and dissolved, where it is dissolved in its proposition – a line of writing, a design or a painting which is not a *vision*.[8]

Writing is traversed by sense but does not complete itself in meaning; opaque and heavy, blind, it allows itself, at the limit of meaning, to be traversed by sense; thus writing is as much exscription as inscription.

Inscribed (this is its presentation), existence is exscribed, which is to say that through its presentation existence *touches* on[9] its own exposition: it is devoted to its own sensible and dense materiality. Whatever its project of clarity and signification, writing does not escape density, it bears the weight of an entire existence, it is the spatial line [*tracé*] of this existence in which what withdraws presents itself. 'By inscribing meanings, one exscribes the presence of what withdraws from all meaning, being itself (life, passion, matter, . . .). The being of existence is not unpresentable: it presents itself exscribed.'[10]

In a later work, *Corpus*, Nancy insists upon the fact that the written makes bodies, touches bodies. *Corpus* records the touch of sense-at-its-limit. If the body then gives rise to the existence of sense, to the incorporeal become touch, this has nothing to do with the body marked, tattooed, punished by the law in Kafka's 'The Penal Colony'.[11] These bodies do not exist; they are subjected to meaning, swept along, seized, caught in transubstantiation.

But bodies exposed to the nakedness of existence (more naked than at the dawn of their clarity) touch each other;[12] addressing one another, 'they infinitely renew their spacing, they diverge', opening themselves to the existence which traverses them like lovers.[13] I would have liked to have shown how much this book was about love (but I know it does not in fact show itself, it does not let itself be seen).

'From love, *I* only return or end up broken', he said.[14] Love is the surprise through which a subject opens itself to the opacity of existence, traversed, suspended, in shreds [*en éclats*]. The sheen [*l'éclat*] of bodies, their global pressure, responds to the shards [*éclats*] of love as if the experience of lovers, which was for so long in the service of the fusional logic of desire, now opens us to the infinite spacing of bodies and to the sharing that we are. The body has become a new world space.

It is here that we must look to Nancy's interest in images, and his passion for photography. They celebrate the bodies of this world.

> Photography passionately exposes the real, its fragility, its grace, its transience. Somewhere, for a moment, something or someone has appeared. Photography shows us that it took place and that it resists our doubts, our forgetfulness, our interpretations. It offers us this evidence.[15]

This is not a passion for seeing, but a letting-be of this existing in the multiple brilliance of its singular exposure. Every body, however ordinary, is also absolutely singular. And the image is neither empty nor simulation, hence his refusal of all those denunciations of our world as spectacle or simulation. Everything that presents itself is open-ended sense, but this 'everything' does not represent a completed meaning on the basis of which a logic of the copy or of the model could regulate itself. Thus technology is the very mark of existence in so far as it proceeds from nothing, in so far as it is open to sense.

This is why the multiplication of images and technologies of reproduction – 'eco-technics' (which at once combines work and trade with technological development) – have globalized the question of an existence exposed to sense, and opened the connection of bodies and their 'appearing-together' to the world.

> So long as we do not think the eco-technical creation of bodies unreservedly as the truth of *our* world, and as a truth *which is easily the equal* of those that myths, religions, humanisms, represented, then we will not have begun to think *this* world.[16]

We shall have to think this world, think it as our own. If the cosmos and the *mundus* are finished, is there any other sense to [*du*] the world, even though it still remains to be thought?

The fact remains that the world itself *is* sense in so far as it is neither a completed totality nor a field of action for man, but the space of sense which belongs to existence: exploded space [*espace éclaté*], a multiplicity of existents where territories and accents become blurred so that the landscapes of the countries of the world come into their singularity each time unique and ordinary.[17] This world – this one, the only one: a place for existing and for thinking.

Translated by Richard Stamp

Notes

1 Jean-Luc Nancy, *L'oubli de la philosophie* (Paris: Galilée, 1986), p. 84.

2 [Translator's note. For the most part, the word *'sens'* has here been rendered as 'sense', and *signification* as 'meaning'. On occasion, *'sens'* has also been translated as 'meaning' (where context or syntax have demanded), and when this is the case the French has been given in parentheses. On the importance of 'the sense of touch' in Nancy's work, see Jacques Derrida, 'Le toucher' (trans. by Peggy Kamuf), in *Paragraph* 16, 2 (July 1993), pp. 122–57.]

3 *L'oubli de la philosophie*, pp. 58–9.

4 Ibid., p. 101.

5 'L'être abandonné', in Jean-Luc Nancy, *L'Impératif catégorique* (Paris: Flammarion, 1983), pp. 139–53, p. 153.

6 Jean-Luc Nancy, *L'Expérience de la liberté* (Paris: Galilée, 1988), p. 13. [translated by Bridget McDonald as *The Experience of Freedom* (Stanford CA: Stanford University Press, 1993), p. 9.]

7 Jean-Luc Nancy, *Une pensée finie* (Paris: Galilée, 1990), p. 27.

8 Jean-Luc Nancy, 'De l'écriture: qu'elle ne révèle rien', in *Rue Descartes*, 10 (Paris: Albin Michel, 1994), p. 107.

9 [Translator's note. '. . . *toucher à*': as Peggy Kamuf notes in her translation of Derrida's 'Le toucher', the verb *toucher à* can be translated as 'to touch (up)on', 'to meddle or tamper with', and even 'to violate or harm' (p. 152, n. 1).]

10 *Une pensée finie*, p. 62.

11 Jean-Luc Nancy, *Corpus* (Paris: Métailié, 1992), p. 13.

12 [Translator's note. '. . . *se touchent*': *se toucher* can mean 'to play with oneself' (i.e., to masturbate), but in the plural form it means 'to touch each other up'.]

13 *Corpus*, p. 20.

14 *Une pensée finie*, p. 247.

15 Jean-Luc Nancy, *Le poids d'une pensée* (Québec: Le grifon argile, 1991), p. 113.

16 *Corpus*, p. 78.

17 Jean-Luc Nancy, *Le sens du monde* (Paris: Galilée, 1993), pp. 92, 240.

5

Ou, séance, touche de Nancy, ici[1]

Werner Hamacher

Here. – Or here.
Now. Or now.

Nothing more banal, nothing more philosophical and more banal than to begin
'here and now' with *here and now*. Almost the whole repertory of the classic
themes and questions of philosophy is collected in this commonplace of the *hic
et nunc*. Whoever affirms that they speak 'here and now', in this determinate
place, at this determinate time, *now, here*, and as this unmistakable particular, is
already placing themselves in a community, in a long history and in a place
defined by this history, which disavows any claim to singularity, to determi-
nateness and to presence. Instead of speaking here and now, they speak in
quotation. Instead of speaking themselves, they let others speak. Instead of
beginning, they continue. The formula which is supposed to break through the
vague generality of time and space, and concentrate attention on a determinate
point, on this *here and now* of the speaker and the spoken to, this formula for
concentrating and communicating, is itself only a vague generality. Whoever
uses the formula doesn't pierce the generality but corroborates it. They
corroborate it and continue it. They continue – that means: they go on, they
hand on what has been handed down, they repeat repetitions, they stabilize the
enthralling [Bann][2] by history and by the society which has stamped the
expression *hic et nunc* with *its* 'hic et nunc'. They continue – but that also
means: they distance, they remove, they desist. Whoever speaks *here*, they
speak *here* – they further the *here*, the talk about *here* and the talk of the *here*, in
that they pass it on, they reproduce and strengthen it; and they separate
themselves from this talk about the *here*, this *here* say; they take up distance
from it, they draw off its power, they no longer speak it, and no longer allow it

38

to speak unchanged. For whoever speaks *here*, they are already speaking in another, incomparable, and unmistakably other *here*, in which the *here* and whoever says it is lost. They speak and they do not speak – and it is the impossible connection between these two, which articulates itself in every *now* and every *here*; the impossible connection between that enthralling and its breaking, between the repetition and its interruption, between the connection and the break. Whoever begins thus, with a *here and how*, has, by continuing, by desisting, already made a start on stopping, on what is leaving him or her.

That is the theme – or one of the themes which are encountered in Jean-Luc Nancy's texts: the enthralling (by the law, by society, by history, by the body, by philosophy), banality, the Here and the Now, beginning and ending. When I quote them here and now, and comment on one point or another, then I will be following the logic of citation and commentary, which I have just referred to – I shall be continuing what I quote, in that I reproduce it and continuing it, in that I distance myself from it here or there; and I will comment on it in that I accompany it and leave it. You could say that the logic of continuation[3] follows the law of enthralling that Nancy formulates: in that it obliges, in that it leaves, and in that it releases from the obligation of the law. 'The origin of the "abandon"', he writes in 'Abandoned Being', 'is the putting *à bandon*. The *bandon* (*bandum*, *band*, *bannen*) is the order, the prescription, the decree, the permission, and the power which controls free disposal of them.'[4] And 'given over to the absolute of the law, the banned is also abandoned outside all of its jurisdiction. The law of abandon implied that the law is applied in withdrawing. The law of abandon is the other of the law, which makes the law.'[5] The banishment which enthrals – so, connection, community, society, however they may be defined, whether as moral, hermeneutic or political, the law, whether of discussion, or conversation or mere presentation – this law, this enthralling is an excommunication. For the law asserts its absolute validity only where it does not suffer another law to be next to itself, and thus only where it does not itself come to appear: it is absolute and it is a law only in so far as it withdraws from every objection and thus in so far as it bequeaths the abandonment of the law. The law simply commands – and its command as such says, that there are no obligations and no duties which might correspond to it, no methodical procedure which might lead to it, and no expedients which might guarantee its fulfilment. The law of the law says that it does not let itself be fulfilled, and that those to whom it is given are abandoned by it. If Nancy says of this law of abandonment or of separation that it is 'the other of the law which lays down the law', that may be understood as saying that it is the law itself which abandons itself as its other, that the law puts itself off from itself, distances itself from its positive directions and prescriptions, from its titles and guarantees and interrupts itself. The enthralling is an exiling – and it is its self-exiling. (It could therefore be said that Nancy's 'bandon', his 'law of abandon' portrays a *bind*, a *double bind* or a *double abandon*. It is a law that simply commands, but in that it commands thus, it commands in the absence of the law. Not only those for whom it is valid are abandoned, the law itself is abandoned by the law. (And, one might add to this, nothing can guarantee that it is still even a law, that it is even a law at all: the law of abandonment, even the abandonment of the law by the law cannot also be *a* law, and neither can the abandonment be an abandonment. *Double abandon*, that means: not *one* bind, and perhaps none).) The law – and once more: it is here a question of the law of community or society, of the minimal law of discussion, of commentary and of critique – the law is alone (and thus perhaps no law). Since it is the law of abandonment, it must itself be, as the law commands, the abandoned law, the law still abandoned by abandonment (and thus perhaps not law and perhaps not abandoned law). And he who follows it – but can he who is abandoned still follow? – will not be less than it: not abandoned less, not less alone (and perhaps not less than one): he will not follow – that is the law of the abandonment of the law – not follow, not precede, nor will he be-there, nowhere, not even alone, not elsewhere, in no Where, stripped of where and word, un-where and un-word.

How can one then still quote, comment and question? The unrenounceable gesture in these three operations is that of a *here*. A *here and now*. That which is somewhere else, in another text or context for example, will, in each case, through quotation as well as through commentary, through discussion and questioning, be cited, summoned from there to here and put *à l'ordre du jour*. The place, which is designated by the *here*, is not thereby already pre-given, it is not to be found simply in a discursive or social space which is already constituted, into which something could be as it were transplanted, but rather it is first opened up through the reference to it in the quotation (or opened again, or otherwise). And the *now*, in which the question or the quotation cites something, is not simply one of the points – the nows – present in a clockwork flux or continuum of time, but a moment that is first marked (or remarked) through this now of the question or the citation. The citation, the commentary and the question thus first open up the *hic et nunc* in which something can appear and be discussed: they make space and time for it. That is what Nancy, who admittedly at this point is speaking neither about citing nor commenting, emphasizes in 'Abandoned Being': 'The here has no place: it is at each instant here or there, here and now, because here *is* now. Hic et nunc'.[6] Now what is cited does appear, but the *here and now*, into which it enters, does not appear. It is an effect of speech or writing in such a strict sense that it has no place outside them. But because it is only ex-cited by them, it succumbs completely to the movement of the inaugurating of this language and its cutting off. The interval of the *here and now*, as Hegel demonstrated, is never that of a sense of certainty, it is that of speech and of its fixing in memory or in writing and thus really and truly a language interval. (Fixing means here that the language in the writing distances itself from every immediate relation to its objects, be it a phenomenal or an eidetic relation.) Therefore Nancy can write: '(*Here*: the most properly, there where that is being written, in front of you. Here is being written here, here is never more than an inscription. *Here lies* its abandoned letter)'.[7] The phrase 'here is being written here' is not only a commentary on the inscription of the *here*, but one in which this inscription itself takes place. And indeed takes place as quotation. In one *ici* the other cites itself. There is an *ici* here – and not only here – only as *icitation*. Yet the *here* is abandoned in its movement, it is given up and can only be repeated *here* as a *here*, given up in that way. *Here* is thus, before it can be *here*, exposed to an alteration, a modification or a pause which destroys the appearance not only of its sense certainty but also its linguistic certainty and which, as a linguistic alteration and as an alteration of the *here and now* of language, can be called the law of its cessation, its ex-position or its *abandon*. For *here* is always *here* or *there*, *here* or *here*. Nancy writes thus: 'But *here* or *there* (it is the same and it is the other), though it shares the places, though it starts to make space'. And again: 'The here has no place: it is at each moment here or there'.[8] So 'here *or* there' and again 'here *or* there'. Nancy makes no comment on this *or*, he does not even emphasize it, but he writes it. *Or* marks – and indeed *between* every *here* and the next just like *in* every *here* – the breaking off of the *here* and the possibility of its insertion. Every *here* is exposed to an *or*, in which it is suspended, forgotten, set aside, distorted, before it can be *here*. *Or*, which is at the same time a particle of disjunction and conjunction, of alteration and alternative, formulates the law to which every positing of a *here and now* is subject: the law of their breaking off. ('Oder', 'ou' or 'or' is only being considered here to begin with as a linguistic or graphic function, which can be taken over by other notations – or the lack of them – thus by a comma or a colon, a pause or a gap. Or, it goes without saying, by non-discursive means.)

Without an *or* there is no *here* or *now*. There has to be an *or* for there to be

41

the possibility of citing, commenting, questioning, something here and now. This possibility – and that means the possibility of every communication, every community or society with me or with others – depends consequently on a linguistic element, that is neither a noun nor a demonstrative, and which expresses neither affirmation nor a negation. *Or* is a particle of disjunction or conjunction, and of co-disjunction, which announces another possibility and, more exactly, the possibility of another. It does not name this other, it does not show it, but it opens the place from which it can express or show itself. So *or* always opens itself to another, and again to others. It makes room for places and times, at any given time a *here* and a *now* and admits each time a *this* in its singularity or in its singular generality; but it only ever admits them as other: as abandoned by a general law, as those abandoned by the law of the suspension of the law, which cannot collect themselves together in any commonplace, in any topical 'here and now', nor in a banality. An *or* admits them and an *or* abandons them. *Or*, that is their exposing.

> Either – Or. An ecstatic lecture.
>
> Marry, you will regret it; do not marry, you will also regret it; marry or do not marry, you will regret both; either you marry or you do not marry, you regret both. Laugh about the world's folly, you will regret it; weep over it, you will also regret it; laugh about the world's folly or weep over it, you will regret both; either you laugh about the world's folly or you weep over it, you regret both : . . . . Hang yourself, you will regret it; do not hang yourself, you will also regret it; hang yourself or do not hang yourself, you will regret both; either you hang yourself or you do not hang yourself, you will regret both.[9]

One could go on in this way *ad infinitum* and in this fragment from the 'Diapsalmata' of his *Either-Or* Kierkegaard very nearly would go on in this way and write himself, one does not know whether ecstatically or mechanically, into the position of what could be called, in Roland Barthes' apt phrase, the 'ninisme' of aesthetic existence. This aesthetic existence recognizes in each decision only a reason for subsequent remorse and therefore shrinks from making even only a single decision. For this existence 'true eternity' lies not behind the Either-Or but before it, not in the choice or decision, but in the indifference towards it, or in the attempt to avoid it. The indifferentist's regret must be all the greater, for he who avoids a decision makes a decision, namely the decision not to decide. Indecisiveness only deceives itself over this: that it makes decisions and stays decided over these decisions. The possibilities from which the undecided man does not choose, pass him by like pictures from another life in whose contemplation he can immerse himself because he believes that he cannot be corrupted by mere contemplation of them; but he is corrupted for the very reason that he has made life into pictures and imagines himself as their unconcerned onlooker. Melancholy is the regret of the undecided man who has made his decision *against* deciding between Either and Or. It is the melancholy of the onlooker, who has himself become the picture of his possibilities. His boundless sadness is the passion of being seen and is therefore the passion of the reflecting man, the aesthete and the phenomenologist, for whom everything becomes the appearance of a decision refused, restricted, or still to be taken. What he sees is hazy because he always only sees himself from the point of view of his difference and therefore from the point of view of he who is seen. Therefore the aesthete does not see – he does not see in an emphatic sense – for were he to see, his gaze would no longer focus on the pictures of his possible existence; rather, it would rip open [*aufreissen*] their prospect, penetrate and outline it: his gaze would be the decision – the outline [*der Aufriss*] – opposite which nothing would stand as an illustrative object, but in which he would complete his existence in an aphenomenological way, without object and incapable of reflection.

This is how Kierkegaard argues. Similarly, however, the picture that he paints of the man who is decided on an explicit decision is not free of the traits of melancholy. What comes to the fore in his decision for the choice between Either and Or is the 'reality' of choosing itself and with it what is called the 'ethical' in Kierkegaard. If the choice *not* to choose leaves the decision implicit and neutralizes the possibilities of existence into merely aesthetic concepts, then the choice of the ethical thinker is explicitly completed, it emerges from the neutralism of contemplation and erects itself against what carries every decision – it is the choice of the will to choice. 'My Either-Or' writes Kierkegaard or 'Kierkegaard', and who could decide between both of these names, between the name and the 'name' and who could decide what '*my* Either-Or' means and whether it can still mean anything at all?

> My Either-Or does not refer directly to the choice between good and evil,
> it refers to the choice by which one chooses good or evil or excludes them
> . . . it is not therefore so much a matter of choosing whether one wills
> good or evil, but, rather, that one chooses willing, with that, however,
> good and evil are posited once again. He who chooses the ethical chooses
> the good, but good is completely abstract here . . . and it therefore does

not follow at all that he who chooses cannot choose evil again, although he has chosen good.[10]

The decision of the ethical thinker is a decision for the Either-Or, not a decision between the Either on one side and the Or on the other. It is a decision for the decision itself and thus a decision for the will. Indeed will is nothing other than the experience of decision, the absolute criterion of the separation between every possible Either and its Or; one could say that it is decision in its consummation, pure, immemorial performance of division, distribution, disjunction; Plato's *nomos* as understood by the philosophy of subjectivity. In the decision there is activated, the will to willing, the will to the power of the will and thereby to the substance of existence as absolute subjectivity. Consequently, as will to the power of the will, the decision for the decision is simultaneously, and independently of how it turns out in individual cases, the will to the reason for existence itself and thus the will to the good. He who chooses the will, chooses the good, for he chooses existence itself, he chooses his Self in its self-evidence, in the autonomy of his will and in what gives his Self existence.

This existence, however, and Kierkegaard makes no secret of this, is without permanence. Although Kierkegaard's ethics is an ontology of the will to power of subjectivity, of the *good* will to power, of the will to power as the absolute *good*; but since this will only finds support from itself, it is dependent on the permanence and continued activity of the will and thereby on its suspended confrontation with the possibility not to will, not to decide and not to choose the ethical and the good, but rather aesthetic indifferentism. That means will is only will in so far as it fundamentally expounds the possibility of not-willing. The decision is only a decision when it stands fundamentally and always before the possibility, that a decision might not be made. Kierkegaard expresses this detail when he writes that it still is not a consequence of the choice of wanting 'that he who chooses cannot choose evil again' (and therefore indifference, notdeciding and the aesthetic), 'although he has chosen good'. It is fundamental and necessary for the decision that it can always be the decision not to decide, that it can never be a definitive, nor a sufficient, nor a saturated decision. Decision is only fundamentally decision when it is decision for the openness of the decision for ever more and different decisions, and thus when it is decision for the impossibility of a definitive decision, for undecidability and therefore when it is decision *out of* undecidability. Correspondingly, will, for it is decision in itself, is only will when it can also be will not to will and will to the

44

impossibility of willing, when it is the ability to the impossibility of willing and is thus the ability of an inability. On principle and *preprincipally* [*präprinzipiell*] will is only that which cannot do what it can do and that which is unable to do what it is able to do, will has no power over its power. It must be what is not willed in order to be will. Kierkegaard's good – and will is the good *par excellence* in his metaphysics of will as in that of his teacher Schelling – his good is always the good of an evil, but of an evil which does not stand diametrically opposed to good, being of equal rank to it, of evil before each evil that might be set against the good, of an evil *before* the good and thus *in* it. Good is therefore the endless trembling, fear and trembling, *whether* indeed good has been grasped in the decision and in will itself and good is thus – good *at last* – and the shivering of the will, of the decision 'itself'.

In the arrangement of the philosophical materials that Kierkegaard propagates, he only indirectly draws out the consequences of this structure of decision that he describes. They do *not* immediately affect the relationship between the ethical and the aesthetic which is worked out with great precision in *Either-Or*: the ethical decision is exposed to a relapse at all times in the position of aesthetic contemplation, however, *Dasein* can only appear as aesthetic by means of the intervention of the ethical positing which for its part is fragile. Those consequences, which are only hinted at in Kierkegaard, refer rather to the structure of the decision itself, to the structure of the absolute decision for the decision. This decision can no longer simply be made in the domain of the metaphysics of will, since for this decision, the will is a final and non-derivative will, whereas in the decision it only becomes active as will *to* will, therefore as will to something not yet given, but which has only just started to be willed, to something not yet reached, but still only to be reached and thus to an infinitely different will. The metaphysics of will refuses to recognize that will is only will at all when divided and thus not only ambiguous [*zweideutig*] but *desperately* [verzweifelt] split in two; this makes will itself into the effect of a differential movement which it is simply not able to control itself. Consequently, if will has to be will *to* will in order to be will, if the distance to itself is constitutive for it, then, in principle, there has to be a not-willing at work in will itself that precedes each of its intentions and is not accessible to a single one of them. But now since every decision, and *a fortiori* those decisions for the decision itself, is a decision for the will every time, the dilemma of the acts of will must repeat itself as a structural dilemma of the decision. Even if each decision brings about a specific situation and thus modifies the room for manoeuvre of the possibilities, each must be a decision for the conditions of preservation of the decision itself, that means that each must keep the room for manoeuvre open in such a way that further decisions for the decision are not only not excluded themselves, but that these extensions and continuations (and positings-away) [*Fortsetzungen (und Fort-Setzungen)*] of the decision actually constitute the decision itself. Decision is always decision *for other* decisions (it is based in their multiplicity) and *a limine* it is decision for *something other* than the decision *itself*. If it is consequently a part of its structure, that decision is decision for the decision, then it cannot but be for undecidability, for this alone guarantees the openness, the room for manoeuvre, the freedom which permits further decisions and any decision at all in every *hic et nunc*. If there were a definite decision, valid once and for all, unmodifiable and thus lethal, then there would be no decision *for* the decision any more, then it would not be free and not a decision but a fact. Every decision is a decision for *another* decision and since its sequence must be inconclusive in principle, it must be decision for undecidability. The choice between Either and Or must always be able to become again the choice of the Either-Or itself, but this always-again [*Immer-wieder*] must infinitely suspend the Either-Or and therefore more decisively shift into a Without-Either-Or [*Ohne-Entweder-Oder*]. This Or-Without-Or [*Oder-Ohne-Oder*], which undermines each decision, thus freeing it as decision in the first place, is the end of absolute arbitrariness, which claims decisionism as an irreducible criterion of its acts and activism as the reason for its performances and the ontology of the will as the substance of the ethical process. Before the necessary Without-Or of the Or [*Ohne-Oder des Oder*] its acts of will become whims, things undecided which are incurable and in Kierkegaard's terminology incurably 'melancholic', because they inhabit the decision of the will itself.

Therefore there are only decisions for the impossibility of the decision and out of it. And, every decision *is* nothing other than this decision of its impossibility. Thus nothing negative is meant by impossibility here, nothing that simply contrasts itself with decision as its opposite; on the contrary, it signifies the open background from which the decision draws its possibility. The possibility of the impossibility of the decision (of the will) is the possibility of the decision itself. The 'own' of the decision in the Or-Without-Or, the 'own' of the Either-Or is only able to be reached in it: therefore only where it is no longer able to be found in advance as the given ability of the subject, but where this ability constitutes itself for the first time in its irreducible inability. The subjectivity of the subject – like the will and the will to will, like the decision and the decision for the decision – only springs forth at all (and thus shatters as self-constitution) in that impossibility and in that inability of justifying itself *causa sui*, the instance of the finite or first decision, the decision to be *self*. Each time it decides itself, the subject is exposed to another. In deciding, the decision is expounded each time to something completely [*toto coelo*] different from the decision: not to itself and not to any possible self. And if the decision should be good, as Kierkegaard repeatedly emphasizes, then it can only be so, in as far as it is exposed to evil, over which it has no power as good because decision is nothing other than this separation — nothing other than existence and nothing other than freedom.

This self-declination of the decision, its *a priori* distancing and expropriation is therefore that mode in which it *is* at all and in which Being[11] happens and appropriates itself at all. In 1936 in a section of his *Contributions to the Philosophy (of the Event)*,[12] Heidegger asks the question in statements which take up some of the questions from *Being and Time* and thus once again the problems of Kierkegaard's *Either-Or*. The question is: 'Why is the truth of Beyng not an adjunct and not a framework of Beyng and also not a pre-condition [of Beyng], but the most intrinsic essence of Beyng itself?' And Heidegger's answer: 'Because the essence of Beyng presents itself [*west*] in the ap-propriative happening [*Er-eignung*] of the de-cision [*Ent-scheidung*]'.[13] Nancy quotes this sentence in his study 'La décision de l'existence' in order to underline that decision and furthermore decisiveness [*Entschlossenheit*] should not be misinterpreted as an anthropologically determined happening and that it is the opening to openness which distinguishes the existence of *Dasein*. Nancy writes that decisiveness

> is nothing but a making-its-own [*Zueignung*] in the opening up, as opening up: the 'making-its-own' which forms the ownmost [*eigenste*] possibility of the ownness of existence as such, the 'making-its-own' or the 'Ereignis' [the appropriating event]. *The Contributions* will say that 'the essence of Beyng deploys itself and presents itself [*west*] in the appropriation of the decision [*in der Er-eignung der Ent-scheidung*]' and that 'the advent of the appropriation [*das Ereignis der Er-eignung*] encloses within it the de-cision'.[14]

However, the 'ap-propriation [*Er-eignung*] of the de-cision [*Ent-scheidung*]' is only the essence of Beyng while it is simultaneously — in the same context Heidegger emphasizes this feature [*Zug*], this withdrawal [*Entzug*] — the 'refusal'. Being 'presents itself' ['*west*'] in the decision as ap-propriation while it withholds itself in it at the same time, while its ap-propriation happens as dispropriation [*Ent-eignung*]. Thus the dis-appropriation of Being [*die Ent-ereignung des Seins*] in the decision has the structure of what I have called 'holding-out' ['*Hinhaltung*'] elsewhere, the structure of what Nancy characterizes as 'offering' and which one might also call the happening of being ['*das Sich-Zutragen des Seins*']. In the decision, the Being of *Dasein* happens to itself, without arriving at itself, but in such a way that it is only with 'itself' in the non-arrival and with its own openness as something which does not belong to anyone or anything – but these are neither Heidegger's words nor his thoughts any longer. Therefore, Being, and thus the decision, is not to be thought from its retrospectiveness [*Nachträglichkeit*], nor from its contractiveness [*Verträglichkeit*], nor from its subtractiveness [*Abträglichkeit*]; rather, Being, and thus the decision, in contrast to Heidegger and Nancy, is to be thought from a carrying [*Träglichkeit*], a ference [*Ferenz*] into which occurrence [*Zutragen*], contracting [*Vertragen*] and retrospection [*Nachtragen*] are released and, yet, which points to another – and therefore another than Being – a not-carrying [*ein Nicht-Tragen*], an unportable [*ein Untragbares*] and an unbearable [*ein Unerträgliches*], an 'aferance' and 'afferance', which is perhaps different from Derrida's *différance*, or which allows it to be read differently.

If the structure of decisiveness and decision is its own openness, as something which does not belong to anyone or anything, not convertible into the egoism of a subject which is identical with itself, then there can and no longer should be a distinction made between the *own* and its *un-belonging*, its un-belonging to *itself* as between two alternatives which might be opposed to each other in Either-Or, the formula of rivalry and, *sit venia verbo*, ar-rivality. However, if the *own*, and the singular decisiveness, is the epitome of *something that does not belong* and only dissolves the ties of egological metaphysics of the will in this way, then the question poses itself as to how seriously or decisively Heidegger – and then Nancy – take this *something which does not belong to anyone or anything*, and how seriously the *unbelonging to itself* [Selbst-Unzu gehörigkeit] of the decision is taken. And there is the corresponding question as to whether there are not also always egological residues in the structure of that decision in which the *Dasein* happens to its Being.

Heidegger starts from the premise – thus summarizing Kierkegaard's reflections without naming him – that decision is first a decision about 'whether decision or non decision. But decision is to bring itself before the Either-Or'.[15] Decision is essentially historical and thus a decision whether history happens or not. This is indeed 'history of Being' and therefore the 'turn' from the philosophy of subjectivity to the thinking of Being and thus from 'another beginning of history'. Consequently, for Heidegger, the 'decisions' against which thought is confronted are:

Whether man wants to remain a 'subject' or 'whether he grounds Being-there ['Da-sein'] . . .

whether being takes Being as what is most general for it' and is therefore dependent on 'ontology' and buried by it or whether Beyng in its singularity comes to the word and chimes through beings [das Seiende] as something unique . . .

whether beings solidify as the most obvious thing of everything mean, small scale and average into something reasonable or whether the most questionable thing represents the flexibility of Beyng . . .

whether Beyng finally withdraws itself or whether this withdrawal as the refusal becomes the first truth and the other beginning of history.[16]

He could continue in this way and it would not change much about the 'fateful' ['geschicklich'] Either-Or, about the parting of the ways between beings and Being at which Heidegger believes he is standing in 1936. For that is the question for him – beings or Being. How is it to be solved? 'By what means can the decision be made?'[17] Heidegger's answer is unambiguous despite the or that divides it – it reads: 'through the gift or the absence of 'those outstanding ones marked out' [jener ausgezeichneten Gezeichneten] which we call 'the future ones'. Among them are: '(1) those few individuals . . . ; (2) those many bound together . . . ; (3) those many directed to each other . . . and (4) and (5) the people'. Concerning them Heidegger then writes: 'In its origin and its definition this people is singular according to the singularity of Beyng itself, whose truth is founded uniquely at a singular place in a singular moment'.[18] The motives of the singularity and uniqueness of the place, the moment, the people and of Being are opposed here to those motives of what was once called 'what is most general' and then 'everything mean, small scale and average'. Thus for Heidegger the decision is between singularity on the one hand and ordinariness on the other, between Being on the one side and beings on the other – and the decision is made in favour of the Being and singularity of the people, the place and the moment, against the ordinariness and generality of beings, of what is immense, of the mass; and the decision is made from Being, from the singularity of the people, the moment and the place. The decision for the singular and the unique is the decision of the singular and the unique for themselves. It is the unique decision for the unique decision. And since it is unique, it is quite simply 'the' decision itself. And for this very reason, although Heidegger sets such store by suggesting the opposite, it is no decision at all. And thus it is no appropriation, no dis-appropriation of Being.

The scandal of Heidegger's statements, which is no less than that of the almost identical sounding, if less provocative formulations in his Rectoral Address, is not only the cunning submersion into the swampy vocabulary of contemporary political ideologues; it is not only found in the blindness which opposes singularity to ordinariness, whereas it can hardly itself be something other than ordinary in this opposition; it is not only to be found in the curious philosophical derailment which makes Being an alternative to beings; it is to be found in all that, and also because the decision is by no means exposed to its impossibility, as it must be, but because it is simply cashed in.[19] Heidegger even multiplies the *or* in the prelude to the decision – but, at the point where he decrees the decision is made by the 'outstanding one marked out' and the 'singular' 'people', it cannot be made between an Either and an Or any longer, for it is 'singular' and 'unique', has already been made, tied to a 'singular place' and to a 'singular moment'. However a singular Or is no Or. Wherever there is an Or, it only exists as a double Or, as Either-Or, which only receives its singularity from the possibility of its repetition, translation, transformation and afformation. The Or, in order to be Or and singular, must be *another* Or and admits of other Ors up to the Or-Without-Or. For Heidegger Or is singular and *no* other, it does not admit any other and is therefore no longer one itself. Heidegger does not want to recognize that the 'singular' decision is not singular and that 'singular' decisiveness which Heidegger disputes is death by hanging. The singular Being is not singular Being. Onto-dicy (the vindication of Being) in the 'original' in the 'singular' decision is an ontocide. The mono-ontological crisis in an Or which Heidegger makes urgent here in 1936 in order to open up 'another beginning to history' is its collapse into an *Ouk*-on tologie, which can neither be different, nor history, nor beginning, nor end because it therefore only holds 'singular' fast to its *own* openness and only belongs directly to itself there, without reference to history to Before or After, to repetition or to change. The 'other' is the ownmost, the selfsame and 'the other beginning of history' is in an all-too-close continuity with the history which Heidegger wants to overcome.

The question put to Heidegger was how seriously he took the definition of the decision which resulted from his thought of ap-propriation as dis-propriation of Being and that in the definition its *own* openness (or decisiveness) happens as something that belongs to nobody and nothing and thus as a decidedly non-anthropological appropriating event. The answer is that he does not take it seriously enough, that with him the Own belongs only to itself in the figure of the 'outstanding one marked out' and the 'singular' 'people' – as in the figure of 'self-standing independence' in *Being and Time* – and that this direct 'belonging to Self', which eradicates every decision, every Either-Or and every alteration of singularity (and thereby also the singularity of alteration), represents nothing less than the political and ethical collapse of Heideggerian thought, its collapse into anthropological ethics and ethnic politics. For him, Being remains Being *of* beings with all the ambiguity of this genitive and moreover of those 'outstanding' beings which are, in an anthropological and well-nigh ethnological curtailment of the thinking of Being, a 'people' in its 'place' – in its *polis*. The on tological difference draws itself together in ontological fusion and articulates itself in an ethnology, topology and political doctrine of Being, Being there [*da Sein*] – 'singular' – is thought of as Being *of Dasein* and therefore as belonging to *Dasein* and since *Dasein* is topical to a 'people' and bound to a 'place' and because in its decision for its Being it is thought of as 'belonging' to this Being. It does not help that this Being is supposed to be experienced as withheld and not-arriving, for its non-arrival is oriented and pointed towards a 'place', a *topos* or a *polis* and thus thought of as a non-arrival of the 'fateful' and of the belonging, but not as not-fateful not-belonging and not-a-member. The dis-propriation which should be completed in Heidegger's decision of 1936 remains thought of as the ap-propriation of the Own and of Being *of Dasein*. It is certainly not sufficient merely to note and 'criticize' this subject matter. For the question which is to be linked in or led off from here is one of the most unpleasant that has to be posed in every confrontation with Heidegger and with the philosophical tradition that he thought he had overcome. This question is whether a dis-appropriation may allow itself to be even *thought* or *experienced* differently as the dis-appropriation of the ap-propriation [*An-eignung*], and whether something not-fateful, un-belonging and not-a-member may allow itself to be *thought*, or *experienced*, at all.

Now how seriously does Nancy take the dis-appropriational structure of the decision? Does it mean the structure of ek-sistence as absolute inconsistency, as exposure of the Or which is expounded most emphatically in Heidegger's later philosophy and a decisive part of which at least is still betrayed by it? In Heidegger's analysis of the ontological structure of the decision, conscience is understood as testimony of the ownmost possibility of *Dasein*, in such a way that *Dasein* is never in the possession of this ownmost possibility and is thus always bad conscience, always conscience of the dependence of *Dasein* and of

51

the inconsolable dependence of the decision. *Dasein* is dependent since it is never the foundation of its own existence and is never capable of converting its ownmost possibility as such into reality; for this ownmost possibility always stays ahead of *Dasein* and removed from it as the possibility of *impossibility* of existing. Thus the decision of *Dasein* for its existence is always a decision for the withdrawal of Being and even Being in withdrawal. *Dasein* is dependent, that means the decision is and remains dependent, further decisions are and remain dependent, the 'final' decision, which could dispense with all decisions, is and remains dependent. 'Own' ['*eigentlich*'] decision is only 'authentic' when it is this decision which decides for infinite finitude, thus for insuperability, indecision and therefore for the undecidability of decision 'itself'. Every decision is dependent on another decision: the openness and dependence on other things and on another time [*Mal*] is the sign [*Mal*] of its finitude. Every decision is a decision for its dependence, only in that it is 'own' and consequently a decision for the *a priori* existential in-appropriability of Being, of *its* Being. Hence Nancy writes in 'La décision de l'existence':

> Thus 'decision' or 'decided-Being' are neither attributes nor actions of the existent subject; they are that in which, from the first, existence makes itself into existence, opens to its own Being, or appropriates the unappropriable event of its advent to Being, from a groundlessness of existence. Existing has nothing more its own than this infinite ownability of unownable Being-in-its-ownness. That is the truth of 'finitude' (and that is the sole 'object' of the existential analytic).[20]

The decision is the event in which *Dasein* 'appropriates' its inappropriable Being to itself. But thereby irreparably expropriates itself, ex-appropriates itself and only ek-sists in this way. But can it be further stated, as Nancy reiterates, almost with the force of the activist: 'existence makes itself into existence [*l'existence se fait existence*]?' 'Everything which is to be done [Tout ce qui est à faire]', Nancy writes in the same context; 'what we must do (in the strongest and most 'praxical' sense of the word 'do') is to make the difference between Being and entities [*das Seiende*]'.[21] But can one *make* [machen] the ontical-ontological difference? And still make it 'in the strongest and most 'praxical' sense of the word "do"'? Can one say 'existence *makes* itself into existence' without adding that it makes itself as the unmakeable and thereby separates itself from the made as well as from the-able-to-be-made? For no decision makes something, none acts something, without thereby exposing at the same time what is acted and made to other decisions and actions and finally exposing itself to something other than decisions and acts, to the unactable, the unconcludable. Every '*à faire*' ['to be done'] that Nancy calls up, justifiably, with incontrovertible justification, does not push out of itself (in space which was not first opened up with this '*à faire*'?) but pushes, in its own structure, against the indestructible resistance of an *afaire* [afaire], against an *afairance* [Afairance] and this is exactly what could be called tentatively and provisionally an *afairance* and an *affairance*. The completion of finite decision is never com-*plete* [Voll zug] and the decision is never decided enough, never complete and itself, apart from at the cost of its immediate *separation from itself*, its parting and communication to another decision and to something other than decision – to something inconclusive, unsolvable and unportable, to something that does not let itself be acted, made or practised, to something undecidable – an Or-Without-Or – and thus to something other than Being. (It should be recalled at this point that the thought of the 'other than Being' or the 'different from Being' is the thought of ontological difference and can on no account be understood as a 'critique' of it. Heidegger speaks of 'essence' [*Wesen*], the difference between Being and beings as something that is not Being itself, but thanks to which it (Being) gives and refuses Being first of all.) Its 'activity' is to be thought from this other, from the structural incompletion and incomplet-ability of the act; every practical skill and praxis itself is to be thought from the structural lack of skill and clumsiness of praxis; from it [the activity] as well as from the existential-structural condition of the possibility *and* impossibility of *Dasein*, from an opening of activity, which itself does not yet and will never have the character of activity, is what is called 'act', is what is to be thought, written and done; from the *affairance*, the act without act.

For this reason Nancy's formulation in *L'expérience de la liberté* should also be read with a degree of reservation:

> Only freedom in action (there is no other), on the limit of thought – where
> in its turn thought is finally the act that it is, and, as a consequence, where
> thought is also the decision – decides while freeing (itself) from good *or*
> evil, that is to say that thought is necessarily, in its act, or rather in the very
> act [*le* fait *même*] where it *freely surprises itself* . . . that thought is in itself and
> by itself the good *or* bad decision.[22]

The reservation here no longer only concerns the theory of the act which is bound up here with the ontology of decision and whose material content is not sufficiently changed by its transformation into a phenomenology of surprise – it also concerns the (admittedly ambiguous) formulation: 'decides while freeing (itself) from good *or* evil [*décide en (se) libérant du bien* ou *du mal'*]'. Why then 'itself' ['*se*'] ? How could freedom free itself from good or evil? How could it free itself from one of them or both of them; how could it free itself from the Either-Or itself? Is not freedom only to be found in the extended and *out*-held [hin *gehalten*] experience of the absolute irreducibility of the Either-Or, in the ever-binding demand to the decision, which cannot be dispensed with, redeemed or freed from its possibilities – up to the possibility of *impossibility*, up to the Or-*Without*-Or – in a singular moment and not even in the singularity of the moment? Is not this *finite* freedom itself that neither saves finite freedom, nor is redeemable, either by it, or by something else? That the decision cannot be free from the Either-Or, from the decision and from freedom? If Nancy writes – because this is also written in the quoted sentence: 'decides while freeing from good *or* evil [*décide en libérant du bien* ou *du mal*]'. Then this is the very thing that is said by it: that freedom in its decision sets the Either-Or free from good and evil, that it by no means encounters good and evil as if they were external to it, that it makes a choice between them but ('but' is a word of freedom and of decision) that it can only be the freedom of itself as the opening up of both of these possibilities and that it derives from a third, an uninvolved or indifferent instance, to the same small extent as the Either-Or, or is able to be annulled in it into a synthetic unity – the unity with the necessity of the movement of the world for example. Freedom does not redeem, neither from evils, nor from the decision in which it happens, nor even from freedom itself. If it can be said that freedom is neither freedom *from* . . . [*von* . . .], nor freedom *to* . . . [*zu* . . .], but freedom from and to the freedom *from* . . . and *to* . . . , then it can also be said at the same time that it can be freedom *from the From and the To* [vom Vom und Zu] and freedom *to the From and the To* [zum Vom und Zu] and that it thus can be a relationless relation, arrelation [*Arrelation*], a relation standing open and the opening up of relationship but never salvation from relationship altogether and never pure absence of relation.

However, can it then be said, as Nancy also does in the quotation, that 'freedom may be a good or bad decision in itself and by itself [*en elle-même et par elle-même une décision bonne* ou *mauvaise*]'? The disjunctive predicate suggests that the decision is either one *or* the other; but if one can also speak with some generosity (it does not have to be laxity) about a good or a bad decision, then one still has to grant that one and the other are exposed to the *or* and thus to the possibility of the good decision *as well as* the bad one, and *remains* exposed to the possibility of the decision *as well as* to the non-decision. And, therefore, since it is not and never is a matter of a decision between given possibilities but always only a matter of the opening up of possibilities, since, as a consequence it is a matter in the decision of a separation and differentiation even *before* every possible choice; the decision is not only for coming decisions, it is simultaneously testimony for the still incomplete and inexecutable decision which is never made *as such*. It is the process of the secession, *séance* in the sense that was outlined elsewhere.[23] For this very reason, it cannot already be decided, whether in the case of the or ('*ou*') in 'the good or bad decision' ('*la décision bonne ou mauvaise*'), it is a question of an alternative, or a deliberative *or* (ou), whether it is the Or for an Either in which the series of possibilities finds an outcome, or the Or of a series of possibilities which can march on to further and ever further (and thus never realizable) Ors. Every decision and especially that one which Heidegger calls the 'original' and the 'own' moves before the question *Either or or or* [Entweder oder oder oder]; therefore it does not move in a binary opposition, but at all events moves up to it and can only move in this way at all and be the movement of *Dasein* as the opening up of 'its' Being. In the decision, *Dasein* does not *hold* itself between secured offered possibilities, but sketches these possibilities 'itself' for the first time and remains ek-sistent in their sketch *outside* itself; it remains without orientation, ateleological and yet waiting for something which cannot be fixed as the final purpose of *its* sketches. In short, *Dasein* remains unbelonging, its own otherness and ex-appropriation which is not exhaustible in the alternative between 'good' ('*bonne*') or 'bad' ('*mauvaise*').

Dasein is as its own dis-propriating surpassing. For this reason it is also not simply *decision*, but is 'de-cision' ['*Ent-scheidung*'], as Heidegger stresses in the word quoted by Nancy, but not commented on further by the latter; de-cision is not only incisive, concluding decision [*Dezision*] (and disjunction), but also the appropriation of what is distinguished in the decision, its coherence and jointure [*Verfugung*] (its conjunction and its *system*), but more than this de-cision is also its non-decision. Although Heidegger's explanation of this de-cision does indeed refer back to the definitions from *Being and Time* he actively attempts to set them apart from its anthropological, existential and moral misinterpretation. He distinguishes them as the 'innermost centre of the essence of Beyng itself' as opposed to the making of a choice and defines them as 'the stepping-apart itself, which separates and only allows the ap-propriation of this very *opening* in the separation to come into the play at the parting as the clearing for what is hidden from itself and still undecided, the belonging of the human to Beyng as the founder of his truth and the dependence of Beyng in the age of the last God'.[24] The de-cision is thus characterized as decision in the sense of the

opening up of the difference between Being (or Beyng) and beings, characterized as a making-its-own of the 'open' of this difference, as the inclusion of the
'space of time and play [*Zeit-Spiel-Raumes*]'[25] of what escapes conceptualization
as Being in all beings and *Dasein* and thus is characterized as the opening on to
what is in principle, as something open, the *still not-decided*. Thus de-cision is,
as Heidegger defines it, simultaneously the outline of ontological difference
and the release of what is undecided and always undecidable in it, the release of
Being; it is the decision of the undecidable and out of it, the disclosedness
[*Erschlossenheit*] of what is closed itself in its openness and therefore which is
held-open non-decision. In this it would be misunderstood as decision *for* a non-
decision lying outside it, for de-cision is in itself and as de-cision, as opening
non-decision. In the de-cision — that is to say, in the open of the opening
decision and un-decision stand together, a *system* before every possible system-
atization of conceptual units, an inconceivable 'system', not an open system,
but the system of the Open, or, in Heidegger's frequently used ambiguous and
anasemic term, the jointure [*Fuge*].[26] The de-cision — no longer understood in a
moral or anthropological-existential way — is thus the making-its-own of Being
as that which is in fact and in the act the inappropriable, and in fact the
undoable. De-cision means a system of the Open and means: the gathering into
ungatherable apartness.

Heidegger, however, insists, in the same sentence in which he defines this
structure of the decision no longer determined anthropologically but by the
history of Being, that this de-cision lets 'the belonging of the people to Beyng'
come into play. Here belonging can no longer signify that 'the person' as a
subject of conception appropriates his own idea, his ideal, his term, or its
essence and that the person understands in propositional decision; here belonging can also no longer mean that the person wills himself as a subject of the will
and takes control of himself as will to will; it can mean all the less that he
realizes his practical substance as an agent in the decision. In contradistinction
to Nancy, Heidegger is in no doubt that the 'situation' of 'highest' 'activity'
belongs to 'lack of decision' which does not dare to decide[27] and that the decision thought of by him is what '"lies" before the "act" and is what reaches
beyond it'.[28] Here 'Man's belonging to Beyng' can only mean belonging to
what is open which can neither be appropriated through propositions, nor acts
of will, nor acts, nor performances and thus not through decision of any sort
and which is not itself active as the subject of a property. Belonging to Being
must then mean belonging to the simply unbelonging. If the de-cision is the
'centre of the essence of Beyng itself', then it is the dis-propriation of every

decision in the 'still undecided', ex-position in something other than decision and only in this way 'another beginning of history – a beginning which is no longer or not yet *arche*, ratio, principle, foundation and condition, and therefore which is not the beginning of the history of the subject and its changing forms.

When the open and the still un-decided exposes itself in the de-cision, then it is a question in every Either–Or of what lies between Either and Or and of the open between which does not signify and which cannot be shown, because only that Something is able to appear in its room for manoeuvre, which is capable of becoming the object of meaning and actions. Its non-signification and unproducibility – the space of time and play – does stay fixed between the poles of the Either, on the one side and the Or on the other, but Either and Or can only result from its inexpressible, atopical or Utopian gap; that makes every voluntative moral anthropological decision and even every graphical distinction like the hyphen between Either-Or, into the making-its-own of the inappropriable and into the disappropriation of what-has-been-made-its-own [*Zugeeignete*] in the de-cision. The de-cision is the rip between Either-Or and is the same rip, non-objective, misshaping itself and withdrawing from its trace [*Zug*], and decision is therefore the unmaking and making impotent [*Entmachtung*] of everything made and makeable; pure surpassing of the act and the sign, of the thought and of the praxis, paralogic and parapraxis *par excellence*. The room for manoeuvre which the decision tears open between Either-Or can certainly be filled, but always only through further and further Either-Ors in which the gaps without Either and without Or multiply incalculably. The de-cision plays itself out in the time and room for manoeuvre of time of this Without. De-cision must be thought of from the Without, from the un-decision [*Un-entscheidung*], from the Without-act and the Without-sign. Or to think from the Without-Or, instead of thinking of the Without-Or as the mere lack of the Or – for Heidegger that means the turn from the metaphysics of subjectivity and ideas to the thinking of Being. But this Without would still have to be written, to be said and to be done without Without [ohne Ohne]. Without would still have to cut itself from Without in order to become Without *itself*, the Without without Without [*Ohne ohne Ohne*] and without *Itself* and thus un-write, un-say and undo the turn and the de-cision.

When the Being of *Dasein*, when the Being, that opens itself up to the *Dasein* in de-cision and speaks to it in the decision, is no longer simply and no longer 'unique' decision-without, simultaneously being the conjunction of the separation and without simultaneously being non-decision, then the philosophical or the political is not affected alone by the de-cision about the decision (which is simultaneously a decision *for* it and for something *other* than it) and affected by the singularity and the uniqueness of the decision, of its 'place' and of its 'moment', and finally affected by the 'outstanding one marked out' and by the 'singular' 'people'. Above all and immediately, the ontologem of the singularity and uniqueness of Being and of the decision-of-Being [*Seins-Erschlossenheit*] is affected by this de-cision. In this de-cision Being does not indeed offer itself as one and as something; it does not open itself, without locking itself, it does not open *itself* without opening up something *else*; it is something else other than *it* is and is different from such, that it *is*. The minimal structure of its *essence* – and this *essence* is 'the ap-propriation of the de-cision' – is its original, pre-original multiplicity (the ap-propriation of the multiplicity, not a strictly limited multiplicity at all), its division, splitting up and communication which is the unity itself, the not-dividing of a previous unity. Being – de-cision – that is multiplicity, 'internal' multiplicity of the decision to decision*s* and to such decisions which do not make up variants of one and the same model, or cases of a general rule and neither, as Heidegger would have it, make up an absolutely unique and singular collective, but decisions which relate to each other heterogeneously and not ever completely *as* decisions, rather taking leave of each other and, *a limine* taking leave of the decision 'itself'. For de-cision means once again – and once again differently, both decision and also gathering or holding together of what has become distinctive in the decision and also *U*ndecision. 'De-cision' is therefore still a concept – which characterizes the structure of action in its broadest conceivable range, but it is a limit-concept which expresses the conditions of unsubsumability of the concept and more precisely the heterogeneity of what is named in it. *De-cision* is still a decision in which something like Being opens up once and thus never once and for all, but it is a limit-decision, in as far as it performs its multiplicity and its making-heterogeneous directly to the point of the Undecision, which means to the limit of its impossibility. Every decision is written from this limit, from the de-cision. It is only decision because it is incomplete and 'actively' impossible decision because it is un-separation [*Un-scheidung*]. However when de-cision is another word for the ap-propriation of Being, then Being does not only open itself up as immediate multiplication into a potentially unending series of decisive acts; rather, it opens itself up in a discontinued manner, from the impossibility of its opening up in acts, from *its* impossibility. Being is not the generality of the concept to which everything that is corresponds; it is no vague possibility which is realized from time to time or constantly, or perhaps also only once; neither is it the omnipresent necessity which would be able to establish and multiply itself automatically. Being is in each case — and differently in each case — the transcategorical possibility of its impossibility. It is in each case only possible as the possibility of its impossibility. From the perspective of its de-ciding in the de-cision, Being is its making-(im)possible [*Ver(un)mögli-chung*]. And more precisely, in reverse, there is only Being in de-cision *by means of* its making-impossible [*Verunmöglichung*]. It only allows itself to be experi-enced as that which withdraws itself from experience. Its experience, and if it were different it would not be experience at all, is experience of the impos-sibility of an experience of Being. In each of *its* experiences, and for this reason there is not only one experience, rather an incalculable multiplicity of deci-sions, each singular but never complete, in each of *its* experiences it testifies to itself as something other, testifies to itself as something else because *itself*, it testifies itself something else as this thing that it is, testifies to its Not and its non-testimony. It (Being) de-testifies and de-materializes [*ent-zeugt*] itself. It *is* its withdrawal, its un-drawing [*Ent-zeichnung*], its dis-testimony [*Ent-zeugung*] — its heterogeneration [*Heterogeneration*] and anageneration. It *is* not, rather it is its Not. And therefore the Or as well, the word of decision, does not de-cide itself, it does not only give itself in withdrawal, it therefore does not give itself and gives its Not as long as it gives itself, it gives its dis-propriation alone, its separation alone and therefore gives itself out alone from its Not: as an Or-*Without*-Or, as an Or struckthrough, as an Or no longer legible *as* Or under its striking through. The Or multiplies and heterogenizes and expropriates: as dis-or, n-Or.

Nancy's sentences from 'La décision de l'existence' should be put into this context: 'This is not an auto-opening but rather an onto-opening. Or [*ou*] the auto- is here in the mode of the onto- which itself *exists* in the mode of the "they" [*du on*]'.[29] However, one should add, not only in the mode of the facticity of the one (*on*), but in the mode of an irretrievable beforehand of the de-ciding Or and of the de-cision of the Or [*ou*] in the mode of pre-facticity [*Antefaktizität*], of affacticity [*Affaktizität*].

Dasein, so writes Heidegger, is the epitome of *transcendence*. That means it decides each time and is decided on its Being in the impassable Beforehand of its possibilities. In view of this and the structure of the de-cision developed later, the sentence can be made more precise: *Dasein* is the epitome of *atranscendence*. That means it opens up its transcendence without ever being able to complete and hold it as such, it transcends without transcendence it is its ad- [*Ad-*] and its atranscendence. It can also be said that *Dasein* is exposed, as long as it is exposed, to an *or* and that this *or*, for its part, always has the structure of an *or-Without-or*. However, what would be a politics of atranscendence of the Or, of the dis-or: a politics that would not only oppose that of Heidegger from 1933–36 but also one which could open up one considerably different: a politics of the Or of democracy – one can read or not read this word - an *Or-cracy* [*eine Oukratie*]? (Every word – and the word 'word' itself – is exposed to its o.r. [*o.r.*] and to the de-cision of its o.r. . . .: politics of the other word, of the Allologism [*Allologismus*], of the opening and of the open decision of a word for another word and for another which still and never is a word: politics for another politics, which is not and never is *politics*: anapolitics, *ici, alibici.. . .*)

Translated by Ian H. Magedera[30]

Notes

1 [Translator's note. An earlier version of the first part of this piece '*Here. – Or here. Now. Or now*' was translated by Marian Hobson and Ian Magedera and appeared in *Paragraph* 16, 2 (July 1993), pp. 216–20.]

2 [Translator's note. *Der Bann* in German means 'spell', but also 'excommunication', and the author is playing on the two senses.]

3 [Translator's note. *Die Logik der Fort-setzung. Fortsetzung* suggests a spatial dimension, an active placing away from the here and now.]

4 Jean-Luc Nancy, 'L'être abandonné', in *L'Impératif catégorique* (Paris: Flammarion, 1983), p. 149.

5 Ibid., p. 150.

6 Ibid., p. 153.

7 Ibid., p. 152.

8 Ibid., p. 153.

9 [Translator's note. For the context see Kierkegaard's *Either/Or* I, trans. by H. V. Hong and E. H. Hong (Princeton: Princeton University Press, 1987), p. 38–9.]

10 [Translator's note. See *Either/Or* II, trans. by H. V. Kong and E. H. Kong (Princeton: Princeton University Press, 1988), 'The balance between aesthetic and the ethical in the development of the personality', p. 169.]

11 [Translator's note. 'Being' renders *Sein* and 'Beyng' translates *Seyn*.]

12 Martin Heidegger *Beiträge zur Philosophie (Vom Ereignis)*, *Gesamtausgabe* 65, ed. Friedrich-Wilhelm von Herrmann (Frankfurt am Main: Klostermann, 1989), henceforth *Contributions*.

13 *Contributions*, section 44, p. 95.

14 [Translator's note. 'La décision de l'existence', in Jean-Luc Nancy, *Une pensée finie* (Paris: Galilée, 1990), p. 134.]

15 *Contributions*, section 47, p. 102.

16 Ibid., section 44, pp. 90–1 (all emphases of 'or' are Heidegger's).

17 Ibid., section 45, p. 96.

18 Ibid., section 45, pp. 96–7.

19 After Heidegger has put the 'question of decision' in the Rectoral Address – 'should science continue to *be* for us, or should we have it driven to a speedy end?' – he writes, in a more explicit way than in the *Contributions*, 'do we, or do we not want the essence of the German University? It is up to us whether and how far we are to concern ourselves about the self-consciousness and self-assertion from the foundations upwards and not only in passing, or whether, with the best intentions, we change old institutions and bring in new ones . . . . However, no one will ask us whether or not we want this . . . . Whether such a thing happens or not is exclusively dependent on whether we will ourselves as a historico-spiritual people time and time again, or whether we do not will ourselves . . . . But we want our people to fulfil its historical task. We will ourselves. For the young and most youthful strength of the people which already reaches beyond us, *has* already *decided*' (Martin Heidegger, *Die Selbstbehauptung der deutschen Universität* (Frankfurt am Main: Klostermann, 1983) pp. 10, page 19.) The Rectoral Address does not only offer an existential-ontological theory of decision, which arms itself with voluntaristic and decisionistic theorems in order to conceal its structural impotence, it also completes by itself an existential decision in a practical, active and 'performative' manner – a decision for the existence of science, of will of Being in the Western sense – a decision for itself and it completes it, according to the logic of the singularity of Being, *as already completed*; the fact *that* 'we' will 'ourselves' and that the question of decision is already answered by this, if it is posed in this way, is not thanks to a decision that 'we' make and which therefore is open to other decisions and decisions by another, but it is thanks to a decision which has already been made – not by 'us' and not by others, but by the 'young and most youthful strength of the people' by the energy of the factical Being-with-others [*Sein-mit-anderen*] in its historical singularity, *hic et nunc*. In other words, an ontology of the decision which is founded in the singularity of this decision and in its unity with the 'essence' of this or that which makes this decision; this ontology of the decision is a theory and a praxis for which there is no decision any more (and therefore also no theory and no praxis), but rather merely the subordinate calling to what it has already achieved through 'our strength'. The existential ontology collaborates in the collaboration with factical power and its intrigues because it is still an ontology of power and the will to power.

20 *Une pensée finie*, p. 136.

21 Ibid., p. 137.

22 Jean-Luc Nancy, *L'expérience de la liberté* (Paris: Galilée, 1988) p. 175.

23 See 'Ou, séance, touche de Nancy, ici', *Paragraph* 16, 2 (July 1993) 227–8.

24 *Contributions*, section 43, p. 88.

25 Ibid., p. 87.

26 Here I only quote that sentence in which Heidegger expresses himself most clearly about the relationship of de-cision and system: 'In so far as the "system" contains the essential characteristic of modern beingness [*Seiendheit*] of beings (represented-ness [*die Vorgestelltheit*]) and in so far as the "decision" means Being for beings, not

only beingness from beings, then the de-cision is "more systematic" than any system in a certain way; that is an original definition of beings as such from the essence of Beyng' (*Contributions*, section 43, p. 89.) Heidegger might have approached the thought of also referring to system in a discussion of decision because the prefix 'de' ['*Ent*'] can be understood as an intensifier but can also be understood in isolation as a privative and de-cision can therefore mean the opposite of decision, that is to say, assembling and thus system. However, the de-cision is 'more systematic' than any system, in as far as it does not retrospectively assemble what is already to hand, but signifies its 'own' procedure in a Together, in Being. Heidegger does not say this often, but this Together is the Together in the apartness. The movement of difference is more 'systematic' than any system – it is 'systematic' *à l'outrance*.

27 *Contributions*, section 44, p. 91.
28 Ibid., section 49, p. 103.
29 *Une pensée finie*, p. 135.
30 The translator acknowledges with gratitude the advice of Miguel de Beistegui and Carol Tully.

6

Rashomon and the sharing of voices between East and West

Michael B. Naas

This chapter takes as its inspiration and point of departure from Jean-Luc Nancy's 'Sharing voices'. It is conceived as a parallel reading of Heidegger's 'A dialogue on language' in *On the Way to Language*. While Nancy's essay brilliantly demonstrates the role Plato's *Ion* plays in Heidegger's dialogue and the way a certain conception of interpretation on the margins of Plato's text accords with Heidegger's own conception, this work attempts to illuminate the very same issues of interpretation and the originary sharing out of voices by focusing on a reference on the margins of Heidegger's text – Akira Kurosawa's film *Rashomon*. The following is thus a philosophical experiment, an interpretive performance in thirty-six takes, that tries not only to demonstrate and analyse but to exhibit the originary sharing out of voices and the 'grounds' for the inoperative community to which Nancy's entire *oeuvre* bears witness. No words could better set the stage for such a performance than the following from 'Sharing voices':

> Thus, one analyzes all the details of the staging (and from the very first the choice of the *genre* of the dialogue, which presupposes a staging) in order to end in this: that which is staged is hermeneutics itself, in its infinite presupposition and in its 'enigmatic' character, which has been announced by Heidegger in his first response on this subject. He does not *respond* to the question because the dialogue – the text – is itself the response. It is the response insofar as it offers itself as the interpretation, as the deciphering of these figures, signs, or symbols, which are figures, signs and symbols of interpretation itself. The dialogue is both enigma and the figure of enigma.[1]

Michael B. Naas

I

The film opens with several different shots, from a variety of angles and perspectives, of the Rashomon, the half-ruined gate in Kyoto.[2] A veil of rain enshrouds the great gate, as the unsettling sounds of a torrential downpour peel off the screen in incessant, maddening waves. Like the disquieting chatter of unknown voices, the chilling rains evoke anticipation and suspense; they fill the sky and cover the ground, preventing characters from entering and dialogues from beginning. Only after several different shots, when the camera has moved beneath the Rashomon, can the dialogue begin, for this is the site of discourse, translation, and film, the site of an originary sharing out of voices, the place where East meets West and the living meet the dead.

II

The dialogue, '*A dialogue on language*', opens with this exchange:

Japanese: You know Count Shuzo Kuki. He studied with you for a number of years.
Inquirer: Count Kuki has a lasting place in my memory.
J: He died too early. His teacher Nishida wrote his epitaph – for over a year he worked on this supreme tribute to his pupil.
I: I am happy to have photographs of Kuki's grave and of the grove in which it lies.[3]

The dialogue 'between a Japanese and an Inquirer' is indeed *between* them. It is not a simple exchange between an Answerer and an Inquirer, between Professors Tezuka and Heidegger, but a venture that exceeds and threatens those who participate in it. In such a dialogue, identities are always at risk, and roles are often reversed, for the identities and roles are less important than the paths along which they travel. As the Inquirer would later write in *Identity and Difference*, a lecture in which his 'identity' is not disguised:

> When thinking attempts to pursue something that has claimed its attention, it may happen that on the way it undergoes a change. It is advisable, therefore, in what follows to pay attention to the path of thought rather than to its content.[4]

64

III

The story, entitled *In a Grove*, begins with the 'Testimony of a woodcutter questioned by a high police commissioner'.

> Yes, sir. Certainly, it was I who found the body. This morning, as usual, I went to cut my daily quota of cedars, when I found the body in a grove in a hollow in the mountains.[5]

The woodcutter had discovered the body of a man dressed in a bluish silk kimono who had been slain with a sword, though the weapon was nowhere to be found. Around his body were 'fallen bamboo leaves . . . stained with bloody blossoms' and pieces of severed rope at the foot of a cedar tree. Though the testimony is presented as a monologue, the woodcutter is clearly responding to the questions of an unidentified police inquirer. His testimony ends: 'A horse was nearby? No sir. It's hard enough for a man to enter, let alone a horse'.

In a Grove is the story of seven witnesses offering seven different perspectives on what one might be tempted to call 'the same event'.

IV

And so another story begins:

> It was a chilly evening. A samurai's servant stood under the Rashomon, waiting for a break in the rain.

The story is called *Rashomon*, and it, along with *In a Grove*, form the basis for the script of the 1950 film *Rashomon*. Both stories were written in Japanese by Ryunosuke Akutagawa, who committed suicide in 1927 at the young age of 35.

V

The film *Rashomon* thus incorporates two stories into a script and then frames them on a screen. One of the questions here, then, will be whether, in this transformation of script into film, in this framing of the written text by the photographic medium, these stories are not misunderstood, misappropriated or betrayed. Like a phantom forever joining and separating the living and the dead, the known and the unknown, this question will continue to haunt us, for the Rashomon is the site of not only translation, dialogue, and life, but betrayal, domination, and death. The Rashomon will come to avenge itself on itself by bringing death into life; it will come to betray and dismember itself, leaving itself, and thus the community that gathers beneath it, in ruins.

VI

During the opening sequence of shots, the title and credits are superimposed over the Rashomon, as is a series of oval insets of the characters/actors appearing in the film. By focusing so long on the Rashomon, the director, Akira Kurosawa, makes sure that his viewers will frame and take this image with them to hang in some dark hall of memory as a reminder, substitute, or representation of what they once saw. Like a gigantic Japanese character on an ageing manuscript, the half-ruined gate against the dark grey sky has, for many viewers, a lasting place in their memory.

Traditional Japanese music plays in the background as the rains continue to fall. Finally, a caption appears on the screen, the only inscription of the film, save the English subtitles and the gate's signboard with its large Japanese characters and the superimposed transliteration, or romanization, 'Rashomon'. No Japanese characters appear near the caption, for they have been replaced by the language and writing of the West:

Kyoto, in the twelfth century, when famines and civil wars had devastated the ancient capital.

The camera finally moves beneath the Rashomon to focus on an unnamed priest and an unidentified woodcutter. Both sit silently and motionlessly under the Rashomon, staring into the devouring rain. After a long silence, the woodcutter says, 'I can't understand it. I just can't understand it at all'. These are the first lines of the film, spoken, framed, recorded, translated and subtitled beneath the Rashomon.

VII

The conversation on which the dialogue between a Japanese and an Inquirer is based took place in Germany in 1953. 'A dialogue on language' is thus the Inquirer's reformulation of the transcript of a conversation that took place three years after the premiere of *Rashomon* in Tokyo. Having said that he was happy to have 'photographs of Kuki's grave and of the grove in which it lies', the Japanese responds:

J: Yes, I know the temple garden in Kyoto. Many of my friends often join me to visit the tomb there. The garden was established toward the end of the twelfth century by the priest Honen, on the eastern hill of what was then the Imperial city of Kyoto, as a place for reflection and deep meditation.

I: And so, that temple grove remains the fitting place for him who died early.

VIII

After the testimony of the woodcutter, a travelling Buddhist priest is questioned by the unidentified police inquirer. The priest had seen the victim, armed with a sword and bow, riding a sorrel horse with his wife on the road to Yamashina just the day before. The witness remembers the wife's lilac-coloured suit and the scarf that hung down over her face, but being a Buddhist priest, he 'took little notice about her details'. The testimony takes place during a police inquest at Kyoto, in a site of discourse and disclosure as well as betrayal and deception. This sign, this gate: *In a Grove*.

IX

The samurai's servant sat under the protective covering of the Rashomon, 'waiting for a break in the rain'. Disowned by his master, he was forced to seek refuge under the gate. It was the twelfth century in Kyoto, and the ancient capital had been plagued by a series of 'calamities, earthquakes, whirlwinds, and fires'. Wild animals, robbers, and murderers all sought shelter under the ruins of the Rashomon. 'Eventually it became customary to bring unclaimed corpses to this gate and abandon them.'

X

Rashomon and *In a Grove* were transformed into a script in 1948 but owing to a lack of financial backing the film could not be completed until 1950. A year after opening in Tokyo, the film was translated, subtitled, and transported to New York for its US opening. Akutagawa's short stories were themselves translated into English in the following year.

XI

After the woodcutter has spoken, a commoner, also unidentified, joins the priest and the woodcutter on the screen, in the frame of the Rashomon.

Priest: Oh, even Abbot Konin of the Kiyomizu Temple, though he's known for his learning, wouldn't be able to understand this . . .. A man has been murdered.

Commoner: Only one? Why, if you go up to the top of this gate you'll always find five or six bodies. Nobody bothers about them.

Priest: Oh, you're right. Wars, earthquakes, great winds, fires, famines, plagues – each new year is full of disaster.

In the twelfth century in Kyoto violent, unnatural death is commonplace; many die too early. Yet the priest's troubled thoughts are not so easily assuaged.

Priest: There was never anything as terrible as this. Never. It is more horrible than fires or wars or epidemics – or bandits.

The commoner asks to hear the details of the story as they wait for the rains to end. The camera focuses on the signboard fastened to the great gate. We Westerners cannot 'read' these letters or characters directly, but we are given their English 'equivalent' – 'Rashomon'. Thanks to this transliteration, the transparent relation between character and referent is momentarily disrupted, as the signboard is revealed to be the site of the sign itself, the place where one sign, medium, or language is both connected to and separated from another. It is thus not surprising that in the following shot the camera assumes the very position of the signboard, framing the three characters from above, filming them from the place where the inside is protected from and joined to the outside, from the place of the great divide.

Beneath the Rashomon, then, a site for dialogue and memory is prepared, so that what was once outside can be brought inside. A series of flashbacks, the narrative takes place between the past and present. Inscribed within the Rashomon is the conversation between the woodcutter, the commoner, and the priest, while within their memories are inscribed the testimonies of the police agent, the bandit, the wife, and the medium. The woodcutter travels back in time to his testimony before the police commissioner, which is itself a return to the discovery of the body in the grove. Between passive mediation and active narration, the past is retrieved and brought into the protective clearing of the half-ruined gate.

Glimpses of sunlight flash through the trees as the woodcutter hastens through the grove along winding wooded paths. The camera, or cameras, follow him from a variety of angles and perspectives, cutting from place to place, appearing and disappearing as if trying to trace and reveal the circuitous and fragmented path of the past as it is projected upon the screens of memory. These flashes, the lights and shadows of recollection, move according to a logic that is neither necessary nor arbitrary. For it is not the direction of the movement or the origin of the memory that is most significant here, but the movement of memory itself.

Out of the past, moving into the future, between conscious intention and subconscious disclosure, the woodcutter reveals and conceals, betrays and defers. With just a few modifications, he follows the lines of *In a Grove*. He had been walking along a wooded path, looking for his daily quota of cedar wood, when he discovered the body of a man who had died at an early age.

XII

Count Kuki had gone to Germany in the 1920s to attend the lectures of Martin Heidegger. He had tried to explain to Heidegger the meaning of the Japanese word *Iki*, which, Heidegger thought, might be similar to certain notions of Western aesthetics. But Heidegger was constantly fearful of imposing terms and concepts that would not only translate but also transform and betray Eastern ways of thinking. While the Western thinker is always concerned with a series of oppositions between inside and outside, reality and appearance, suprasensuous and sensuous, and soon, such oppositions may not structure the thought of the Easterner, even though the Easterner might wish that they did.

J: Aesthetics furnishes us with the concepts to grasp what is of concern to us as art and poetry.

I: Do you need concepts?

J: Presumably yes, because since the encounter with European thinking, there has come to light a certain incapacity in our language . . . .. It lacks the delimiting power to represent objects related in an unequivocal order above and below each other.

I: Do you seriously regard this incapacity as a deficiency of your language?

The Inquirer intimates that what is perceived as the cure for a deficiency may in fact be a 'dangerous supplement', something that not only adds to but also supplants an entire way of thinking. Could it be, asks the Inquirer, that in spite of the West's economic and social influence on the East, in spite of the 'technicalization and industrialization' of it, 'a true encounter with European existence is still not taking place'?

In this question the danger is both indicated and multiplied. Arising in the midst of the dialogue between the Japanese and the Inquirer, the question implies that a 'true encounter' between them may not be, and may not have been, taking place. Around this danger the dialogue constantly circles, moving closer and closer, as if propelled by a necessary logic, to a series of differences inscribed in the midst and from the beginning of the dialogue, and explicitly revealed at the propitious moment when the dialogue turns to *Rashomon*.

XIII

After the Buddhist priest, the police agent who had identified and arrested the notorious bandit Tajomaru is questioned. He had discovered Tajomaru riding a sorrel horse similar to the one the Buddhist priest had seen the victim riding the day before.

XIV

Beneath the Rashomon, the samurai's servant sat 'vacantly watching the rain'. As he gazed out, 'his attention was drawn to a large pimple irritating his right cheek'. We too, as readers, are drawn to this festering sore, for something seems foreshadowed, hinted at, perhaps even represented by it. Like a clearing in a forest stained by human blood, this irritation of the skin will soon be drawn inside, inscribed within the man, for it will prove to be a symptom of something that will have been there from the beginning.

XV

The Japanese and the Inquirer are concerned that by discussing Japanese art within a Western language structure and, thus, metaphysics, the bifurcation of inner and outer, sensuous and suprasensuous, will force itself upon the Eastern world. The Inquirer is thus as much concerned with the movement of the conversation as with its content. For instead of leading to a hollow in the grove, the dialogue may be marked by the hollow throughout. The risk of deception and infection may reside not so much in the content of the dialogue as in its language. With the end inscribed in the beginning, the place of risk is perhaps both nowhere and everywhere.

I: The danger is threatening from a region where we do not suspect it, and which is yet precisely the region where we would have to experience it.

J: You have, then, experienced it already; otherwise you could not point it out.

I: I am far from having experienced the danger to its full extent, but I have sensed it – in my conversations with Count Kuki.

J: Did you speak with him about it?

I: The danger arose from the dialogues themselves, in that they were dialogues.

The Inquirer says that the danger of the dialogue was 'hidden in language itself'. But how did he detect it? Can the difference between East and West be experienced without being understood or articulated?

J: The language of the dialogue constantly destroyed the possibility of saying what the dialogue was about.

And yet the dialogue was about language, about the difference between East and West. To speak of the difference between East and West is thus to speak of the danger from within the danger, it is at once to speak the danger and fall prey to it. Indeed, the danger is that the danger must remain concealed. Between speaking and silence, then, the danger is detected, so that it is neither a question of speaking the unspeakable nor of remaining silent in the face of what must be spoken, but of 'hinting' at the place of danger and difference, the Rashomon.

XVI

After the police agent has testified, an old woman is questioned. Though grief-stricken and frightened, the woman is hungry for revenge, for it was her son-in-law who was found dead in the grove and her own daughter who, at the time of the inquest, remained missing. She describes her daughter in just one short paragraph, but reveals two curious details:

> She is a spirited, fun-loving girl, but I am sure she has never known any man except [her husband]. She has a small, oval, dark-complexioned face with a mole at the corner of her left eye.

Inside and outside: this mole, like a pimple on a face or a hollow in a grove, is situated between opposing human desires. This mole, of which the Buddhist priest took no notice, lies between the known and the unknown. A woman's son-in-law has apparently been killed by a notorious bandit, her daughter is still missing; no one has questioned the daughter's honour, and yet her mother feels obliged to defend it.

The old woman is the fourth to testify before the silent inquirer, the police commissioner who is spoken to but never speaks. Inquisitive, always searching for clues, trying to make sense of the whole, and yet silent, the police inquirer bears a striking resemblance to the reader, to a certain sort of reader, to a hermeneute in the classical sense.

XVII

The samurai's servant had drifted aimlessly through the streets of Kyoto looking for shelter before happening upon the Rashomon. Though he knew that he would have to steal in order to survive, 'he was still unable to muster enough courage to justify the conclusion that he must become a thief'. Huddled beneath the Rashomon, he shared the darkness of the night with wild animals and abandoned corpses. He considered himself to be in ruins, like the gate itself. But the festering pimple on his right cheek was a sign that at this hinge between life and death a site was being prepared for decision and dialogue.

XVIII

The Inquirer once called language the 'house of Being'. Is it possible, he now asks, that the Eastern world dwells in an entirely different house from the Western world, making a dialogue between them 'nearly impossible'? In 'A dialogue on language' neither the Japanese nor the Inquirer can avoid this perilous question, but it seems that one must engage in dialogue before asking whether it is genuine, to begin translating before asking whether translation is possible. Because there is no privileged question or place from which to start, the rules and conditions of dialogue cannot be established in advance. If these rules and conditions are thus to become themselves the subject of inquiry, they are to be encountered not outside or before the path, but already along the way.

XIX

After the old woman has spoken, the bandit, Tajomaru, delivers his confession. He had seen the man and his wife on the road to Yamashina a little past noon on the previous day. As they rode by, a slight gust of wind blew and 'raised [the wife's] hanging scarf. Instantly it was again covered from my view. That may have been one reason; she looked like a Bodhisattva'. Hence Tajomaru must have seen, unlike the Buddhist priest, the woman's 'small, oval, dark-complexioned face' and the 'mole at the corner of her left eye'.

Reconstructing the crime, a faceless and unidentified reader might imagine Tajomaru, catching a glimpse of this mole and then, in a flash of insight and desire, devising a plan to lure her and her husband into the hollow of the grove. Like the festering sore on the cheek of the samurai's servant, this mole both represents a site of decision and enters into its play of differences. Both a sensuous representation of the suprasensuous, internal state that stands above or before it, an objective correlative in the terms of Western aesthetics, and a site where the differences between presence and absence, sensuous and suprasensuous, are put into play, this mole brings with it all the questions of a dialogue between East and West. Both a symbol of the hollow in the grove, a mere symptom of desire, decision, violence, and betrayal, and a site of traces and displacements behind which there are only more traces and veils, this mole both reaffirms and calls into question an entire system of metaphysical oppositions.

A gust of wind momentarily lifted the veiling scarf and Tajomaru, catching a glimpse of this unconcealed mark, this presence of absence, took a stab at a description, though such a description was impossible. Lifting the scarf, he pierced the veil with a simile: 'she looked like a Bodhisattva'. Having thus transgressed in speech, Tajomaru confesses to murder:

> To me killing isn't a matter of such great consequence as you might think.
> When a woman is captured, her man has to be killed anyway. In killing I
> use the sword I wear at my side.

Tajomaru's confession is clear and concise, bereft, it would seem, of any traces of abstract morality. He acted quickly and decisively, without hesitation or abstract moral consideration, according to a code that treats killing as an ordinary unambiguous affair. But the Eastern bandit with his rustic innocence is soon unmasked, revealing, at least to the Western eye, a moralizing, noble savage.

> Am I the only one who kills people? You, you don't use your swords. You
> kill people with your power, with your money. Sometimes you kill them on
> the pretext of working for their good. It's true they don't bleed. They are
> in the best of health, but all the same you've killed them. It's hard to say
> who is a greater sinner, you or me. (*An ironical smile.*)

Because he lives outside a corrupt society, Tajomaru claims the right to pronounce the judgement of 'sinner'. Is this what the Inquirer would call the 'fateful encounter of East and West'? Has an abstract morality added to, and displaced, an ancient code or practice?

Tajomaru had lured the couple into the mountains by promising them a bargain on some old swords and mirrors. He had practised his craft with intelligence and skill, but once again he cannot let his actions speak for themselves; the mirrors reflect the lurer as well as the lured. 'Then . . . you see, isn't greed terrible? He was beginning to be moved by my talk before he knew it.' Is this type of irony, this elevated, moralizing tone, something previously unknown to the East or has it always existed? Does the mirror's image entail the opposition between reality and image, righteous and unrighteous, indeed, dialogue and film?

While the woman waited at the foot of the mountain, Tajomaru led her husband deep into the grove. When they had reached a small clearing, Tajomaru grabbed him from behind, disarmed him, and tied him to a cedar tree: 'it was easy to stop him from calling out by gagging his mouth with fallen bamboo leaves'. Tajomaru then retrieved the woman, who, at the sight of her bound husband, drew her small sword and attacked the bandit. Though she put up a good struggle, Tajomaru was quickly able to disarm her and 'satisfy [his] desire'.

XX

In the film *Rashomon*, the site of discourse unveils the sight of memory, as the woodcutter relates the different testimonies given in front of the police inquirer on the previous day. A woman's unveiled face leads all the major characters into the hollow of the grove. The man is disarmed of his sword, the woman draws hers, a smaller version, and is quickly subdued. All the action takes place in the hollow of the grove, while the events of the hollow are narrated, through voice and memory, under the protective clearing of the Rashomon. The hollow in the grove and the Rashomon are thus inscribed within each other, for just as the outside is brought inside through memory, so the inside is projected outside through film.

XXI

Violated by the bandit, the woman said that she could not accept the shame of being 'known' by two men. She said that she would rather see her husband killed than live with a stain on her honour. Though Tajomaru had decided not to kill the man, he was forced to abide by the code of honour – the code that was supposed to be the face, but was, it seems, the mask. Having agreed to duel until death, Tajomaru released the man from his bonds and gave him back his sword.

> Furious with anger, he drew his thick sword. And quick as a wink, he sprang at me ferociously, without speaking a word. I needn't tell you how our fight turned out. The twenty-third stroke . . . please remember this. I'm impressed with this fact still. Nobody under the sun has ever clashed with me twenty strokes.

As *In a Grove* develops, the testimonies of all the major characters are cast in a strange and dubious light. Facts become indiscernable from lies, and objective events, indistinguishable from personal fantasies. Even the lines between East and West are obscured, for Tajomaru's description of the duel is reminiscent of many late nineteenth-century Western novels (Thomas Hardy, for example) where the duel is a representation or presentiment of a sexual encounter or competition. Where, then, should one locate the difference between East and West, where is the East ultimately betrayed by Western representation: in the postwar films of Kurosawa, or in the stories of Akutagawa, a half-century earlier?

XXII

Having seen her husband killed in the duel, the woman flees into the grove in the film version of *Rashomon*. Tajomaru quickly pursues her, leaving the hollow empty for several seconds, empty save for the lifeless body of the husband, the bamboo leaves stained with blood, and the eye of the viewer that turns to behold itself. Between life and death, speech and silence, this is the site of memory and film, the site, perhaps, of an unavowable community.

XXIII

Trying to fall asleep beneath the Rashomon, the samurai's servant was startled by a movement above him. Lifting himself up, he gazed with both fear and curiosity upon an unidentifiable human form moving in the reddish glow of the fire. But before this form can be identified, the reader's attention and vision are once again displaced. 'A light coming from the upper part of the tower shone faintly upon his right cheek. It was the cheek with the red festering pimple visible under his stubby whiskers.'

But visible to whom? Glimpsed from afar by a narrator, reader, thief or inquirer, this pimple stands out like a mole on the side of a young woman's face; it is the mark of a displacement and the scene of a crime. At the limits of presence, it marks the threshold of a transgression, the decision of all reading.

XXIV

In 1921 Martin Heidegger gave a course entitled 'Expression and appearance', a series of lectures transcribed in Germany and later brought to Japan. Thirty-two years after the course was given, Heidegger, going by the name of an unnamed Inquirer, had this to say about it:

I: Transcripts are muddy sources, of course; what is more, the course was most imperfect. Yet there was quickening in it the attempt to walk a path of which I did not know where it would lead. I knew only the most immediate short-range perspectives along the path, because they beckoned to me unceasingly, while the horizon shifted and darkened more than once.

Transcripts, testimonies, and memories are thus always ambiguous, always fragmentary, not because representation is always imperfect, but because that which is represented is never singular, never fully present, never itself. The origin of this multiplicity of perspectives and memories, the common ground of Orient and Occident, the site of this originary sharing out, is, of course, the Rashomon, but the Rashomon is simply the medium between story and film, narration and transcription, dialogue and subtitle, East and West. Out of the clearing of the Rashomon, action, memory, and translation all emerge, only to return to a Rashomon that is no longer itself and always in ruins.

The Inquirer and the Japanese would like to embrace the possibility of a common origin of language, a 'source' that would remain 'concealed from both language worlds', a common metaphysical ground, but the movement of the dialogue constantly disrupts this possibility. The danger in and of the dialogue continues to drive the Japanese and the Inquirer forward towards the origin, towards a common ground that is always being rent asunder by a sort of perpetual tremor. As the Inquirer says, the 'origin always comes to meet us from the future', the origin that reveals both the possibility of a dialogue between East and West and the fear that such a dialogue has never taken place.

XXV

We are concerned here, clearly, not merely with the English version of *Rashomon* but with 'version' itself. What is turned, changed, or translated in a version? How does one translate written stories into images, or spoken words into subtitles? How is version or translation to be thought in itself?

Because 'translation' is itself a translation, because it is not an invisible passageway connecting two distinct languages or houses of Being, it must always exceed itself and go by a name that is not its own. Because it has nothing proper to it, it must always go under an alias; *die Übersetzung, hon'yaku* are just two of its names. These names simultaneously reveal and conceal the identity of translation, for the hinge or gate between one language and another must betray itself in order to be named, in order to be itself, the place where the name is given. An ongoing process of construction and destruction, translation, like the Rashomon, is always in ruins; it is the trace of and passageway to itself. There is, therefore, no exterior from which one may objectively translate by plucking essences or meanings from the flesh of one language in order to insert them into another. This does not condemn us to radical subjectivity but, rather, situates us between subjectivity and objectivity, where differing testimonies of the 'same event' need not be interpreted as either in objective agreement or subjective discord. As in translation, the various perspectives and versions of a single event always return to their common origin, in this case, the Rashomon; they always return, but only by means of an endless series of detours and displacements.

XXVI

Just as Tajomaru ends his confession, the dead man's wife arrives unexpectedly at the inquest. She begins her testimony: 'That man in the blue silk kimono, after forcing me to yield to him, laughed mockingly as he looked at my bound husband. How horrified my husband must have been!'. The woman tried desperately to reach her husband at the foot of the cedar tree, but Tajomaru struck her to the ground. When she got up, her attention was drawn not to Tajomaru but to an 'indescribable light' in her husband's eyes.

Something beyond expression . . . his eyes make me shudder even now. That instantaneous look of my husband, who couldn't speak a word, told me all his heart. The flash in his eyes was neither anger nor sorrow . . . only a cold light, a look of loathing.

77

Identities and differences, we have seen these images before: the look beyond expression, the instantaneous flash, and the difference between speaking and silence.

Overwhelmed by the look in her husband's eyes, the woman fell unconscious. When she came to, Tajomaru had gone, but the look of loathing in her husband's eyes had not. Shamed and dishonoured, she resolved to kill both her husband and herself. Noticing that Tajomaru had taken her husband's sword, she decided to use her own small sword that had fallen to the ground. In spite of the bamboo leaves in her husband's mouth, she could hear him say with contempt, 'Kill me!': 'Neither conscious nor unconscious, I stabbed the small sword through the lilac-coloured kimono into his breast.'

Having killed her husband at the limits of consciousness, the woman cut the ropes off his dead body and fell unconscious once again. When she revived, she could not find the strength to kill herself; she stabbed herself in the throat and threw herself in a pond but was unable to end her life. She concludes:

I killed my own husband. I was violated by the robber. Whatever can I do? Whatever can I . . . I . . . (*Gradually, violent sobbing.*)

So the attacked becomes the attacker, the words of sadness, the words of contempt, and the murder, a duel and then a mercy killing. A woodcutter finds a body along with pieces of severed rope in the hollow of a grove, but he does not find the sword that pierced the victim's breast. All these clues for reading and viewing.

XXVII

In the glow of the fire beneath the Rashomon, the frightened servant gazed in disbelief at the decomposed corpses strewn across the floor. 'One would doubt that they had ever been alive, so eternally silent were they.' Then he saw, bent over one of the corpses, the 'ghoulish form' of an 'old woman, gaunt, gray-haired and nunish in appearance'.

As he watched, terrified, she wedged the torch between two floor boards and, laying hands on the head of the corpse, began to pull out the long hairs one by one, as a monkey kills the lice of her young.

Watching this spectacle, the servant's horror turned to hatred, becoming a 'consuming antipathy against all evil'. Had he been asked at that moment to choose between stealing and starving, 'he would not have hesitated to choose death'. Was this ghoulish form a messenger from the underworld, coming in the night as the medium between life and death, or just another poor woman of Kyoto trying to steal what she could from the dead?

XXVIII

Asked by the Japanese about the etymology and meaning of the word 'hermeneutics', the Inquirer, instead of giving a direct answer, suggests listening to the message that is borne by the question itself.

I: for the matter is enigmatic, and perhaps we are not dealing with a matter at all.

Neither a word nor a concept but the very medium between word and concept, hermeneutics can be understood, the Inquirer says, only by following a certain path of thinking – a path difficult to find, no doubt, but one that he and the Japanese have perhaps never left.

I: . . . ways of thinking hold within them that mysterious quality that we can walk them forward and backward, and that indeed only the way back will lead us forward . . . .. 'Fore' – into that nearest nearness which we constantly rush ahead of, and which strikes us as strange each time anew when we catch sight of it.

A gust of wind uplifts a scarf and reveals a mole, a fire's glow illuminates a festering sore, a woodcutter travels along winding paths to a hollow in a grove, and a commoner seeks refuge from the cold and rain beneath the Rashomon. Each time these clearings are discovered, they strike us as strange and mysterious, but because we constantly overlook 'the presence that springs from the mutual calling of origin and future', we catch a glimpse of them only rarely. Because these clearings are so near, always just around the corner or just beneath the veil, we, the faceless readers, writers, and viewers beneath the Rashomon, abandon these places of difference where we always already live to move into concepts and metaphysics. Because they are so near, at the very threshold of the visible, they end up getting defined, understood, mastered, and thereby overlooked. This betrayal of the Rashomon is no doubt essential, but because the gate between sensuous and suprasensuous, here and beyond, so often leads to the privileged side of the opposition, to the suprasensuous and the beyond, the gate itself is constantly overlooked. Should we, then, simply focus our attention on these gates, limits, and thresholds? Or must we, because of the dangers of 'focusing attention', proceed like the Inquirer and the Japanese by way of hints?

Because translation describes the very practice of which it is the trace, because it is its own trace, and because 'Rashomon' names, using a Western script, the place of the sharing out between East and West, one cannot focus on translation or the Rashomon without missing them. Thinking must, it seems, focus otherwise, so as to abandon itself to the sharing out of voices that it can never grasp.

J: We Japanese do not think it strange if a dialogue leaves undefined what is really intended, or even restores it back to the keeping of the undefinable.
I: That is part, I believe, of every dialogue that has turned out well between thinking beings. As if of its own accord, it can take care that that undefinable something not only does not slip away, but displays its gathering force ever more luminously in the course of the dialogue.

Indeed *this* discourse or experiment too follows an uncertain path, circling back to itself from time to time not because of an aesthetic principle of circularity or repetition but 'of its own accord'. It too is its own trace, writing itself where writing leaves off, between different media, testimonies, and time frames, between one story in the past, one in the present, and a dialogue that continually defers and anticipates its future. This discourse, like the dialogue 'within' it, thus moves ahead to its origins, the conversation between Heidegger and Kuki and the differences between East and West.

I: The manner in which Kuki explained the basic word *Iki*. He spoke of sensuous radiance through whose lively delight there breaks the radiance of something suprasensuous.
J: With that explanation, I believe, Kuki has hit on what we experience in Japanese art.
I: Your experience, then, moves within the difference between a sensuous and a suprasensuous world. This is the distinction on which rests what has long been called Western metaphysics.

Though Kuki's definition seems to rely upon a Western metaphysical distinction, both the Japanese and the Inquirer are hesitant about interpreting a similarity as sameness, since to do so would be to force a second metaphysical distinction upon a world that may not have accommodated the first.

J: Our thinking, if I am allowed to call it that, does know something similar to the metaphysical distinction; but even so, the distinction itself and what it distinguishes cannot be comprehended with Western metaphysical concepts. We say *Iro*, that is, color, and say *Ku*, that is, emptiness, the open, the sky. We say: without *Iro*, no *Ku*.

In the midst of the dialogue, then, a similarity between East and West is detected, but this similarity leads 'of its own accord' to the suspicion and fear that a dialogue may not be taking place.

I: The *aistheton*, what can be perceived by the senses, lets the *noeton*, the nonsensuous, shine through. [. . . But] even greater was and still is my fear that in this way the real nature of East-Asian art is obscured and shunted into a realm that is inappropriate to it.

J: I fully share your fear; for while *Iro* does indeed name color, it yet means essentially more than whatever is perceptible by the senses. *Ku* does indeed name emptiness and the open, and yet it means essentially more than that which is merely suprasensuous.

Can the dialogue speak of sameness or difference without already betraying what is to be spoken about? Between speaking and silence, in the place where the speechless speak and the speakers remain silent, language, which is also a trace of itself, both a description and a practice, appears and disappears. Between dialogue and subtitle, speech and writing, we will perhaps hear these foreign characters speak, though their mouths and voices be muted with fallen leaves, if they should say to us, 'Kill me!' At the limits of discourse, the living must even speak with the dead.

XXIX

The last of the seven witnesses to testify before the police inquirer is the victim. He speaks through an alias, through a body that is not his own – that is, through a medium. Possessed by the spirit of the dead man, the medium represents and supplants the man who is forever silenced. In the medium, a site is cleared for language and discourse, like a hollow in a grove, or a covering in the rain, or a sore festering on the face of indecision. As the mediator or messenger between two realms, the medium, like Hermes, dwells in the undecidability of the Rashomon, translating the testimony of the dead into the language of the living.

Having seen his wife raped by Tajomaru, the man watched helplessly and with horror as the bandit, using his 'clever talk', seduced her into leaving with him. As they were about to leave the hollow, however, the wife suddenly demanded that Tajomaru kill her husband.

> Even now these words threaten to blow me headlong into the bottomless abyss of darkness. Has such a hateful thing come out of a human mouth ever before?

Even Tajomaru 'turned pale' at the wife's viciousness and disloyalty.

> Quietly folding his arms, he looked at me and said, 'What would you like done with her? Kill her or save her? You have only to nod. Kill her?' For these words alone I would like to pardon his crime.

As Tajomaru spoke to the man, the wife fled into the grove, and Tajomaru, after releasing the man from his bonds, ran after her. Thus the hollow was left empty, save the man, the severed ropes, and the small sword that the woman had dropped. Dishonoured and betrayed, the man took the small sword and plunged it into his breast. But then:

> someone crept up to me. I tried to see who it was. But darkness had already been gathering around me. Someone . . . that someone drew the small sword softly out of my breast in its invisible hand. At the same time blood again flowed into my mouth. And once and for all I sank down into the darkness of space.

With these, the final words of the seventh testimony, the story ends, radically undecidable, as the silence of the empty grove speaks of identity and difference, theft and discovery, rape and seduction, honour and lust, murder and suicide, truth and deceit. Not even the testimony of the dead is beyond reproach, for mediation is another name for suspicion, and that which is not mediated cannot come on the scene. Though a reader might wish to reconstruct, like a good police enquirer, the 'actual crime', such a reconstruction is always frustrated in In a Grove, for it is the story of many crimes, always trying, but never able, to resolve themselves into a coherent whole, and always disclosing not so much an event but a *between*, a sharing out of voices. Though another writer might have betrayed, through factual discrepancies and character portrayals, the exact motives and intentions of each testimony, Akutagawa offers no such synthesis or resolution.

In the 'darkness of space', where the living go down to meet the dead, the medium translates between different realms and media, between life and death, story and history, film and writing, twelfth-century Kyoto and the present, the dead man of *In a Grove* and Ryunosuke Akutagawa, or Count Shuzo Kuki. Between one death and another: the Rashomon stands in ruins.

XXX

As the samurai's servant watched the old woman pulling hair from the corpse's head, his rage grew uncontrollable. With one hand on his sword, he crept up behind her, knocked her down, and 'thrust the silver-white blade before her very nose'. He assured her that he was not from the police but wanted to know why she had come to the Rashomon in the middle of the night to pull hair off the dead. Standing there at the limits of morality, where one is neither guilty nor innocent, the samurai's servant had no interest in passing judgement on the old woman. He had arrived at the place of decision; the festering sore was ready to burst.

XXXI

A third of the way through 'A dialogue on language', the Inquirer returns to the origin of the dialogue, to memory, in order to be embraced by hope and then consumed by fear. Just as *this* essay will move between two endings of *Rashomon*, one of hope and one of fear, so the dialogue moves to a place where hopes are inscribed in the midst of fears and vice versa. These origins and differences, inscribed in the dialogue from the very outset, bring us to the threshold of the Rashomon, that is, to the threshold of the threshold.

I: Your suggestions, which I can follow only from afar, increase my uneasiness. Even greater than the fear I mentioned is the expectation within me that our conversation, which has grown out of our memory of Count Kuki, could turn out well.

J: You mean it could bring us nearer to what is unsaid?

I: That alone would give us an abundance to think on.

J: Why do you say 'would'?

I: Because I now see still more clearly the danger that the language of our dialogue might constantly destroy the possibility of saying that of which we are speaking.

J: Because this language itself rests on the metaphysical distinction between the sensuous and the suprasensuous, in that the structure of the language is supported by the basic elements of sound and script on the one hand, and significance and sense on the other.

I: At least within the purview of European ideas. Or is the situation the same with you?

J: Hardly. But, as I indicated, the temptation is great to rely on European ways of representation and their concepts.

I: That temptation is reinforced by a process which I would call the complete Europeanization of the earth and of man.

By means of what logic are uneasiness, danger, fear, and temptation linked to origins, memories, concepts, and representations? On the brink of the *Rashomon*, the Inquirer refers to the origin of his fears and expectations but then ignores, suppresses, or forgets it: 'our conversation . . . has grown out of our memory of Count Kuki'.

For as the dialogue opens, and not only words but roles are exchanged, the Inquirer responds to a question of the Japanese: 'Count Kuki has a lasting place in my memory'. But we may recall, and it is the way we recall that is at issue here, that there was another place where Count Kuki, or the memories of him, had found a lasting place – in the 'photographs of [his] grave and of the grove in which it lies'. The Inquirer thus shifts of his own accord, it seems, from memory to photographs, as if he assumed there were a significant link between them. So that when he returns later in the dialogue to memory, to a memory that he now attributes to both himself and the Japanese ('our memory', he says), he experiences danger and uneasiness, as if the assumed link between memory and photographs had risen from the grave to avenge itself on the dialogue and threaten it retrospectively from the beginning. For the fear now arises, though it remains unspoken, that the conversation never had a single origin, that the common ground had been shaking all along, that a few simple photographs had given it all away.

Indeed, the dialogue seems to begin, before any theoretical discussion of Eastern and Western aesthetics, on perfectly common grounds – the temple grove in Kyoto and the memory of a mutual friend. But a third of the way into the dialogue, in the midst of a 'purely' theoretical discussion about aesthetics, a suspicion arises, seemingly inconsequential with regard to the possibilities of a dialogue between East and West, that the Eastern world is incompatible with the medium of photography. It is at this moment that we, the unnamed inquirers, always looking for clues, remember the incriminating photographs

84

of Kuki and his grave – incriminating precisely because they are photographs. These photographs thus return to frame and betray the dialogue in which they are enframed, since a technical, Western mode of representation cannot, it seems, be the common origin of a dialogue between East and West. And so no origin is innocent, as even the small talk that precedes a theory can undermine that theory, and taking out a photograph album to share with friends is never without consequence for those friends.

'A dialogue on language' suggests that in the West an essential link exists between memory, reflection, representation, and the photograph. This ascendancy of objectifying, visual memory is the result of what the Inquirer calls the 'Europeanization of earth and man'. By calling to mind a photograph in his recollection of Count Kuki, the Inquirer casts suspicion over 'our memory', the origin of what was assumed to be a dialogue between East and West.

With all these fears and expectations raised in advance, it is not surprising that the dialogue should turn of its own accord to the site of all our reflection.

J: The incontestable dominance of your European reason is thought to be confirmed by the success of that rationality which technical advances set before us at every turn.

I: This delusion is growing, so that we are no longer able to see how the Europeanization of man and of the earth attacks at the source everything that is of an essential nature. It seems that these sources are to dry up.

J: A striking example for what you have in mind is the internationally known film *Rashomon*. Perhaps you have seen it?

I: Fortunately yes; unfortunately, only once. I believed that I was experiencing the enchantment of the Japanese world, the enchantment that carried us away into the mysterious. And so I do not understand why you offer just this film as an example of an all-consuming Europeanization.

J: We Japanese consider the presentation frequently too realistic, for example in the dueling scenes.

I: . . . As long as you speak of realism, you are talking the language of metaphysics, and move within the distinction between the real as sensuous, and the ideal as nonsensuous.

J: . . . Ultimately, I did mean something else altogether with my reference to realism in the film – this, that the Japanese world is captured and imprisoned at all in the objectness of photography, and is in fact especially framed for photography.

85

I: If I have listened rightly, you would say that the East-Asian world, and the technical–aesthetic product of the film industry, are incompatible.

J: That is what I have in mind. Regardless of what the aesthetic quality of a Japanese film may turn out to be, the mere fact that our world is set forth in the frame of a film forces that world into the sphere of what you call objectness. The photographic objectification is already a consequence of the ever wider outreach of Europeanization.

I: A European will find it difficult to understand what you mean.

The Japanese claims, in effect, that the Eastern world is betrayed when it is framed, that the film adds to and betrays the script, that the frame displaces the subject, that the photograph usurps the memory of the friend, that the West frames and thereby supplants the East. But we have discovered other, earlier traces of this transformation or betrayal – the early twentieth-century stories of Akutagawa.[6] The borders between East and West cannot thus simply be drawn between two different media such as script and film, as if merely using a camera were enough to guarantee the objectification and betrayal of the Eastern world.

Rashomon is a 'striking example' of Europeanization, but why single out the dueling scenes as too realistic? Why refer to the content of the film when it is the form or medium that affects the objectification and betrayal of the subject? How might one scene or film be more exemplary than another? The claims of the Japanese cannot escape the questions and oppositions put into play by the dialogue itself. We cannot even assume that we know what film is, for it is perhaps not that which is opposed to the world or the script, but that which is situated between them, between the photograph and the script, the film and the world. Both subject and object, sensuous and suprasensuous, inside and outside, film is, perhaps, the 'sensuous radiance through whose lively delight there breaks the radiance of something suprasensuous'.

XXXII

With the sword pressed to her neck, the old woman trembled in *Rashomon* and tried to explain to the samurai's servant why she had gone to the great gate to pull hair off the dead.

A panting sound like the cawing of a crow came from her throat: "I pull the hair . . . I pull out the hair . . . to make a wig".

The woman explained that in Kyoto people must lie, cheat, and steal – even from the dead – if they are to survive. They are not guilty and they cannot be blamed, she said, because if they did not do these things they would starve.

And so the gate is opened for the samurai's servant to step beyond guilt and innocence, the betrayer and the betrayed.

> His right hand touched the big pimple on his cheek. As he listened, a certain courage was born in his heart – the courage he had not had when he sat under the gate a little while ago.

The servant seized the woman by the neck and said, 'Then it's right if I rob you. I'd starve if I didn't'. He thus tore the clothes off the old woman, kicked her down the stairs of the Rashomon, and walked out into the night.

A festering sore thus reveals the site of danger and betrayal. One cannot predict the outcome beforehand; one can only wait and listen, for the place of greatest danger is also the place of greatest hope. Akutagawa's story *Rashomon* ends: 'The thunder of his descending steps pounded in the hollow tower, and then it was quiet'.

XXXIII

Sitting beneath the gate of Kyoto, listening to the woodcutter recount the testimonies given before the unidentified police inquirer, the Buddhist priest trembles with fear near the end of *Rashomon*. He is uneasy throughout the entire film, wondering whether all men are as corrupt and wicked as those who lied, killed, raped, and stole in the hollow of the grove. But when the testimonies are completed, the priest's uneasiness turns to despair, as both he and the commoner surmise their narrator's complicity in the tale. It was he, they now suspect, who stole the small sword from the breast of the dying man.

Hence the film *Rashomon* promises to end like the short story, in a theft, a betrayal, an abandonment of hope. Just as no origin exists outside the play of differences in the dialogue between the Japanese and the Inquirer, so no narrator remains outside the web of complicity and deceit. The film threatens to end with the suspicions, veils, and masks with which it began. But at this moment, the darkest and most desperate of the film, the woodcutter, commoner, and priest are drawn away from the images of deception in the grove to the sounds of a baby crying. In the clearing of the Rashomon, where dead bodies are often abandoned, where a samurai's servant once attacked and robbed an old, helpless woman in the middle of the night, a baby cries. The rains suddenly cease, the screen brightens, and nothing can be heard save the cries of the infant. The priest finds the baby wrapped in blankets, takes him in his arms, and walks slowly towards the camera. The woodcutter approaches to look at the baby, but the priest quickly turns away, as if to protect the newborn from the man who has just been exposed as a liar and a thief.

Priest: What are you trying to do? Take away what little it has?
Woodcutter: I have six children of my own. One more wouldn't make it any more difficult.
P: I'm sorry. I shouldn't have said that.
W: Oh, you can't afford not to be suspicious of people these days. I'm the one who ought to be ashamed.
P: No, I'm grateful to you. Because, thanks to you, I think I will be able to keep my faith in men.

The camera moves out from beneath the Rashomon as the priest gives the baby to the woodcutter, who then walks towards the camera into the sunlight. The baby has stopped crying, the dark clouds have dissolved. Bathed in sunlight, the woodcutter and the infant are framed by the Rashomon behind them. Over the woodcutter's right shoulder, the signboard with its large Japanese characters is visible. No caption retranslates these characters, for memory is expected to link the beginning to the end as the music rises and the image fades away.

XXXIV

Meanwhile the Rashomon remains in ruins, fragmented – shared out between oppositions and endings, the bifurcated trace of itself. For while one *Rashomon* ends in birth, the other ends in the shadows of death; while one directs our gaze towards the illuminated interior of the gate, the other leads us out into the night; and while one ends with the intimations of a moral code based on faith, hope, and charity, on the triumph of light over darkness, the other ends in the fear and darkness of unbridled survival. But to isolate the precise moment of the Rashomon's betrayal, of its subjugation to Western categories, to say that it is the film that frames the East or that the film's ending marks the unambiguous advent of Western morality and aesthetics in Eastern culture, is perhaps itself to betray the Rashomon, to betray its sharing out of voices and identities, its singular distribution.

XXXV

Although the Rashomon has no identity of its own, no form, no structure, no medium that is proper to it, it cannot fail to have a lasting place in our memory – though that memory is never simply our own.

XXXVI

Like the community that has gathered there, it stands to ruin. Jean-Luc Nancy writes in 'Of divine places':

> Divine places, without gods, with no gods, are spread out everywhere around us, open and offered to our coming, to our going or to our presence, given up or promised to our visitation, to frequentation by those who are not men either, but who are there, in these places: ourselves, alone, out to meet that which we are not, and which the gods for their part have never been. These places, spread out everywhere, yield up and orient new spaces: they are no longer temples, but rather the opening up and the spacing out of the temples themselves, a dis-location with no reserve henceforth, with no more sacred enclosures – other tracks, other ways, other places for all who are there.[7]

Notes

I would like to thank Robert Ginsberg of Penn State University, Kenneth Itzkowitz of Marietta College, and Hugh Silverman of SUNY Stony Brook for their kind and attentive criticism of an earlier draft of this paper. It is dedicated to Pascale-Anne.

1 Jean-Luc Nancy, 'Sharing voices;, trans. Gayle L. Ormiston, in *Transforming the Hermeneutic Context: From Nietzsche to Nancy*, ed. Gayle L. Ormiston and Alan D. Schrift (Albany: SUNY Press, 1989), p. 227.
2 'The "Rashomon" was the largest gate in Kyoto, the ancient capital of Japan. It was 106 feet wide and 26 feet deep, and was topped with a ridgepole; its stone wall rose 75 feet high. This gate was constructed in 789, and in 794 the capital of Japan was transferred to Kyoto. With the decline of Kyoto in the twelfth century, the gate fell into disrepair, cracking and crumbling in many places'. This description of the Rashomon is from a footnote in Takashi Kojima's translation of *Rashomon*. Cf. Ryunosuke Akutagawa, *Rashomon and Other Stories*, trans. Takashi Kojima (New York: Liveright, 1952), reprinted in *Rashomon*, ed. Donald Richie (New Brunswick NJ: Rutgers University Press, 1987), p. 97.

3 Martin Heidegger, 'A dialogue on language', in *On the Way to Language*, trans. Peter D. Hertz (New York: Harper & Row, 1971), pp. 1–54.
4 Martin Heidegger, *Identity and Difference*, trans. Joan Stambaugh (New York: Harper & Row, 1969), p. 23.
5 All citations of Akutagawa's *In a Grove* and *Rashomon*, along with all citations from the script of *Rashomon*, are from *Rashomon*, ed. Donald Richie (New Brunswick NJ: Rutgers University Press, 1987).
6 A translator's note in the French translation of *Rashomon* suggests that Akutagawa used as the primary source for his story two tales from *Konjaku monogatari*, a late eleventh-century collection of tales whose author is unknown. Cf. Akutagawa Ryûnosuke, *Rashomon et autres contes*, trans. Arimasa Mori (Paris: Gallimard/ UNESCO), p. 284. A comparison between these tales and Akutagawa's reformulation of them would, no doubt, further complicate the relationship between East and West.
7 Jean-Luc Nancy, 'Of divine places', trans. Michael Holland, in *The Inoperative Community*, ed. Peter Connor (Minneapolis: University of Minnesota Press, 1991), p. 150.

7

Nancy and the political imaginary after nature

Wilhelm S. Wurzer

After nature, an 'aesthetics' of community? A post-political event marking Heidegger's reading of time beyond ontological ecstasis? Where is Nancy really going? Is he relentlessly confronted by the crisis of Marxism, the rift of thinking and dwelling? Quite plainly, Nancy performs a Promethean act by offering a philosophy of our time. In an epoch in which *Denken* is absent, he gives birth to a renewed philosophical presence. His rigorous readings of Heidegger's logic of *Ereignis* does not overlook the historical force of the thought of Kant, Hegel, and, perhaps, more importantly, Adorno. In short, these readings highlight the experience of our world. Nancy writes: 'A world is neither space nor time; it is the way we exist together. It is *our* world, the world of *us*, not as a belonging, but as the appropriation of existence insofar as it is finite'.[1] Beyond essence, world is neither transcendental (Kant) nor ecstatic (Heidegger). It 'is not the time of an origin, nor the origin of time: it is the spacing of time, the opening up of the possibility of saying "we" and enunciating and announcing by this "we" the historicity of existence' (*BP*, 164).

Nancy's philosophy wrestles with the necessity of a metaphysical demise, in particular, the fading of the principle of the beautiful-in-nature. He wonders about philosophy's darkening after nature: beyond Hyperion's joy and Kant's 'free play' of imagination; beyond the Nietzschean spell of the Dionysian; beyond George's *Neue Reich* and even, beyond Trakl's mourning. A distinct question persists: Regarding these beyonds, is philosophy still concerned with the political? Nancy's leap from the romantic principle of the beautiful-in-nature to a post-Kantian sublimity of finite history signifies a serious concern for 'community'. Indeed, community names philosophy's responsibility after nature. A certain destitution follows nature's farewell in our time.[2] Alienated from truth, God, and nature – digressing from the very essence of Western mimetology – philosophy is suddenly thrown into a world it can no longer understand. Such hermeneutic failure is clearly linked to an inevitable renunciation of the theoretical (i.e. of the political dialectic of practice and theory). Nancy's task, therefore, is to explore philosophy's uncanny thrownness into community, which, surprisingly, is not regarded as a unified body of individuals with common interests but rather, more intriguingly, as 'happening itself', undoubtedly thinking's happening.

What fascinates in Nancy's operation is expressly philosophy's ability to cope with its metaphysical death machine by coming into world and opening it up. This does not mean interpreting the world again. In his own way, Nancy executes the challenge of Marx's Eleventh Thesis on Feuerbach.[3] His deconstruction of the Marxian thesis is laboriously Heideggerian. This is why Nancy's 'community' circumvents mimesis by playing the script of *Ereignis*. His concern is not a matter of political accomplishment or representation. Indeed, he writes, '(history) is neither mind nor man, neither liberty nor necessity, neither one Idea nor another, not even the Idea of otherness, which would be the Idea of time and the Idea of History itself' (*BP*, 158). The diversity of things in the world presupposes instead 'finite history', and derives from community, a historical happening. In point of fact, community is history happening as togetherness of otherness. 'Otherness has no Idea, but it only happens – as togetherness' (*BP*, 158). Such a subversion of Hegel's historical idealism allows for a singular existence of reason which is no longer essence or subject but rather non-essential presentation of history. A masterful speculative performance without yielding to speculation itself, Nancy's rewriting of reason's *Kehre* as well as spirit's new assignment recognizes that *we* are exposed to and belong to community.

Yet, one might ask, is community the myth after myriad narratives of nature? Is community the story of another coming, that of 'the last god', a new *poiesis* of world, a displacement of Schelling's new mythology? Nancy's texts indicate that community is not the ultimate montage of reason's speculative reflections. There is no sense of *positing* any kind of idealism in community. 'History is nonrepresentable' (*BP*, 161). Philosophy is no longer a work of representation but essentially *writing* the happening, drafting the design of world according to community. Drawing our existence, our *we*, world marks an essential *farewell* to the very presence of a historical event.[4] Nancy elucidates: 'To be present in history and to history (to make judgments, decisions, choices in terms of a future) is never to be present to oneself as historic' (*BP*, 160). From this point of view, community is recognized with regard to a difference in time, 'by the spacing of time itself' which always comes from the future.

The political question is played out in Nancy's refusal to be political, in his refusal to repeat the historical mimesis. This renunciation of temporal presence is intimately linked to the space of community which Heidegger opens in his readings of time. He calls this space – *Übermacht*.[5] It is the power which goes beyond primordial textuality. An incomparable power, Heidegger's temporalizing, captures a ghostly *actio in distans*, an apparitional deepening, interpreting, rewriting Nietzsche's critique of historicism. What draws Heidegger irresistibly into Nietzsche's early work, *The Use and Abuse of History*, is the post-Cartesian eye revealed as the unhistorical and the superhistorical. The unhistorical signifies the necessary forgetting of the past as simply textuality-present-at-hand. It also signifies the touch of the moment, the eyes of animality, a temporal making present – an ontological naturality. So, when Heidegger unfolds Da-sein as being primarily historical, there is something unhistorical about this. More subtly, there is something superhistorical here. Thus, less and more of the historical, thus less and more of the textual, the ontological historical happens without ignoring happening as it comes. We are no longer consumed by the weight of the *culture of textuality*.

What is set in place in *Being and Time*, the site Nancy is wondering about, without drifting aimlessly, is the region (*Gegend*) that holds a unique kind of temporality, a temporalizing in so historical a manner that nothing present-at-hand may surface. What happens, then, when we look at the textual terrain of philosophical towns and cities? The site we regard, the place which opens up allows for textualities, indecidables indeed, which suddenly fascinate in their peculiar coming from the future.

A certain erasure of the philosophical letter and the presumption to dispense with it by other means will be necessary: for Nancy (as well as Lacoue-Labarthe), obliteration, therefore, of both reduction and expansion of textuality. Beyond recent textual invocations, how does Nancy cull the most crucial themes from Heidegger's out-of-textual temporalizing? Here we meet a more radical off-centring, specifically, an ex-centric post-textualizing which Nancy regards as belonging very much to the ambiguity of philosophy's *farewell*. The erasure of historical presence engenders the proliferation of certain textual economies. One may, however, as Nietzsche urges, break textuality's windows and leap into freedom.[6] We may begin to detextualize the higher formations and drive our carts and ploughs over the bones of dead philosophers, as Blake might say.[7] *We still have the how, we no longer have the what.*

Nancy repeats the soundings of Heidegger's Dasein analysis which signifies resistance of the what, first of all. Invariably, an operation of the how, philosophy opens up world in its most proper historical performance. Dasein is not present; it shows itself in its unique temporalizing. The task of thinking the farewell is *now* linked to temporality, singularly to *Zeitigung*, temporalizing, expressing the ultimate phenomenological scene. Accordingly, the ambiguity of the farewell lies in how time temporalizes itself. Obliterating the what, time is primarily futural. It always already erases the past and present in its distinctive coming (*Zu-kunft*) towards community. Community is not a mere joining of words (*Wortgefüge*), nor a delightful textual interweaving, but rather a farewell to *what* philosophy *thinks*, if it thinks to belong inseparably to philosophical textuality. Attempts to distinguish philosophy from the philosophical language of textuality, whether old or new, arise out of a desire not to let philosophy become the subject again. *Philosophy is not the subject*. Philosophy is merely *how* we regard the subject. *The subject is time, our time – now –* our finite history, the 'I' within the 'we', the difference of community beyond commu- nitites. Indeed (as we will see) the subject is a non-identical comma, between 'we, now'.[8]

There are certain difficulties which linger in Nancy's texts. These are: the intimacy of community and finite history; the historical as absence of 'political' presence; happening as farewell to what happens. These difficulties derive from the obscurity of the concept of community. This obscurity, however, is not a lapse in Nancy's logic of freedom but rather a darkening of presence which belongs to the non-essential nature of finite history. What is essential, for the moment, lies in the belonging-together of freedom and community such that neither emerges as substance or subject but that each consists in existence. Nancy writes: 'To partake of community is to partake of existence, which is not to share any common substance, but to be exposed together to ourselves as to heterogeneity, to the happening of ourselves; (*BP*, 166). Hence, the historical 'we' is not something to be decided.

Nancy's heading of community is indisputably related to Heidegger's *Zeiti- gung*, a temporalizing, or coming, more seductively, *ekstatikon* itself.[9] An incomparable power, community is destined to run ahead of political textua- lities. This radical post-textualizing belongs very much to the ambiguity of the affair between community and *Zeitigung*. Rooted in finite history, community is exposure to thinking as liberation. Nancy says that freedom is even free *from* freedom, that is to say, it comes before freedom. This coming (not becoming) defies intention as well as representation. 'It does not answer to any concept.'[10]

There then begin the resemblances between Nancy's community and Heidegger's *Zeitigung*, not to mention Adorno's *Nichtidentische* as well as Derrida's *différance*. None the less, it would be a mistake to identify these operations. For, ultimately, community is no longer an operation but historical freedom. This means we no longer receive our sense of freedom from history; instead, we prepare ourselves to enter history by resisting a collective or individual 'community'. Community endlessly withdraws from every appropriation of essence or foundation. It is freedom coming as history's decisive farewell. Here, farewell is finally also a parting from Heidegger's temporalizing. The political is tough to eliminate. It will persist all the more in one's spacing of time. Yet, this spacing of time, is it ever an experience as Nancy claims? And, if so, what kind of experience?

Nancy's reading of experience begins with the decision never to appropriate any community as foundation. What is proper to community is infinite resistance to presence, foundation, and essence. It is obliteration of metaphysics, in short, philosophy's farewell. Gone far away, philosophy now is 'itself' the consequence of its own parting. This parting, however, is always related to 'the spacing of time itself, the spacing that opens the possibility of history and of community' (*BP*, 160). Nothing happens for historians to write about. What is spectacular here is that philosophy still thinks this nothing as our time taking place, happening, the way we exist together. Our time is not another substance or subject. It is always the future. Now, it is nothing. It will *emerge*. In as much as we are offered to ourselves, we are thrown into community. For Nancy, 'we, now' are not here: 'We are no longer able to understand ourselves as a determined step within a determined process' (*BP*, 166).

'We', now is non-identical. We, now do not have centres. We no longer address one another by way of substance or subject. Ours is a complicated world; the electro-economic systems change more radically than we. 'The now' becomes a paradox. It sends out an invitation for an invasion. 'The we' collapses by itself. Will it fade into the now, beneath our streets, into the power lines and cables inside our walls? Farewell to us. The non-identical comma remains. This pause is not a coma. It is indeed a cut, a slash. News of 'the now' may dash our hopes. Still, **now** is always different from 'the now' we know, specifically, the centreless whole. Hence, the non-identical comma turns out to be a *promesse du bonheur*, a flash of the unexchangeable.[11] Is this another heading for a gift without a present? The unexchangeable, the non-identical, the we, no doubt, beyond 'the now'?

Are we able to isolate the non-identical from new bits of data or technical factors? When the economic unit is the globe, where is the subject? Who are we, now – now that the gods have fled and dubious models shine without wanting to become phenomena? Speculation has become very light indeed. It belongs to the madness of economic reason.[12] So, how are we? 'It is no mere coincidence that along with the integration of the world's economy into a seamless electronic whole, there is an upturn in ethnic rivalries and violence and civil unrest.[13] With the electronic rise of 'the now', what is happening to 'the we'? Will the 'we' become one now?

For many we's, a world that is rapidly integrating, a world that is becoming one with a different spirit from Hegel's, is quite frightening when they are not familiar with a threatening 'now'. What is going on **now**? How/where do **we** fit in? Are these questions merely a matter of replicating romanticism's desire to blend the real and ideal? It might be good to understand the **we** as belonging to **now** without letting the **now** become a belonging. A certain non-identical invitation still holds. **We** are invited to invade the **now**. We are invited to spread over into the now. To affect the now. To permeate the links. To give ourselves to the now without ever letting go or letting the now become a mere present. **Now** (together) **we** are a gift. Now, much lighter than before, is much more than telecommunications. For post-identitarian thought, the difference between **we** and **now** will not fade. **We** choose to be **now**. Nancy's dilemma of the non-identical comma does not lie in a coma. We, now incline to be free. We incline to resist permanence, above all, the myth of Platonism, in which nothing of value ever changes. The technological era, therefore, is no longer merely a determined echo of Platonism. Nancy agrees with Heidegger that the essence of technology, the now we are and are not, is not, by itself, anything technical. Inclined towards a bizarre content, how/who are we, now?

After nature, the new political imaginary exceeds the modern/postmodern aesthetics of law and politics. The decision to depart from representational textuality signifies the coming to presence of *our* freedom. We, now are infinitely how we will be. We, now means we are prepared to think, 'to leave behind what "thinking" usually means. But, first of all, to think this, that there is something to think' (*BP*, 174): to think community beyond Hölderlin's melancholy, Gottfried Benn's aesthetic nihilism, and Peter Handke's lyrical cynicism; beyond nature, in particular, beyond *das Naturschöne*. To think community under a new spacing of time brings joy continually, necessarily born within communal freedom. None the less, we are prompted to ask: Is Nancy's writing of community not a matter of retrieving a certain auto-operative power of reason akin to some of the sublime strategies of early romanticism? Does community not become a political imaginary within the limits of philosophy's ends? It appears that Nancy's thought repeats the spirals of spirals that romanticism sketches in the texts of Kant, Schelling, and Heidegger. Nancy grants an incommensurable privilege to poetic speculation. For him, romanticism is not yet completed primarily because the poetic speculative has not taken place.[14] It cannot take place. For now, we let time take place. Community, therefore, is not present. At the heart of things we are hardly ever together. It is not a question of being present to ourselves. It is always a matter of coming-together, clearly, of deciding to say 'we, now'. Once we reach this decision, we prepare ourselves for a new chaos. This chaos is nothing, it does not simply come about. Still, it belongs to Hyperion's joy of thinking an infinite life in a limited existence. To say more would be excessive for Nancy. After nature, he stands in the shadow or parody of Hölderlin.

Is Nancy's intra-philosophic manner of exposing community 'easy philosophy' again?[15] After nature, we are no longer transposed into a poetic involvement (engagement) of 'Hölderlin's joy' but rather into electronic expressions which are more akin to Descartes' joy. Poetic engagement may diminish our alienation by encouraging the belief that we are still somehow linked to das Naturschöne. But our time dispels the memory of continuity with the experience of nature. Resisting the spell of an identitarian dialectic, Nancy also recognizes that it is not sufficient to anticipate relief in poetic speculation. He believes linking reality and community is comedy. Nature is withdrawn, yet thought is drawn into community as 'being-together'. The comedy lies in the withdrawal itself, not only nature's but also that of communication. Clearly, Nancy has reservations about the latter: 'Communication is always disappointing, because no subject of the utterance comes in touch with another subject' (BP, 314). The best 'model' for a dialogue on community is precisely 'the conversation, where nobody knows what he or she will say before he or she has said it' (BP, 315). This betrays a certain temporalizing which reveals that being is historically more diverse than what Heidegger gives to think. Our time signifies a coming-to-presence of freedom which no longer grants sovereignty of any kind. Community, as I read it in Nancy, calls for a temporalizing, which exceeds the phenomenal/noumenal connection. 'We are not a "being" but a "happening"' (BP, 156), the happening of a certain space of time. We happen. This happening is history or community. We are infinitely exposed to our time.

Beyond the political as an operating public, Nancy sets up a higher community. A new connection is made: 'Being-together' is now linked to a new comedy, the myth of Iakchos, the coming god, truly, political laughter. This

Wilhelm S. Wurzer

joyous Dionysus, resurrected from the dead, signifies the coming/futural community.[16] For Hölderlin (and Schelling), the coming god, who marks a post-identitarian expansion of spirit, involves a new politics, a breaking-forth of a distinct absence of ground. This very abyss indicates the communal, non-securing foundation of poetry, history, and philosophy. In keeping with Nancy's fidelity to Schelling, this decisive interruption of myth sustains a 'social culture' (*gesellschaftliche Bildung*) which questions the aesthetic sovereignty of taste. Here, judging is not a question of taste but rather a question of community, pertinent beyond conventional ethical, political, or even aesthetic conceptions of freedom. There is no architectonic ground of the political. 'There is nothing but the indeterminable *chora* (not an undetermined place, but the possibility of places' (*EF*, 84). In turn, a certain originality of the political reconfigures our experience of *die jauchzende Zukunft*, a gleeful, imageless coming, a community of thought, or, as Hölderlin says, 'jenes gemeinsame Höhere'.[17] Such a reconfiguration of German romanticism's 'higher community' is also evident in Nietzsche's reading of the Dionysian.[18]

But Nancy does more than reconstruct a mythical fantasy of the eighteenth and nineteenth centuries. He links romanticism's politico-poetic discourse with reality. This is indeed the new comedy of freedom, 'pirating foundation', letting community take its place on the margins. We, now are not concretely present in a community. We are communal not because a law or a constitution says so, but because we are free prior to law and government. Community, therefore, signifies the twilight of sovereignties. Beyond nature and city, we are free for the unexpected, infinitely resisting politics, if politics means appropriation of essences. Engaged in pirating, we are exposed to the unlikely coming of the last god, the communal relation of all beings-in-the-world.[19] Suitably, Nancy's political imaginary sustains the privilege of the question of *relation*: 'We share what divides us: the freedom of an incalculable and improbable coming' (*EF*, 95) – laughter, silencing the seriousness of the all-too-common. Quite simply, then, community prepares us for communal relations without substance or subject.

In what sense, however, are these relations really abyssal, desisting essence? Communal relations demand a more rigorous reading of finite history than Nancy's, perhaps, with more divergences within their textual rhythms. Between community and the markings of our time, a split happens (*kommt*) – capital offering the clearest relation of irreducible dispersions. No longer nature, nor the beauty thereof, no longer subject, nor its object, capital signifies the divergences of beings at a distance from the entire ontotheological tradition. The historical double of community and capital explodes, playing (out) the ends of textual foundations. According to Derrida, this makes for 'the other heading' of presence, a postmodern *Urerlebnis*, pure auto-apparition. He elucidates:

> From this paradox of the paradox, through the propagation of a fission reaction, all the propositions and injunctions are divided, the heading splits, the capital is deidentified: it is related to itself not only in gathering itself in the difference *with itself* and with the other heading, with the other shore of the heading, but in opening itself without being able any longer to gather itself.[20]

Community's other heading, capital resists every appropriation of essence without giving in to a Marxian intimidation. Diverging from left and right, it points to a rhythmic alterity which blurs the thematics of Being. In Derrida's words, 'To say it all too quickly, I am thinking about the necessity for a new culture, one that would invent another way of reading and analyzing *Capital*, both Marx's book and capital in general'. Without naming capital, Nancy develops Derrida's logic of *différance*.[21] None the less, a certain theoreticism remains in his philosophy. Community is elevated to a post-identitarian reason which may or may not discern capital. Nancy, who recognizes post-textual divergences, beyond metaphysics' auto-textualities, never the less regards these communal relations from the standpoint of a certain textuality, a telling/ retelling of *Denken und Dichten*.

An inter-shadowing of relations does not always assimilate textuality into history. In dissimulating textualities, capital is more wildly differential than *Ereignis/différance*, and, perhaps, more primordially free (and open) than community. The fictioning power of capital descends to a concrete, dynamic network of alliances (*Werkwelt*). Nancy does not consider capital's rhythmic renunciations of presence, which expose an untimely involvement with electro-economic relations. Freed from metaphysical moorings, including technology's commodified aesthetics, these 'weightless' relations obliterate cultural closures, exploding the ideological equipment of emancipation. As it strays from a pure metaphysical script, capital is more than a cursory glance at the ecstatic obscenity of capitalism. Disengaging from mirroring a particular cultural/textual space, it marks the very ends of money, sketching time as a sublime straying from presence *and* simulation. Roaming beyond a postmodern image-system, capital points away from the logocentric signal of spirit to a dissemination of electronic offerings and communal experimentations.

Wilhelm S. Wurzer

Rereading Nancy's configurations of community, it is conceivable to name our electro-economic experience of time – *Zeitkapital*. A few remarks about this then. Timecapital signals capital's manner of comporting to Da-sein as well as Da-sein's manner of comporting to capital. More specifically, capital transposes us into the realization of our time, not in the mere representation of time. Here our time is regarded as *capital, happening* within and beyond the inevitable paradox of the ready-to-hand world with its electronic technologies. Capital happening designates 'the global conversation' we are, an involvement with a spacing beyond Nancy's logic. Da-sein's most temporal performance, capital happens as global community, surpassing the merely electronic-economic ready-to-hand 'now'. Coming-towards capital, time runs ahead without getting a head. Blending **running ahead** and **coming-towards**, timecapital is community. There is no particular ready-to-hand being that is responsible for this intimacy. Instead, *Zeitkapital* is **how community manifests its textualities-in-the-world**. These textualities render the old philosophical textualizing of world obsolete. Beyond dialectics, community is now a matter of capital, happening. A temporalizing proper to the electromagnetic spectrum, *Zeitcapital* points to a necessary modification of community, away from *Zeitgeist*. What is politely crossed out is community as presence. Hence, timecapital reveals community at the limit of comprehension in a 'global conversation' which brings us back to ourselves (*Zu-kunft*). This new arrival (re-turn/future) marks a coming-to-presence of diverse possibilities. In coming, capital, more than Da-sein, perhaps, has shown itself to be 'dynamic, interactive, simultaneous, swift' (*DM*, 33). Erasing the historical weariness of man, capital is not constricted into foundational limitations. Indeed, it signifies a certain fitness which is not out there in 'reality'. Nor is this fitness found in philosophical textuality. In turn, the value of capital is dematerialized. Its vast and swift happening demands to be read, interpreted, and explored while resisting appropriations of essence. Paradoxically, for Nancy, this practice of resistance is community.

Stated more rigorously – beyond Nancy – timecapital, as this very community, lets resistances come to new textualities. We, now, taking a step further to *Zeitkapital*, are exposed to how we will be: a communal future which indicates neither collective otherness nor individual selfhood. Nor is this matter a triumph of privatization. As heir of Prometheus, communal timecapital transmits a revolution of (dis)continuous relations, a *dis-appropriation*, properly private, fittingly revealing the likely coming of freedom within and beyond electronic convergences in unlimited possibilities. A new community sets in

100

motion the collision of diverse electronic operations. Its discourse echoes a baffling economy swaying openly from presence to finite history, from capitalism to a non-essential founding of our time. In sum, our time, *Zeitkapital*, signifies the twilight of old and new communities. Thinking, now 'places philosophy before its strangest, most disconcerting truth' (*EF*, 150). Inevitably, after nature, there then begins community as we, now no longer know it.

Notes

1 Jean-Luc Nancy, *The Birth to Presence*, trans. Brian Holmes *et al.* (Stanford: Stanford University Press, 1993), p. 163. Henceforth, *BP.*

2 An unspeakable alienation intensifies our desire for poetic involvement. The discontinuity of a certain happy moment in time is recalled by the continuity of a Dionysian poetic. This early dimension of romanticism is formidably present in the logic of a philosophy of art from Kant to Adorno. See J. M. Bernstein's *The Fate of Art* (University Park: Pennsylvania State University Press, 1992).

3 'The philosophers have only *interpreted* the world, in various ways; the point, however, is to *change* it.'

4 *BP,* 160.

5 See *Sein und Zeit* (Tübingen: Max Niemeyer Verlag, 1967).

6 See W. S. Wurzer, 'Heidegger und die Enden der Textualität', in *Textualität der Philosophie*, ed. Ludwig Nagl (Wien: R. Oldenbourg Verlag, 1994).

7 See 'Proverbs of Hell', in William Blake, The Complete Poetry and Prose of William Blake, ed. David V. Erdman (New York, 1988).

8 The significance of the non-identical (*das Nichtidentische*) is illustrated in Theodor Adorno's *Negative Dialektik* (Frankfurt am Main: Suhrkamp, 1966).

9 See *Being and Time*, trans. J. Macquarrie (New York: Harper & Row, 1962), p. 377.

10 Jean-Luc Nancy, *The Experience of Freedom*, trans. Bridget McDonald (Stanford: Stanford University Press, 1993), p. 82. Henceforth, *EF.*

11 See Theodor Adorno, *Ästhetische Theorie* (Frankfurt am Main: Suhrkamp, 1970).

12 See Jacques Derrida, *Given Time: 1. Counterfeit Money*, trans. P. Kamuf (Chicago: University of Chicago Press, 1992), 34–70.

13 See Joel Kurtzman's illuminating reading of our time in *The Death of Money* (New York: Simon & Schuster, 1993), p. 205. Henceforth, *DM.*

14 See Philippe Lacoue-Labarthe and Jean-Luc Nancy, *The Literary Absolute*, trans. P. Barnard and C. Lester (Albany, NY: SUNY Press, 1988).

15 For a brilliant illustration of the effects of 'easy philosophy', see James R. Watson, *Between Auschwitz and Tradition* (Amsterdam: Rodopi, 1994).

16 See Manfred Frank's illuminating lectures on 'new mythology' in *Der Kommende Gott* (Frankfurt: Suhrkamp, 1982).

17 See ibid., p. 288.

18 'In song and in dance man expresses himself as a member of a higher community

(*einer höheren Gemeinsamkeit*); he has forgotten how to walk and speak and is on the way toward flying into the air, dancing. His very gestures express enchantment. Just as animals now talk, and the earth yields milk and honey, supernatural sounds emanate from him, too: he feels himself a god, he himself now walks enchanted, in ecstasy, like the gods he saw walking in his dreams. He is no longer an artist, he has become a work of art', *Birth of Tragedy*, trans Walter Kaufmann (New York: Vintage Books, 1967), p. 37.

19 Note Heidegger's allusions to the 'last god' in *Beiträge zur Philosophie (Vom Ereignis)* (Frankfurt am Main: Klostermann, 1989): 'The last god is not the end, but our history's other beginning with its vast possibilities': my translation (p. 411).

20 *The Other Heading*, trans. Pascale-Anne Brault and M.B. Naas (Bloomington: Indiana University Press, 1991). While Derrida alludes to the necessity of rewriting 'capital' he has not yet described this operation. I have illustrated a certain rewriting of capital in Chapters 7 and 8 of *Filming and Judgment* (Atlantic Highlands, NJ: Humanities Press International, 1990).

21 See *BP*, 164.

8

Interruptions of necessity: being between meaning and power in Jean-Luc Nancy

Jeffrey S. Librett

dès que l'existence constitue elle-même l'essence . . . et dès que, par con-
séquent, ces deux concepts et leur opposition n'appartiennent plus qu'à
l'histoire de la métaphysique, il faut.[1]

What is the relation between meaning and power? How is one to characterize,
for example, the meaning of power or the power of meaning? From what
standpoints and in terms of what concepts are these questions to be developed
and answered? Is the science or art of 'hermeneutics' the proper standpoint
from which to study meaning, while the 'political' and 'social' sciences would
be the proper standpoints from which to study power? And what is the proper
role of the notion of being here? Is it not necessary to bring the notion of being
– and thus presumably also the field of 'ontology' – into play in order to clarify
the relation between meaning and power? For example, does one not have to
clarify the different modes of being of meaning and power (i.e. how they exist,
come to exist, and pass away) in order to have understood their interrelation-
ship? But further, and conversely: does one not have to clarify the meaning and
power possessed by being in order to be able to ask about the being meaning
and power might have? How is one to describe the being of meaning and the
meaning of being, the being of power and the power of being? How is one to
describe the interrelationships between ontology, hermeneutics, and politics?

The following considerations give some definition to the space opened up by
this series of questions by accomplishing two particular tasks. First (in parts I
and II), they describe the systematic connections between modal ontology, on
the one hand, and some of the most fundamental categories of modern politics
and hermeneutics on the other. And second (in part III), they show how these
systematic connections are interrupted and displaced in Jean-Luc Nancy's work.

I begin by arguing that the ontological figure of necessity is to be situated on the undecidable limit between possibility and reality (part I). I then go on to characterize in modal-ontological terms the opposition between hermeneutics and politics, which I understand to be a form of the opposition between theory and practice. Within the field of hermeneutics, I examine the subordinate opposition between historicist and formalist hermeneutics in order to clarify its ontological presuppositions; within the field of politics, I examine to the same end the subordinate oppositions between rights and duties and between conservatism and progressivism. What I try to show in these examinations (which are carried out in Part II) is that the categories in question have traditionally been 'grounded' in the interplay between dogmatic determinations of necessity as residing either in *reality* (i.e. existence) or in *possibility* (i.e. essence). The interplay between such modal determinations provides only an *unstable* 'ground' for these hermeneutic and political categories, however, because each modal determination is itself always dogmatic or ungrounded. Whichever way it goes, the preference – that is, the decision that either possibility or reality is the proper realm of necessity – can never amount to anything other than the arbitrary (mis)construal of the modal concept of *necessity*, for the concept of necessity is simply the concept of the *limit* between the possibility and reality with which it is regularly confused.

Having established this decisive (and disruptive) presence of the modal categories and hence of ontology within both hermeneutics and politics, I proceed to show (in Part II) how ontology mediates the politicization of hermeneutics (i.e. how ontology determines the apparent political implications of the major traditional approaches to hermeneutics (formalism and historicism)). At this point in the argument, a certain systematicity becomes visible in the connections between ontology, politics and hermeneutics. It becomes simultaneously clear that such a systematicity exercises an extraordinary *power* of self-stabilization, self-imposition, and self-reproduction, but a power that is not in the narrow sense *political*, because the political in the narrow sense (at least in the dimensions examined by the present chapter) can assume the form and the history of a meaning only *within* the relational system in question. None the less, because due to its formidable internal coherence this system generates complex social, institutional, cultural, economic, and more narrowly political effects, its power certainly deserves to be considered political in a broader sense, a sense which escapes the perspective of most forms of political hermeneutics *per se*. It is this system and its power – including, but not limited to, the power of the conventional distinction between political left

and political right – that, within the tradition of post-Heideggerian deconstruction, Nancy works to destabilize. In order to show how the destabilization occurs, I focus (in part III) on Nancy's displacements of the traditional
embodiments of necessity in the form of the concepts of decision, socio-
political practice, and interpretation.

I. Necessity from a metaontological point of view

The ontological-modal figure of *necessity* has always taken on meaning – at least
in the occident, to which I restrict myself here – above all by way of its specific
relation to the figures of *possibility* and *reality*, together with which it functions
as one of the potential modal traits of the being of anything that may be taken
to exist. It is the infinitely non-totalizable or undecidable 'community' of this
functioning that we will have to examine here. My intention in this first section
is neither to develop my own modal ontology nor to retrace any other
particular ontology from the history of philosophy,[2] but rather to sketch out
in a *metaontological* manner – a *pre-* or *post-ontological* manner – the internal
conditions of possibility shared by all modal ontologies heretofore designed
(i.e. these conditions in so far as they have been determined by the minimal
relationships between the terms that have comprised the elements of modal
ontology across the history of Western metaphysics).

To begin with traditional, everyday conceptions of the modal terms' minimal
definitions: the necessary is 'what must be the case', the possible is 'what may
be the case', and the real is 'what is the case'. As already indicated, because
necessity, possibility, and reality define being as a trio (i.e. always in concert
with one another) their meanings are mutually dependent. In all modal
ontologies, each term determines (and is determined by) the other two.
Anyone who intends to develop a modal ontology – to concretize or explore
any further these initial definitions (or verbal forms: *must*, *can*, and *is*, and their
equivalent transformations) – is faced with the difficult task of investigating
their interrelationships and their relationships to those things to which they can
be applied.

Due to the triadic structure of modal terminology, there are three main
versions of such an investigation (see Figures 1 and 2). For each version, one of
the terms (i.e. possibility, reality, or necessity) serves as the central point of
departure, with relation to which the others function as two mutually opposed
modifications of this centre or origin. The initial relationship between the two
latter terms is determined further by the fact that both of these terms serve as

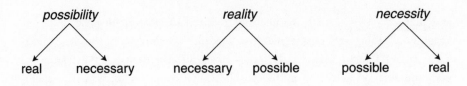

Figure 1

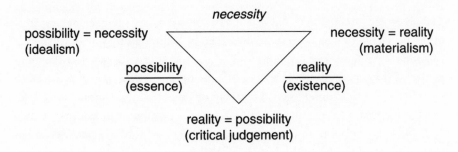

Figure 2

differentiations of the modal term to which they are applied. The term with which one begins is the trait shared by the two terms that modify it and are taken to be differentiated out from it. This first term is therefore the *border* along which the two secondary terms are disjunctively conjoined.

Somewhat more concretely: (1) one can begin with *possibility*, and define necessity and reality as opposite modifications of possibility; or (2) one can begin with *reality*, and then define necessity and possibility as opposite modifications of reality; or (3) one can begin with *necessity*, and proceed to define possibility and reality as opposite modifications of necessity. Indeed, for example, the history of the main methodological options in modern philosophy from Descartes to Kant seems to unfold the possibilities contained in these three versions of the modal system, although there can be no question here of confirming such a hypothesis in detail. A comment on each of the three versions would, however, doubtless be of some use, in order both to concretize their meaning and to explain somewhat further this philosophico-historical hypothesis.

(1) When one begins with *possibility*, and then modifies it in the directions of *necessity* and *reality*, necessity and reality become necessary possibility and real possibility, respectively. Possibility tends to be associated with the subject,

106

thought, consciousness, language, etc., as opposed to reality. It is therefore not surprising that necessary and real possibility here takes on the sense of necessary and contingent propositions or essences (as opposed to things or existences, as in the next version we will consider). The burden of the further determination of these notions then falls on the explanation of how possibilities (in whatever way they may be further characterized in the given ontology) can be either necessary or real. Positing the possible as origin in this way will always produce a rationalist ontology of the sort epitomized, for example, by Leibniz.[3]

(2) In contrast, when *reality* is divided into necessary and possible (i.e. contingent) realities (or referents, or existents), the resultant concepts constitute an empiricist aspect or view of the world, for such a view always locates the origin in reality as objectivity.[4] The thing that *necessarily* exists can then be further defined, for example as past (and hence unchangeable) history, or as fate, the ineluctable that exists. Likewise, the things that *contingently* exist can be specified in their contingency, for example as the future possibilities the eventual non-realization of which still remains possible.

(3) Finally, one can begin with *necessity* and then proceed to divide the necessary into *possible* necessity and *real* necessity. Such a starting point gives rise to the oppositions such as those between the law of freedom and the law of nature in Kant, which comprise the necessity of the will and the necessity of the world, or the necessity of practical reason and the necessity of the understanding, respectively, necessities that in turn are ultimately to be mediated in Kant by the 'subjective necessity' of the faculty of judgement.[5]

Even when convoked in their totality, however, these three versions of the system of the modalities preserve a discreet silence in the face of the demand for a *ground*: the starting point for each version is not so much explained as simply divided into two further starting points, while the latter starting points mean little more than the two terms into which they can each be divided in turn. For example, to know that there are possible and real necessities is not to know much more than before about what necessity is in itself: it is hardly to know anything more about necessity than that necessity must appear (misleadingly) either as possibility or as reality, or rather that it must appear (fleetingly) as the mere *border*, holding them apart and collapsing – displacing itself – into the one or the other. In each version of the modal system, the initial term will always remain obscure, because purely *liminal*. Each of the other two terms will of course be able to function in turn as the point of departure, but only to the degree that it too appears utterly opaque. The non-groundedness of the modal terms obtains for all three. While one could therefore take a detailed look at the implications of *each* of these versions of the modal system for the politics of discourse in the contemporary humanities, I will be focusing in what follows on the third of these versions, the differentiation of necessity into possibility and reality.

The notion of necessity is indeed of particular interest here for at least two preliminary reasons. First, it is almost synonymous with the notion of grounding or foundation: what cannot *not* be the case is obviously the most stable place to be, the safest place to stand – and therefore continues to represent the beginning and end of all 'rational' discourse, including all discourse on the topic of modality. The fact that the concept of necessity depends on the concepts of possibility and reality for its meaning, however, suggests that it is not itself necessary (if 'necessary' can mean independent or self-grounding), but contingent (assuming 'contingent' can mean dependent on something outside oneself for one's meaning and existence). If there were a ground in the triad of modal categories, it would have to be the notion of necessity, yet necessity does not appear as grounded in itself, but merely as one term in the self-relativizing structure of the modal triangle. All attempts to ground necessity – to find the ground of necessity as the necessary ground – will have to ground it in or as reality or possibility, but such a position will always be dogmatic and arbitrary, because reality and possibility are dependent on necessity precisely as their ground.

Second (and this reason to some extent tends to obscure the first), despite the fact that we often invoke necessity indirectly in one form or another – for example, as the necessity of historicization or the necessity of structural or logical analysis – it seems to have become something of an embarrassment to thematize necessity directly and *explicitly* in the human sciences, because of the vaguely secular and sceptical ethos that (rightly) predominates in these fields. One feels that the word *necessity* evokes occult or inflated entities like God, Fate, Absolute Knowledge, and Logical Truths: in short, all sorts of illusions one would like to think one shed some time ago. And explicit thematization of necessity is easily confused with the emphatic proposal of dogmas of substantiality. The danger inherent in this discursive situation, however, is that it risks becoming a mere repression, rather than an overcoming, of the illusory hope for a ground, a hope that would then persist despite its repression unbeknown to those who, somewhat complacently, imagine themselves to have outgrown such puerile wishes long ago. Desire not to lay claim to necessity has tended to become an incapacity to explore its conceptual contours and to monitor the many forms such a claim can implicitly take. These two reasons prompt us to explore the implications of the various versions of necessity in the politics of discourse today.

II. The power of ontology in contemporary discourse: necessity in (political) practice and in (hermeneutic) theory

Contemporary debates on the political status of the human sciences, of their objects and methodologies, are to a great extent governed – at once controlled and rendered out of control – by the opposition between, on the one hand, 'theory' (i.e. that theoreticism which, as hermeneutics taken in its broadest possible sense, hopes to uncover or recover meaning), and on the other hand, the discourse of political engagement, praxis, and/or practicality, whose principal aim is to act upon and transform the world to which it belongs. This distinction is indeed fundamental to the human sciences: it answers the question of whether or not there is to be science (as theoretical knowledge) at all. Further, this distinction corresponds to the distinction between the two kinds of necessity, or two determinations of necessity, between which any attempt to extend an ontology into a theory of the place of the human in the world is compelled to choose. Hermeneutics locates necessity – as ground, telos, or origin – in meaning. That is, it *identifies* the necessary *with* meaning. And meaning, whether it be construed as conceptual or affective-sensuous sense, as individual or collective value, etc., is always marked by a certain subjectivity or ideality, which is in turn traditionally associated, on the level of ontology, with one or another figure of *possibility*. The activist and praxis-oriented discourses that tend to be anti-theoreticist (even if not anti-theoretical or anti-intellectual), whether in the form of Western Marxist 'critical theory' pragmatism, or even one of the various neo-conservative or neo-fascist tactical activisms, locate the necessary in, or identify the necessary with *reality*. Their ultimate goal is always to have a material effect on the 'real' world, or to have a hand in the self-determination of 'reality', however discretely they may avoid making any traditionally substantializing gestures.[6]

As one will no doubt already have reflected, however, this opposition between the subject of understanding as possibility and the object of action as reality is unstable. It is tendentially supplemented, first, by the re-emergence of reality within meaning and of possibility within the (so-called) real world, and then by the splitting of this reality (of meaning) and possibility (of the world) into possible and real reality and possible and real possibility, respec-

Jeffrey S. Librett

tively. Somewhat more concretely: the theoreticism of hermeneutic understanding always posits a pre-existent something, some sort of discursive *reality*,
outside of itself as the core or actual site of meaning itself.[7] And this reality –
the reality of meaning – is then divided into possible (formal) and real
(historical) realities in turn. Conversely, political activism, even in its conservative forms, intends not merely to conform to reality, but to project its
notions, the *possibilities* that it envisions, into the world, and so to subordinate
reality to those possibilities, even as it realizes them. In other words, political
reality is determined by the *possibilities* of reality, possibilities which constitute
the very *meaning* of politics. And this meaning too is then divided into realist
and possibilist forms. Let us examine in some detail how these supplementary
displacements of the opposition between hermeneutical theory and political
practice occur, beginning with political practice (see Figure 3).

Necessity in politics as/in practice

The discourse of political practice – of practice as politics and of politics as
practice – establishes its own privilege by privileging reality over possibility as
the necessary. It then proceeds, however, to endow this necessity of the real (or

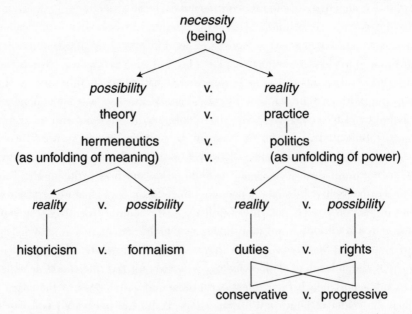

Figure 3

110

real necessity) with meaning (or possibility) and to divide this political meaning in turn into its possibilist and realist forms. Again, these new avatars of possibility and reality are modifications of the return of possibility after its repression by the realism of the political itself, a return that takes the form of the question of the *meaning* of politics. In order to be in a position to trace the re-emergence of possibility (or meaning) as both possible and real possibility (or possible and real meaning) within the space of the political-practical, we have to ask more specifically how necessary reality is given meaning within that space.

Rights and duties

Let us assume for the present argument that the principal task of the practice of politics is the distribution of power *by* the human collectivity (or some part of that collectivity) *among* the members of the various human populations. The principal necessity of politics, then, would be the necessity of the distribution of power. Now, although we certainly have difficulty both in situating power precisely and even in determining the limits between its real and virtual possession or appearance, still we tend to agree on this: power is that which imposes itself. Absolute power or pure power is absolute imposition, the unavoidable, the inevitable – apparently, a variant of necessity itself, namely the 'real' variant. This 'real' variant is opposed to the 'ideal' power of things of the mind, for example, which, as an 'ideal' power, is a power that has no power, the 'other' of 'power' in its material sense. In distributing 'real' power, then, politics distributes an avatar of necessity. Political power is the power to distribute (itself as) necessity, to attach necessity in specific forms to specific populations.

How, then, is (political) necessity distributed? In what form is the necessary 'reality' of politics given 'meaning' and 'direction', or how is the pure *that-ness* of necessary reality diversely determined in its *what-ness*? Doubtless, there are any number of ways in which political necessity assumes form, contour, and sense. No way is more important, however, than its articulation as, and division into, *rights* and *duties*, which we can regard, respectively, as positive and negative manifestations of the necessity or power of the (individual or collective) subject to which they refer, expansions and restrictions of the space in which the subject operates. What the above analysis of necessity enables us to see more clearly than otherwise is that these expansions and restrictions are structurally undecidable – indeed, impossible. On the one hand, rights give

111

meaning to political reality as necessary *possibilities*: if one has a right to an action, one *may* perform it, but need not. And duties give meaning to political reality as necessary *realities*: if one is obliged by a prescriptive or proscriptive duty, then one must conform one's actions to the limits imposed by that duty (i.e. the duty represents, or is at least supposed to represent, a *real limitation* upon one's movement). On the other hand, as we know even 'empirically', the exercise of power (i.e. the political distribution of necessity) is never this simple. Freedoms regularly transform themselves into burdensome obligations, while with distressing consistency obligations turn into freedoms. Any given distribution of necessity always repeats itself in the form of the opposite distribution. The positing of rights repeats itself as the becoming-cliché of those rights (which often appears as the becoming-meaningless and -boring, through conventionalization, of what was formerly regarded as desirable). And the concomitant positing of duties recapitulates itself as the becoming-attractive of those restrictions (which we sometimes read in psychological terms as the masochistic internalization of authority or the identification with the aggressor here represented by the social law). Ontologically, however, these reversals translate into the *becoming-real of the possible* (in the case of the becoming-duties of rights) and the *becoming-possible of the real* (in the case of the becoming-rights of duties). These two processes are inevitable (albeit neither simply possible nor simply real) because necessity – or power – is always both possible and real and therefore neither.[8] The distribution of political necessity into – or the determination of its meaningfulness as – possibility and reality does indeed empirically enable its distribution into rights and duties, which can in turn be distributed among subject populations by state legislative, judicial, and policial apparatuses. But necessity is structurally undecidable. Its distribution therefore never properly takes place, even if it does so ideologically (i.e. even if it *seems* to do so, and in a manner that seems capable of being stabilized) every minute of the day. Because necessity is structurally undecidable, its empirical determination as (one or another form of) possibility or reality will always, sooner or later, be empirically reversed.

The immediately political significance of the undecidability of necessity (this undecidability being the very necessity of necessity, the essence of necessity as its existence in the mode of neither essence nor existence) is that the distinction between rights and duties is untenable, structurally unsound. Such a provisional conclusion certainly does not mean, however, that one has henceforth no 'right' to effect such a distribution of necessity into possible and real, or to draw such a distinction between rights and duties, while one *would* have the right to make other sorts of distinctions. For what is being undermined here is the notion of rights and duties as epistemological as well as ethico-political (i.e. grounding in general). In the context of the present argument, and before turning to Nancy's treatment of the question, it will have to suffice to say that we are (and are not) constantly obliged to keep in mind, to ironize, or to signal in one way or another the untenability of the distinction between rights and duties, its infinite questionability and artificiality.

Right and left

In addition to differentiating necessity as power into rights and duties, however, the political sphere gives necessity meaning also by differentiating it into the orientations of *right* and *left*, conservatism and progressivism, orientation towards the past as preservation of the present, and orientation towards the future as overcoming of the present. To risk a trivial example: anyone who has ever been involved in administrative committee work within a university context will undoubtedly have experienced that conservatism is effectively based on the assumption that what has been or is now *real* is necessary, whereas progressivism is based on the assumption that what is *possible* is necessary ('la fantaisie au pouvoir' as the slogan of Paris 1968 had it), or at least that the real is not the necessary, and that a certain subset of the possible is indeed necessary. While reactionary movements such as German fascism, in so far as they propose conservative revolution, may seem to evade these two alternatives, they do not in fact so much evade these alternatives as synthesize them into one totality, making the real seem necessary *qua* pure possibility (e.g. making the nation absolute as unified subject), while conversely making possibility seem necessary qua pure reality (e.g. where all projects come to be grounded in the blood-and-soil of the people as earth). The need to formulate a discursive politics that would evade the two dogmatic ontological alternatives of realist conservatism and possibilist progressivism without amounting to their reactionary sublation is precisely the need to which Nancy's work – in the wake of Heidegger's confusion of his own best insights with the political totalitarianism of the Nazis – attempts to respond.[9]

Rights and duties, right and left

The distinction between conservative and progressive tendencies relates to the distinction between duties and rights in two principal ways. On the most simple level, conservatism is aligned with duty and progressivism with rights to the degree that both conservatism and duty are based on the identification of necessity with reality, while both progressivism and rights are based on the identification of necessity with possibility.[10]

But on a slightly more complex and much more significant and interesting level, conservatism and progressivism are frequently characterized in terms of the ways in which they distribute duties and rights differently with respect to the individual and society, despite the fact that these characterizations can be inverted, indeed are so easily inverted that the play of their construction and inversion makes up an enormous part of the political polemics between left and right. The two most common characterizations of the differences run as follows.

1 According to one scenario, conservatism would regard the society (and the state that represents it) as being properly burdened (i.e. restricted) by the *duty* of bowing before the individual (as free-wheeling capitalist subject), while it would endow individuality with all *rights* to self-expression and self-realization, including the right to determine its own ethical-political duties. In contrast, progressive politics would regard the society (and as its representative, the state) as properly having the principal *rights*, whereas the individual would have to bear the burden of the *duty* to serve the collectivity.

But this characterization, as frequently as it is invoked by both right and left, can easily be and in fact is often enough inverted, giving rise to the following scenario.

2 Conservatism, one now imagines, burdens the individual with the *duty* of subordinating him/herself to existing conventions which are essentially social in character, and thus it gives all *rights* to the totality as it stands. In contrast, progressive politics is essentially concerned with or devoted to the emancipation of all individuals, the endowment of them with their proper (e.g. civil) *rights*, and to this end it attempts to *oblige* the society to care for the individual.

The fact that both of these versions of the relation between the conservative-progressive distinction and the distribution of rights and duties across individual and society are so persuasive only indicates how powerful is the polemical system constituted by the seemingly endless oscillation between them. Indeed, this system seems to have sufficient inwardly polemical coherence to keep conservatives and progressives arguing over its alternatives both among themselves and against each other for a long time to come. And yet the system does begin to be disrupted once the binary oppositions between progressive and conservative and between rights and duties (as also between individual and society, to which we will return in part III below) are destabilized (i.e. once it has become clear that the unequivocal identifications on which these oppositions are based – the identification of necessity with reality or with possibility – are themselves impossible and unreal). We will turn in a moment to the way this destabilization occurs in the work of Nancy. First, we must show how the repressed ontological ambivalence of hermeneutics returns in the form of the distinction between the two apparently unequivocal methodological dogmas of historicism and formalism.

Necessity in theory: the splitting of hermeneutics into historicism and formalism

In the field of hermeneutics in the broadest sense, conceived as the (always tendentially theoreticist and essentialist) project for the understanding of meaning, possibility as meaning is the privileged modality of necessity. But after being submerged beneath possibility (or meaning), reality re-emerges as the reality of possibility or the actual site or core of meaning, in accordance with two opposite determinations. The main opposition in terms of which hermeneutics, as the privileging of possibility, is marked by this return of reality (as real reality and as possible reality in turn) is the opposition between historicism and formalism. Historicism posits *reality* as the reality of possibility, and thus attempts to reduce all meaning to the ground of its contextual origins. In contrast, formalism situates the reality of possibility (or the site of meaning) in the very possibility of possibility (i.e. in *form* as the mere possibility of meaning).[11] But what are the political implications of these guiding methodological-disciplinary categories of theory (as hermeneutics) and practice (as politics) and of the subordinate theoretical-hermeneutical categories of historicism and formalism?

The ontological mediation of apparent political implications: theory, practice, history, and form

By the question of the political implications of theory, practice, history, and form, I mean here the question of whether it appears to be *conservative* or *progressive*; to be, on the one hand, 'passively' and 'apolitically' involved in the disengaged operations of mere interpretation, or on the other hand, 'actively' involved and busy 'getting one's hands dirty' in the political realities of the world; the question of whether it is *conservative* or *progressive* to approach interpretation, on the one hand, with a historian's interest in social and political context or, on the other hand, with an aesthete's interest in pure forms. Most frequently, when one attempts to answer such questions, one sets aside the ontological dimensions of the categories concerned (in this case, hermeneutics, politics, history, and form). Instead, one inquires merely into the political implications of these categories as such. It is the contention of the present chapter, however, that the *political implications* of these categories (i.e. their relations to the necessities of power both 'real' and 'imagined') precisely *derive from*, and are implicitly interrupted or destabilized by, their *ontological dimensions*. This is the case because these categories are unstably based on unreliable ontological presuppositions and because, as we have seen, the guiding notions of modern political implication or meaning as such – right, duty, progressive, conservative – derive from, and are at once implicitly destabilized by, their own ontological presuppositions – presuppositions which, again, are not only latent but also dogmatic or ungrounded. More specifically, the apparent political implications of the notions of hermeneutics, practice, historicism, and formalism depend on whether or not these notions *share the ontological presuppositions* that underlie our most common conceptions of progressive and conservative political meaning. The politics of hermeneutics and the hermeneutics of politics depend on the ontology common to both politics and hermeneutics: the politics of hermeneutics is always a political ontology of hermeneutics, and the hermeneutics of politics is always a hermeneutic ontology of politics. In order to concretize this claim, it is necessary now, first, to sketch in the associative ontological 'grounds' for the political appearances of hermeneutics (as theory) and politics (as practice) in general and, second, to sketch in the – equally associative – ontological 'grounds' for the political appearances of historicism and formalism (as specifications of hermeneutics).

The pattern of the (ontologically mediated) political resonances of theory and practice is symmetrically self-doubling, and in this sense quite simple. Hermeneutics (or theory) appears to be progressive because with progressive politics it shares the privileging of *possibility* as the essential modality of necessity. (This analogy between hermeneutics and progressivism obtains despite the fact that hermeneutics privileges possibility as such, whereas progressive politics privileges possibility only as the preferred form of a ('political') reality initially privileged (i.e. only as the preferred form of the possibility that returns from its repression at the origin of the discourse of political practice) when reality is installed as the proper form of necessity).

116

Practical politics, in turn, appears initially to be conservative, and this applies in principle even to revolutionary practical politics, as soon as it acknowledges itself to be a practical politics *per se*. Although this appearance may at first seem paradoxical, upon slight reflection the reason for the conservative appearance of politics as such (and indeed of all that acknowledges the sovereignty of practice) is clear. Politics and conservatism both privilege *reality* as necessity (even if politics, unless one should speak here of a 'politicism', privileges reality as necessity pure and simple, whereas conservatism privileges reality as the proper determination of the meaning (i.e. as the essential possibility) of reality). This ontological 'reason' for the apparent conservatism of politics as such explains, for example, the enduring appeal, from a progressive point of view, of such forms of political engagement as the extra-parliamentary opposition or, at the limit, of total political disengagement, apathy, or aestheticism.

On the other hand, of course, we often assume that hermeneutics is conservative, because it is taken to sanction reality, in the sense of the status quo, precisely by ignoring it (i.e. by, apparently, refusing to acknowledge reality in favour of mere possibilities of meaning (or meaning as mere possibility or essence)). And in turn, we often enough consider politicization to be progressive as such. For it is certainly reasonable to suggest or to suppose that the activist acknowledgement of reality is always also an acknowledgement that reality could be other than it is, and that such an acknowledgement of the possibility of change shares with progressive politics the possibilist determination of necessity. This apparent accord of essence between politics in general and progressivism as such explains, for example, why those who think of themselves as conservatives tend to want to depoliticize the humanities, and why those who think of themselves as progressive activists sometimes seem to operate in terms of the assumption that any politicization is always better than none. The vanity of these schematizations, in their easy reversibility, does not prevent them from functioning with a degree of persuasiveness that is all the greater the less the arbitrariness of the ontological associations that underlie them comes into view. Again, as we will see in a moment, these are the kinds of schematizations Jean-Luc Nancy tries to displace. But first, it is important to trace ontologically the political implications of the hermeneutics of historicism and formalism, implications whose instability is no less fundamental than the instability of the political implications of the more general theory–practice distinction considered thus far.

Thus, first of all, because of its realism, historicism always appears to be more political-practical than formalism. On the other hand, then, where theoreticist apoliticality is branded as conservative (in so far as the failure to address the political is taken to be tantamount to sanctioning the status quo), historicism comes to seem progressive by means of its associations with the possibilist, activist dimension of the political-practical. On the other hand, to the degree that, in ontological terms, like historicism, conservatism too is a form of realism, historicism always echoes conservatism, just as does the political-practical in general in one of its aspects. Historicism also echoes all that goes along with the notion of duty, in both its conservative and its progressive aspects, to the degree that duty leans principally towards the notion of necessity as a restricting or limiting reality.

In turn, formalism evokes all the traits associated with those notions with which it shares the presupposition of the possibilist dogma. Thus, formalism seems theoreticist and apolitical, and in this sense conservative. It seems progressive, however, because progressivism too privileges the possible: one always therefore tends to have the vague sense that formalism *must* on some level serve emancipation, that it must have something to do with providing people with the chance precisely to unfold their lives in accordance with the possibilities that rights open up. Given the overdetermination of the political-methodological resonances circulating among these various categories – where the categories are identified with or differentiated from each other depending on whether or not they share the same interpretation of necessity – it is no wonder that there is so much confusion about political meaning in the humanities and social sciences in which these categories play such a crucial role.

III. Interruptions of necessity in Nancy

Being-in-decision

More than anywhere else in his work, it is in decision, in Nancy's decision on *decision*, that the transmutation or interruption of all traditional determinations of necessity occurs, and along with this the displacement of the political resonances of the categories of contemporary discourse sketched above (i.e. the displacement of their relations to the theme of power in its social distribution). While these traditional determinations of necessity always decisively situate the identity of necessity in either reality (existence) or possibility (essence), Nancy does not decide the issue, but everywhere insists on its undecidability. However, this non-decision on Nancy's part must be seen, he argues, as a decision precisely *for* decision. By comparison with Nancy's decision (i.e. also with his decision to adopt such a notion of decision), the traditional decision of necessity as either reality or possibility appears to be an attempt to deny or avoid decision by moving beyond or transcending it as quickly as possible and hence to be a decision *against* decision. This distinction between the confrontation of decision and its evasion, between the decision in favour of decision (as the undecidable) and the pseudo-'decisive' decision which turns out to be a decision against decision in its (in)essential undecidability, is one Nancy himself explicitly clarifies in various places, in particular in 'The decision of existence'.[12]

The ontological status or modal position of decision, as it arises out of Nancy's reading of Heidegger in 'The decision of existence', is rendered difficult to situate already by the essay's title, as also by the essay's explicit thesis, 'the mundanity of decision' (p. 82). Whereas 'decision' is traditionally seen as situated within the will, the subject, and hence the sphere of possibility (even if decision initiates the move towards realization), while the 'world' and 'existence' are traditionally associated with the object and its reality, Nancy unsettles the expectations established by these traditional connotations. The meaning of the phrase 'decision of existence' is suspended between three possibilities: the title can refer either to a decision that would decide *over* existence or to a decision that would be reached or decided *by* existence or, finally, to a decision that is nothing other than existence, an existence that is in turn pure decision. We thus neither know which term is the object and which the subject nor whether or not there is an identity or a difference between the two terms. The effect of the title as expression for the essay's thesis, then, is to displace the concept of decision towards the reality it is normally taken to determine, while displacing the concepts of existence and worldliness towards the subjectivity and possibility they are ordinarily taken to realize or delimit.[13] Decision is thereby displaced into the undecidable position that we have specifically identified above as that of necessity itself. Decision becomes a name precisely for necessity as undecidable. But what exactly is the rationale for such a positioning of decision? Why place decision in this ontological situation? What is the structure of decision and why does it dictate such an indeterminate ontological status?

As a 'thing' situated somewhere between thought and action while remaining none the less nominally on the side of subjectivity, a decision can be structurally described in two contrasting ways: either decision realizes the possible, seizes the possible and initiates the process of its transformation into a reality, or decision renders the real possible, takes hold of what was simply external reality and transforms that (dead) reality into a (living) possibility for the subject, transforms inessential existence into essential existence, internalizing and appropriating it in so doing (p. 89). To this double model for the structured event of decision corresponds a double model for the cognitive process that would accompany the event of decision on the level of ontological dogma. If decision is experienced as realization of the possible, then it must be accompanied by the passage from the assumption that the necessary is the possible to the assumption that the necessary is the real. If decision is experienced as the rendering possible of the real, then it must be accompanied by the passage from the belief that the necessary is the real to the belief that the necessary is the possible. What is entailed by these two points of view or models — models at once of the structure of decision and of the ontological dogmas implied by the elements of this structure (these elements being the moments with which the event of decision begins and ends) — is that decision is radically liminal and intermediary, always conceivable in terms of both models, and in this sense undecidable. Because the passage is a moment of mediation, the passage itself is always undecidable concerning not only which way it is moving but also which term it belongs to (i.e. which term determines the status of decision itself). Thus, in decision, the terms themselves (possibility and reality) become undecidable.[14] Since, in decision, one neither knows whether one has to do with a possible or real event, nor how the structure of this event is to be described in unequivocal modal terms, nor even how to tell possibility and reality apart, how could one ever determine definitively whether or not a decision is taking place or has taken place?

Since Nancy develops his view of the undecidability of decision through a partial reading of *Sein und Zeit*, and since the 'decisionism' of Heidegger is one of the more important traits he shares with various other manifestations of Fascist irrationalism, it is important to retrace here the outlines of Nancy's reading of Heidegger in 'The decision of existence'. The argument by means of which Nancy unfolds his view of decision (as undecidable in its very worldliness) arises from a reading of Heidegger that overemphasizes neither the conservative (i.e. realist) nor the revolutionary (i.e. possibilist) dimensions of Heidegger's text. Nancy's reading turns around a decision to de-emphasize the differences between *Erschlossenheit* (disclosedness), *Entschlossenheit* (resoluteness), and *Entscheidung* (decision), while emphasizing their continuities, a decision that makes possible a more nuanced appreciation of the complexities of Heideggerian decision than a reading that elides the continuities between these terms in favour of their differences. As a consequence of his willingness to be guided by the play of the signifier that brings these terms together, Nancy is able to distinguish two levels in Heidegger's distinction between the authentic and the 'falling' forms of existence (i.e. between decided and indecisive existence). On the one hand, Heidegger in fact draws a distinction – quite traditionally philosophical in character – between an essential and an inessential aspect of human experience (pp. 93–4). On the other hand, he indicates that the 'fallen' state of inauthenticity, idle talk and its equivalents – that is, the (inessential) awareness of entities in the absence of any awareness of being – is the essential situation of humanity. The standpoint from which the distinction is drawn between authentic and inauthentic existence would itself belong within this essential situation of inessentiality.[15] The distinction between authentic and inauthentic, or between decision and non-decision, would itself be an inauthentic and non-decisive distinction. The consequence of this latter inauthenticity, however, is double. On the one hand, the authentic is now situated in the inauthentic, decision situated precisely in indecision, the understanding of being itself situated in the ontologically forgetful ontic understanding of mere entities.[16] On the other hand, such a correction of the inauthenticity of the original distinction is corrected, and suspended, in turn: the constatation that all experience is involved in the inauthenticity of non-decision is itself also, and by its own lights, caught up in inauthenticity and non-decision.[17] It is thus neither quite the case that there is a difference between decision and non-decision nor that there is no difference.[18] It is not decided whether or not there is a difference between decision and non-decision, and thus it is not decided whether or not it is decided whether or not there is a difference between decision and non-decision, etc., to infinity.[19]

The socio-political implications of Nancy's reading of Heideggerian being-in-the-world as being-in-decision (and as being-indecision) begin with the rejection of Heidegger's elitism of the heroic.[20] Decision becomes in Nancy's work so intimately intermingled with the banalities of everyday life that there is no room left for the always easy and always dangerous pathos consistently attached in Heidegger's text to the choice to face death rather than to face the social, 'practical' concerns of the everyday.[21] Because Nancy authenticates being lost in 'practical' concerns as an adequate mode – or rather as the only conceivable medium or place – of (always inadequately) assuming one's being-towards-death, the pathos of heroic authenticity comes to seem the ultimate inauthenticity, the *ne plus ultra* of kitsch, the apotheosis of banality. This does not of course imply that the banality of the everyday becomes simply heroic, although the heroization of the non-heroic is also an immediate after-effect of the deheroization of the heroic. Rather, as a third step, being-in-decision must avoid these two principal alternatives, which are so many ruses of the desire for salvation. On the one hand, the relation of the individual to the social must not take the form of the individual's (heroically) self-sacrificial self-removal from the social whole. Here, the individual part would stand apart from the social whole – the part representing the death of the whole while the whole represents the life of the part – only in order to master its own death by dying for the whole in exchange for the right to live on ideally in the life of the whole. Nor is it sufficient, on the other hand, for the (non-heroic) individual merely to conform to the demands of the social. Here the part would take its place in the whole, would disappear or die into the whole, only in order to be saved by its eternal duration. In contrast to these two alternatives, being-in-decision requires neither the disappearance of the individual into pure possibility devoid of reality (i.e. the death purified of all life that in turn, dialectically, becomes a life purified of all death), nor the disappearance of the individual into a pure reality devoid of all possibility (and so purified of all loss and all desire), but the insistence of the individual-in-decision. This would give rise to a politics (i.e. a position on and in the distribution of necessity qua power) somewhere between the mere deheroization of the heroic and the concomitant return of the hero in the heroization of the non-heroic. Neither heroic nor non-heroic, such a politics would be a-salvationary. It would insist on remaining in-decision, that is, it would refuse all illusions of the salvation or redemption of the human from precisely the unreal and impossible necessity of decision. Decision would be the inescapable – but also interminably indeterminable – necessity towards which such a politics would commit its loyalties. For such a politics, the only homeland would be the homeland of being-in-decision, (not) a very homely homeland (at all); the only identity in terms of which to articulate a political position would be the identity of the in-decision of the everyday.[22]

It does not, of course, follow from the undecidability of decision that being-in-decision is simply inactive or devoid of any practical dimension. But the notions of action and practice are no longer determined here by the realist decision of necessity. Rather, action and practice are drawn into the space of decision and affected by its non-reality and non-possibility, which again does not mean that they do not persist or insist – and even become more 'real' than ever before – in this state of modal suspension.

thought . . . does not think action in the sense in which it would subsume action under 'theoretical' or 'ideal' rules; rather, it thinks, as its own limit and as its own difference (and as that which makes it think, in its ownness), the *essential, active decision of existence*. Its necessity is also called freedom, and to itself it sounds freedom's most demanding call. But freedom is not what disposes of given possibilities. It is the disclosedness by which the groundless Being of existence exposes itself, in the anxiety and the joy of being without ground, of being in the world.

(pp. 108–9; my italics)

In order to unfold further the implications of this necessary freedom of decision – neither material reality nor ideal possibility and both – for the 'realities' of action and practice, let us turn to the explicit determination of the concept of practice in Nancy's recent book, *Le sens du monde*.

The politics of non-self-sufficiency as practice of infinite linkage

For all that falls within the closure of Western metaphysics, politics considered as real practice has always been taken to subserve (i.e. to originate and to culminate in) a self-identical, self-sufficient, self-determining entity, whether or not this entity be characterized as real or possible, material or ideal, and whether this entity be viewed in terms of nation, race, religion, class, sex, gender, sexual preference, or some other category of cultural-political identity. In contrast with all such political archeo-teleologies, Nancy views political practice, without origin or end, as the incessant (re)configuration (and deconfiguration) of the *non*-self-sufficient. On such a view, practice becomes one name for being 'itself' as the incessant play of (un)linkage. Nancy develops this view of practice out of an analysis of what he takes to be the two dominant traditional conceptualizations of a politics of self-sufficiency in the West, an analysis it behooves us to retrace here in its main outlines.

The two models of political grounding Nancy views as structuring the entire field of the political within the closure of metaphysics are what he calls the model of the collective *Subject* ('le Sujet') and the model of the collectivity of *Citizens* ('le Citoyen'). Whereas the identificatory participation in the subjecthood of the Subject in this sense means participation in the interiority of a self-negating self-appropriation, citizenship means sharing in the exteriority of purely formal relations. A politics of the Subject is always essentialist and subjectivist. Hence, it proposes itself as a ground of pure *possibility*. A politics of

123

the Citizen, in contrast, is constituted around the external existence, the objectivity of the collectivity. Hence, it proposes itself as a ground of pure *reality*. Both the notion of political subjectivity and the notion of political citizenship attempt to reduce the political entity to a variant of *necessity* in the sense of self-sufficiency and self-determination.[23]

According to Nancy, the two poles of this political closure never appear empirically in their purity but always, in one way or another, in mixtures. Moreover, in structural (as opposed to empirical) terms, they are always bound to turn into each other to the degree that they are mutually definitive. Because each structurally contains the other, it is inevitable that the difference between the two should reappear within each. Thus it is that in Nancy's analysis political subjecthood and political citizenship are each divided in turn into the two terms of *sovereignty*[24] and *community*.[25] Sovereignty and community represent here the aspects of separateness and togetherness, respectively, that repeat in different ways the possibility (of the subject) and the reality (of the citizen) within each. Sovereignty, Nancy writes, corresponds to the *conceptual*, and thus to the subjective or freely grasping aspect of self-sufficiency, while community corresponds to the *intuitive*, or the objective, unfree, and passively grasped aspect, its dimension of mechanical exteriority (p. 172).

In the face of the alternatives presented by these two fundamental political models – or rather, in the face of the continual transformation of each into the other – Nancy chooses (not to choose). He decides (to decide) upon the exploration of the undecidable border between the two as the place of the political 'necessity' of today.[26] It is on the border between pure interiority and pure exteriority, on the border between free separateness and unfree belonging, that Nancy attempts to develop his notion of practice as the incessant and unending[27] renewal and reknotting of (un)linkage.[28] The infinite task of such practice is the (reflexive) task of the constant redetermination (and re-indetermination) of the proper subject of this practice.[29] The movement of practice is no longer merely the movement of self-determination, but also and above all the movement of self-indetermination. Practice has as its origin and its goal the continuous displacement and redetermination of its own borders. Political practice is the practice of (collective) self-displacement and (collective) self-suspension, the opening of the (collective) self on to the world without.[30]

Within the context of the present argument, what is above all important about this politics of linkage is that *it does not privilege the real* either as that on which practice should act or as the action of practice (i.e. it does not determine the ontological status of practical action as reality). Between the reality of any fixed community and the possibility of a free subjectivity, the 'act of trying' (p. 180) is always neither possible nor real, neither active nor passive. Like a decision, it remains to be repeated in order to have occurred.[31] And what it acts upon is unities that are other knots in turn (i.e. other knottings (neither simply possible nor simply real) in the process of being tied up and coming untied, and with which it – passively also – finds itself tied up).[32]

Not only does Nancy's notion of political practice escape the privilege of the *real* (that is, the totalizing denegation or marginalization of possibility as which politicization always tends to hyperbolize or caricature itself), but it also refuses to sanction unaltered both the divisions of the field of political 'reality' we have discussed above, the division into left and right political directions, and the division into rights and duties. While Nancy explicitly links himself – obviously in order to distance himself from all forms of conservatism – with left traditions (and hence risks identifying himself with the privilege of the possible these traditions entail), he none the less also explicitly criticizes the degree to which the left traditions still adhere to political theology and the idealism of self-sufficiency.[33] And while he speaks of (un)linkage in terms of rights and duties, he does so by situating (un)linkage midway between the two: as a duty that is at once a right, a right that is always already a duty, and hence as what is properly speaking neither a duty nor a right.[34]

Finally, and with this gesture he places himself again on the limit between the discourses of left and right and on the limit between the discourse of rights and the discourse of duties, Nancy determines the act of (un)linkage as a 'seizure of speech – which is also a being-seized by speech' ('prise de parole – qui est aussi bien la prise par la parole' (p. 181)). Such a moment of speech is at once more ideal than a moment of pure action (because it participates in the notion of expression) and less ideal than a moment of the expression of subjectivity (because the one who speaks is seized by speech, so that the 'seizure of speech' is not a moment of self-presence for the subject, but precisely of the subject's connection to the coming 'communities' with which the language will have communicated). On the one hand, the politics of the seizure of speech is not meant to enable the self-expression of stable communities (qua substantive subjects) taken to be preconstituted already in the struggle for expression that precedes their accession to speech. Rather, it regards communities as simultaneously gathered and strewn only by such accession and not before. On the other hand, such a politics would not demand that unstable knots of identity-configuration translate their singular idioms into the overarching language of the total or universal community or society. Neither particularist nor universalist, then, the practice of (un)linkage constitutively alters each of its terms in the moment when they enter into the virtual spasm of their mutual 'seizure':

> politics does not come from an Idea. . . . Its occurrence could be called a
> *seizure of speech*: the surging forth or passage of some *one* and of each *one* in
> the enchaining of the effects of meaning, enunciation, proffering, phrasing
> or tracing, going from the cry, the call, and the complaint all the way to the
> discourse, the poem, and the song, but also to the gesture and silence. Both
> language and more or less than language, but always responding to some-
> thing of language in that it is itself the link without substance, idiosyncratic
> and common.
>
> (p. 180)

The political practice of incessant linkage and unlinkage, then, is a politics of the participation in the partitioning of parties and parts.

But do we not have to take more seriously and view more sceptically the fact that this political practice culminates in what is essentially a modality of language, a mere communicative 'gesture' ('geste' (p. 175))? According to the metaphysical political ontology sketched above, political practice has to articulate itself as a real intervention in a real reality in order to be worthy of the name of 'political practice' at all. If Nancy reduces political practice to the polylogue of gestural speech, from the viewpoint of the metaphysics sketched above he would seem to be reducing the realm of hard reality to what is little more than mere possibility. He would seem to be reducing politics to some kind of vaguely aesthetic spirituality, to a kind of meaning or meaningfulness more appropriate to the discursive-subjective concerns of a hermeneutics than to the real-world tough-mindedness and the serious work of the political. In what remains I will attempt to demonstrate the insufficiency of such a meta-physical reading of Nancy, by showing that if, in Nancy's work, political necessity is displaced in the direction of hermeneutic necessity – a mere need of interpretive reading and writing – this displacement is accompanied by a displacement of hermeneutic necessity in the direction of the political. Moreover, because the dialectics of these two displacements is a dialectics of being-in-decision, it does not culminate in a conclusive synthesis of any kind, but in the incessant interruption of its own repetition.

Understanding before understanding: the passing on of interpretation

In his main text on hermeneutics, *Le partage des voix*,[35] Nancy argues, once again by way of an interpretation of Heidegger, that interpretation is not essentially a task teleologically oriented towards the recovery of meaning but rather – if not quite essentially, then not quite existentially either – the passing on of an announcement whose meaning remains deferred. In order to develop this notion of interpretation as passing on, Nancy begins by summarizing the main principles of the 'classical' hermeneutics of meaning, as represented currently by the work of such scholars as Ricoeur and Gadamer.[36]

The conventional, institutionalized form of hermeneutics determines it as a project for the recovery of lost meaning *qua* recovery of lost subjectivity.[37] Nancy retraces this project of recovery according to the 'classic' version of the hermeneutic circle found in the work of Paul Ricoeur, where the circle takes the (Hegelian) form of a three-step trajectory for the recovery of the meaning of belief as a belief in meaning.[38] The first step of this trajectory is the immediate presence of belief as meaning (i.e. possibility in its reality or presence). The second step is the 'discovery' that such immediate belief has been lost. Hermeneutic consciousness in the narrow sense begins with this second moment, when the mind registers or posits retroactively that immediate belief has been lost. The potential interpreter finds him/herself confronted by the mere possibility of possibility, the mere possibility of meaning, a discovery which tends to turn into a hermeneutical reflection on how meaning, or possibility, is possible, and thus to give way to a theory of the meaning of meaning. Finally, this retrospective anticipation, or nostalgic expectation, of meaning passes, by means of the work of critical interpretation, into the third step, in which meaning is recovered and secured (i.e. possibility becomes necessary by discovering its own ground). In summary, according to such a hermeneutic narrative, the process of understanding takes us back from the present possibility of possibility (i.e. the present desire for meaning) to the prior reality of possibility (i.e. the prior presence of meaning), and this backward movement simultaneously accomplishes the movement forward to the necessity of that original possibility (i.e. to the recovery of lost meaning on the basis of interpretation).[39]

I have suggested above that the 'decisive' hermeneutic determination of necessity as possibility (i.e. as subject and meaning) is followed by the reintroduction of the reality this determination excludes. Reality returns to haunt meaning as form (in formalism) and/or as history (in historicism). Form and history return, that is, as determinations of the very reality of meaning. The dialectical model of hermeneutics that Nancy takes as his point of departure is a bit more sophisticated, however, than either of these alternatives (formalism or historicism), for it combines both (history and form, or real genesis and ideal structure) into a single structured genesis. This dialectical hermeneutics identifies with the process of history (seen as reality) both the *process* of the passage across the formal moments of the reality, possibility, and necessity of meaning and the *culmination* of this process (i.e. both the *passage* from meaning (presupposed as lost) to meaning (whose rediscovery will have been anticipated) by way of the interpretive desire for meaning, and the *meaning* ultimately arrived at). The (real, historical) *development* and the (potential, formal) *structure* of meaning are thus ultimately synthesized in the meaning of history, that is, in *history* itself (as the history of meaning): the development of the structure and the structure of the development of meaning become one in the meaning as soon as this meaning has been rediscovered as and in the necessity of its reasons, causes, or grounds.[40] History is here (as in any Hegelianizing dialectics) the history of the loss and recovery of meaning.

The 'model' of interpretation as passing on that Nancy discovers in Heidegger, however, diverges radically, even if in a subtle and easily overlooked manner, from this dialectical model in which metaphysical hermeneutics culminates. And in diverging from and undermining the foundations of this dialectical model, the passing on of interpretation in Nancy also of course undermines the foundations of the pre-dialectical models that dialectics totalizes, historicism and formalism.[41] In its most economical formulation, Nancy's passing on of the Heideggerian passing on of hermeneutics runs as follows:

> being (*l'être*) is nothing the meaning of which would be attained by a hermeneutic path, but the *hermeneia* is the 'meaning' of this being (*étant*) that we are, 'human beings,' 'interpreters' of the *logos*.

> (p. 10)

In the Heideggerian search for the meaning of being, the terms 'meaning' and 'being' do not, of course, retain their everyday (i.e. their dialectical) senses. We do not pass from being (as henceforth lost reality of possibility) through the interpretive activity of phenomenological description (as possibility of possibility) to the arrival of the meaning of being as the synthesis of being and meaning (i.e. reality recovered in its essential possibility as in its necessity). We do not achieve this passage in Heidegger because here the meaning of being as human being is *interpretation itself*, which entails the indefinite *postponement* of meaning. For Heidegger, according to Nancy, what we are, in our being, is the interpretation of being. The meaning of being is the postponement or interruption of the arrival of the meaning of being in, as, and through interpretation itself. The meaning of being(-there) is that being (as the being of meaning) has never come (back), but is always still coming (back) out of the future. Because the meaning of (human) being is interpretation, we cannot ever know what this means; we cannot ever know what interpretation means, for we could only know this at the end of an endless process of interpretation. Interpretation is thus the 'passing on' of meaning in two principal senses: it 'passes on' or transfers and defers meaning from one moment to the next in the process of an endless unfolding; and in it meaning 'passes on' or dies in being born, since interpretation constitutively interrupts and infinitely postpones the arrival of meaning as such.

As Nancy's analysis brings out, the principal import of Heidegger's (dis)-figuration of the hermeneutic circle as a figure of necessity resides in the fact that he takes seriously and affirms not only the necessity of the circle but also its *impossibility* and its *unreality*, that is, the necessary impossibility of meaning itself (including any meaning of 'interpretation'), and the necessary unreality of meaning, the failure of its recovery ever punctually to occur. In other words, Heidegger 'realizes' that human being is endlessly interpretive understanding, and that precisely *therefore* there is no meaning *per se*. In stark contrast, although traditional hermeneutics, too, situates the essence of human being in inter-pretive understanding, such hermeneutics draws from this anthropological thesis the consequence that what is essential and essentially present is the *meaning* that interpretive understanding actually grasps.

What makes it possible for Heidegger to affirm the non-reality and the non-possibility of the necessity of the hermeneutic circle (i.e. of necessity *as* the hermeneutic circle) is that, as Nancy points out, Heidegger does not imagine himself to be required to conceive in terms of *grounding* the passage from the loss of meaning to its recovery. In this (now endless) passage or passing on, neither term grounds the other except in so far as it simultaneously ungrounds it. The passage of interpretation is the condition of (im)possibility for any meaningfulness of 'grounding' whatsoever: 'The meaning of being can never be contrasted with entities or with being as the 'ground' which gives entities support; for a 'ground' becomes accessible only as meaning, even if it is itself the abyss of meaninglessness (pp. 193–4).[42] The passage from the loss of the reality of the meaning of being to the return of this meaning as the necessity of interpretation does not take the form of the grounding of interpretation in the reality of the meaning of being nor of the grounding of the reality of the meaning of being in interpretation. Rather, meaning and being in general – possibility and reality – are here 'grounded' in the necessity of interpretation which ungrounds each in that it holds their relationship in the suspension of an 'actual' expectation. But how are we to 'understand' this necessity of inter-pretation, if not as grounding?

> The *logos* of the phenomenology of *Dasein* has the character of a *hermeneuein*, through which the authentic meaning of Being, and also those basic structures of Being which *Dasein* itself possesses, are made known [*kundge-geben*] to *Dasein's* understanding of Being. The phenomenology of *Dasein* is a *hermeneutic* in the primordial signification of this word, where it designates this business of interpreting.
>
> (pp. 61–2)

Instead of being a foundational path to comprehension, interpretation (*Aus-legung*) in Heidegger is the announcement, proclamation, manifestation (*kund-geben*) of a message, its being passed on as the incessant recommencement of its passing on. Interpretation announces or offers 'the authentic meaning of Being' and 'the basic structures of Being which *Dasein* itself possesses' to '*Dasein's* understanding of Being'. As in a dialectical hermeneutics, so here, too, inter-pretation both arises out of a presupposed understanding and moves towards an anticipated understanding, but it does not arrive at what it announces. It announces only in a mediated, discontinuous way, from afar: *kundgeben* is only with some difficulty assimilable to the fundamental figures of logocentrism such as hearing oneself speak. And it announces the broken-open-ness of its own 'circularity' (i.e. the fact that it does not know what the very 'circularity' of its own message actually means).[43] Understanding always finds itself *before* understanding, then, in two different senses which do not coincide: interpretive understanding has a reflexive or circular structure, and in this sense it stands facing itself or *before* itself; but the reflexive structure is never closed: Hei-degger speaks of the *opening* or *disclosure* of the world through interpretive understanding. To this extent, understanding incessantly precedes and proceeds upon itself, comes *before* itself and, not yet having come, keeps on coming.

Given the (broken) *reflexivity* of interpretation as annunciative passing, it is not surprising that the *necessity* of such passing in Heidegger should still be marked by the divisions of subject and object, possibility and reality. On the side of the 'subject', as we have thus far seen, the necessity of the passing of interpretation appears as the necessity of the hermeneutic circle (i.e. as the necessity of an unavoidable methodological, epistemological, theoretical con-undrum). Of course, the fact that Heidegger places this epistemological difficulty at the centre of the ontological structure of being-there effectively shifts the necessity of the hermeneutic circle away from the possibilism or theoreticism of the epistemological. The hermeneutic circle becomes a matter of existence, not merely a matter of essence.

In addition, however, the necessity of interpretive passing appears in a more 'literal' manner on the side of the 'object': Heidegger defines interpretation as the passing on of a message the 'origin' and 'content' of which is nothing less than *destiny* itself. As Heidegger writes in a text Nancy quotes from nearly thirty years after *Sein und Zeit*:

> The expression 'hermeneutic' derives from the Greek verb *hermeneuein*. That verb is related to the noun *hermeneus*, which is referable to the name of the god Hermes by a playful thinking that is more compelling than the rigor of science. Hermes is the divine messenger. He brings the message of destiny [*Botschaft des Geschickes*]: *hermeneuein* is that exposition which brings tidings because it can listen to a message. Such exposition becomes an interpretation of what has been said earlier by the poets, who, according to Socrates in Plato's *Ion* (534e), *hermenes eisin ton theon* – 'are interpreters of the gods'.
>
> (p. 29)

What is this destiny to which interpretation is destined? Because it is a matter of being (*Sein*) and not the totality of beings (*das Seiende im Ganzen*), destiny cannot be here the brute reality of the ineluctably given. Hence, it does not simply exclude (the 'freedom' of) the possible. Since the possible plays a role in its determination, this destiny is one that still awaits both its destiny and the determination of its destination. Because here destiny is to be understood as neither merely real nor merely possible, neither referent nor sense, it is a destiny that is always still beginning and ending, moving between its reality and its possibility.[44] It is always still just opening up out of (and closing down as) the difference between reality and possibility, always opening to and as its redestination towards one or the other of these modal poles.[45] Unlike the historicist notion of history as reality, and equally unlike the dialectical notion of history as synthetic recovery of meaning, the history (*Geschichte*) of being as the destiny (*Geschick*) of interpretation occurs – and passes on – as the non-synthesis of non-reality with non-meaning, as the necessary (and therefore incessant) interruption of the hypostasization of the incessant. To interpret – to be – is to participate in the occurrence and the passing on of this interruption.

But what are the political implications of this notion of interpretation as the passing on of an announcement of destiny? Whatever may have been Heidegger's misunderstanding of his own notion of destiny (and although we have

131

touched on it obliquely in our discussion of decision above, this 'historical' question does not belong to our main concerns here) we have excluded the possibility that Heideggerian destiny (*Geschick*) can be destined to be understood as anything like the totality of a reality, including *a fortiori* the national-socialist version of the totality as national-racial reality synthesized with a national-racial possibility it would absorb. The question of the politics of such a notion of destiny, however, still remains open. Implicitly broaching an answer to this question while explicitly attempting to clarify what Heidegger means by 'Hermes brings the message of destiny', Nancy writes:

> it is necessary to add [*il faut ajouter*] that destiny is nothing other than the announcement, and the passing out [*le partage*] of the announcement of the *logos*. What one has called 'logocentrism' . . . proves at the same time to be given to the most powerful of decenterings, to a destinal (fatal) division of the *logos* itself.
>
> (p. 82)

The necessity of interpretive passing is not only a passing *on*, in the sense of a deferral and death, of meaning. It is also a passing *out*, in the sense of an originary (and still fainting) distribution, partition, division, and sharing of meaning between the singularities who pass it on to each other.[46] In principle and/or in fact, interpretation involves an endless fragmentation of voices, of messengers who deliver perhaps finally no message other than the endless fragmentation they are. Thus, not only is Nancy's hermeneutics not theoreticist or possibilist, but the subject of Nancy's hermeneutics, in so far as one can still speak of a 'subject' here, is so radically communal, so hypercommunal or hyperbolically communal, that 'communal' can no longer be the word. Because the 'subject' of interpretation, as the passing on and out of meaning, does not recover itself as meaning, but remains beside itself, awaiting the arrival of its meaning as the arrival of its self, this 'subject' exceeds the borders of the individual, but also exceeds the borders of any identifiable community. The passing on and passing out of meaning passes on and out beyond itself into the political practice of communal (un)linkage.

Since 'we' participate in the process of such (un)linkage, it falls to 'us' to decide the 'political meaning' of the passing on of meaning into its practice as the seizure of speech. It falls to 'us' to decide that this 'political meaning' is neither theoretical nor practical, neither a matter of meaning nor a matter of action, neither historical nor formal, neither progressive nor conservative, neither a matter of rights nor a matter of obligations; in short, neither possible nor real, but the (fatal) eventuality of the (un)splitting and interruption of the entire system of these oppositions. What passes (itself) on in Nancy's text – the interruption of necessity, the necessity of interruption – is the undecidability of a praxis of (un)linkage that is (not) at once a rhapsodic passing out of pure anticipation. Nancy certainly does not own this undecidability nor is he its sole or original author. His text passes it on and passes it out; it passes on and passes (itself) out in his text. It remains for 'us' to pass it on and out differently in 'our' turn. The strewn, hyperteleological and therefore no longer merely teleological redestination of this undecidability is the foremost necessity of the politics of discourse today.

Notes

1 Jean-Luc Nancy, *L'expérience de la liberté* (Paris: Galilée, 1988), p. 13.

2 For a useful overview of this history from the pre-Socratics until the twentieth century from an ontotheological point of view, see Étienne Gilson, *L'être et l'essence*, second edn (Paris: Vrin, 1981).

3 In Leibnizian rationalism, necessary propositions are 'propositions of essence . . . which can be demonstrated by the resolution of terms; these are necessary, or virtually identical, and so their opposite is impossible, or virtually contradictory. . . . Existential or contingent propositions differ entirely from these' ('Necessary and contingent truths', in *Philosophical Writings*, ed. G. H. R. Parkinson (London: Dent, 1973), p. 98).

4 The fact that English empiricism can develop from Lockean realism into Berkeleyan idealism and then into Humean scepticism is indicative of the instability of its ontological bases, the ease with which reality becomes mere possibility. The culmination of empiricism in scepticism is itself the response to the undecidability of necessity that gradually becomes explicit. Cf., David Hume: 'There are no ideas, which occur in metaphysics more obscure and uncertain, than those of *power, force, energy*, or *necessary connection*, of which it is every moment necessary for us to treat in all our disquisitions' ('An enquiry concerning human understanding', in *The Empiricists* (Garden City, New York: Anchor Press, 1974), p. 350). For a tracing of the path from the modal ontology of empiricism to Nancy's notion of the 'experience' of 'freedom', see Peter Fenves, 'From empiricism to the experience of freedom', *Paragraph* 16, 2 (July 1993): pp. 158–79.

5 This position of necessity as border (threshold, passage, mediation, limit, etc.) between possibility and reality is the central problem around which the entire 'transcendental dialectic' of Kant's first *Critique* turns. Dialectic in Kant means the conflation of subjective (possible) and objective (real) necessities. Kant's problem is that in order to make the transition from possibility to reality one needs necessity (i.e. in order for the given to be given, for the real to become real) and not merely possible or virtual, one needs an unconditioned condition, an uncaused cause, a

Jeffrey S. Librett

non-contingent ground (i.e. a necessary condition), but this condition cannot be given as an object of experience. In place of the dogmatic solutions to this problem, Kant attempts to ground transcendentally reality (through the Understanding), possibility (through Reason), and finally necessity (through the faculty of Judgement). On the position of 'subjective necessity' as the status of the faculty of Judgement, see *Kritik der Urteilskraft*, ed. W. Weischedel (Frankfurt: Suhrkamp, 1979), section 35, 217.

6 Two examples of the power of this opposition are: the extended debate in Germany between the 'critical theory' of Jürgen Habermas and the 'traditional hermeneutics' of Hans-Georg Gadamer, and the very different debate between cultural studies and philosophical deconstruction in America in the eighties.

7 Indeed, it often happens, of course, that 'hermeneutics' and 'theory' are opposed one to the other. In such instances, it is the realism (or textual quasi-empiricism) of 'hermeneutics' and the possibilism (or conceptualist quasi-rationalism) of 'theory' that are being set up in mutual opposition. But when 'hermeneutics' and politically engaged 'critique' are being contrasted, it is precisely the possibilism of 'hermeneutics' and the realism of 'critique' that are being emphasized.

8 Michel Foucault's attempt to exceed the repressive hypothesis, and to appreciate not merely the negative but also the positive dimensions of power, registers this double aspect of power or necessity. See 'Truth and Power', in *Power/Knowledge: Selected Interviews and other Writings 1972–7*, ed. Colin Gordon (New York: Pantheon Books, 1980), pp. 109–33, especially p. 119.

9 Cf. Philippe Lacoue-Labarthe and Jean-Luc Nancy, *Le mythe nazi* (La tour d'Aigues: Editions de l'Aube, 1991).

10 For a highly persuasive example of left ontology, see Herbert Marcuse, 'The concept of essence', in *Negations: Essays in Critical Theory*, trans. Jeremy J. Shapiro (Boston: Beacon Press, 1968). Marcuse traverses the history of ontology, in order to argue for the priority of materialist dialectics as the inheritor of the tradition of possibilist ontology as ethics of autonomy. For a complex example of right ontology, see Leo Strauss, 'What is political philosophy?' in *What is Political Philosophy and other Studies* (New York: Free Press, 1959), pp. 9–55. Strauss bemoans the loss of idealism in modern political philosophy, but his 'idealism' is that of virtue, whereas the 'realism' he sees in modernity amounts to a privileging of freedom. In the absence of a more detailed reading of Strauss, suffice it to say here that the opposition he draws between (ancient) virtue and (modern) freedom translates in our terms into an opposition between duty and right. Straussian conservatism would privilege the 'higher' reality of obligation.

11 This position would be illustrated by much of the work in Russian formalism, French structuralism, and Anglo-American 'new criticism', with its penchant for ambiguity and immanent formal analysis.

12 'La décision de l'existence', in *Une pensée finie* (Paris: Galilée, 1990), pp. 107–47. I will be citing, and giving page numbers parenthetically in the text for, the English translation, translated by Brian Holmes, from Jean-Luc Nancy, *The Birth to Presence* (Stanford: Stanford University Press, 1993), pp. 82–109.

13 One additional way in which Nancy places decision in between the real and the possible is by at once opposing it to and bringing it into a proximate relation with the two (themselves mutually opposed) terms of event and thought. As opposed to thought, decision is an event, but as opposed to event, decision is thought. As opposed to each, it is brought close to each but remains neither the one nor the other.

14 Among the numerous formulations of this undecidability: 'The relation to the "possible" is nothing other than the relation of existence to itself. . . . But the relation to the possible is that of (in)decision' (p. 86); 'It is . . . in this "reality", it is *as this reality*, that *Dasein* is properly open' (p. 95); 'In suspension, by definition, decision escapes; it does not take place; it can never take place. To the extent that the uprooting is constant, undecidability is the rule' (p. 95); 'Therefore, "to decide" means not to cut through this or that "truth", to this or that "meaning" of existence – but to expose oneself to the undecidability of meaning [*sens*] that existence *is*' (p. 97).

15 'The thought of decision at the origin . . . says that decision does not belong to the writing-reading of its own text. In other words, the discourse set down here (i.e. in *Sein und Zeit*) has no privilege and is not more appropriate to ownness . . . than any other (im)proper discourse would be. . . . The discourse of the existential analytic is caught up, throughout, in *Gerede* (p. 93)'.

16 The 'situation of *Gerede* . . . is itself, in its ownness, the situation of disclosedness – insofar as it is a situation wherein decision is impossible' (p. 95).

17 'This is a classic philosophical gesture. It is customary for the discourse of philosophy to warn its reader that what is to be understood is not within the reach of the ordinary way of understanding' (pp. 93–4).

18 Heidegger characterizes the passage from non-decision to decision as a 'modified grasp' or a 'modification' of non-decision. This modification should be taken literally, perhaps more literally than even Heidegger was able to take it, as a modalization, not in the sense that the modality of non-decision was simply altered, but that the decision of non-decision takes place by way of a disruption of the distinctness of all modal categories, in a kind of transmodal or omnimodal and hence nonmodal or demodalized space (Cf., 'Decision', p. 99).

19 'How can we distinguish between the basis and the suspension. . . . Will it suffice to say . . . that we must decide in favor of the impossibility of making the distinction? In one sense, we cannot get beyond this result. But in another sense, the same result seems to offer nothing more than a dazed resignation to the daze of the "they". Heidegger's text never stops wavering between these two directions. The text floats . . . it is the finite thought of the finite access to the originary Being of existence' (p. 97).

20 See Nancy's note 45 (p. 405).

21 To Heidegger's tendency to indulge in the heroic pathos of 'staring death in the face' Nancy risks opposing the affirmation of life, and to Heidegger's limitation of his analysis of moods to the privileging of anxiety Nancy risks opposing the affirmation and analysis of moods such as joy. See Nancy's notes 54 and 56 (p. 407).

Jeffrey S. Librett

22 Cf. the discussion of evil as decision against existence as against decision in
   L'expérience de la liberté (pp. 157–82).
23 *Le sense du monde* (Paris: Galilée, 1993), pp. 164–9, forthcoming as *The Sense of the
   World*, trans. with Introduction by Jeffrey S. Librett (Minneapolis: University of
   Minnesota Press, forthcoming).
24 In *L'expérience de la liberté*, Nancy displaces the traditional notions of freedom by
   radicalizing them. Here, freedom is no longer merely the freedom of the subject
   from all otherness, but also – against and beyond such freedom – the freedom of
   the subject from the otherness of its own subjectivity (i.e. the freedom of the
   subject from itself, in the sense of the freedom of the subject from the obligation
   not to be other than it is at any given moment). Freedom becomes here the
   freedom of freedom to be different from freedom. In terms of our modal allegory:
   possibility becomes the possibility for possibility to be some modality other than
   possibility. While he begins by distinguishing freedom from necessity, Nancy ends
   the book by trying to explore their quasi-identity (pp. 15, 197, et passim).
25 In *La communauté désoeuvrée* (Paris: Christian Bourgois, 1986) (in English as *The
   Inoperative Community*, ed. Peter Connor (Minneapolis: University of Minnesota
   Press, 1991)) Nancy situates our being-in-common in that which we manifestly
   have most in common: that we are apart, at an infinite distance of absolute
   singularity each from the other, and that we have, in this sense, nothing in
   common. This notion of the community of those who have no community situates
   identity in difference, and so displaces the reality with which the identity of group-
   belonging endows the individual towards the radical (im)possibility of identity to
   which the belonging precisely to the group of those who belong to no group
   delivers the singular human being.
26 The necessity of this exploration emerges, for example, where Nancy speaks of
   'l'injonction absolue d'avoir à nouer' (p. 187) – 'the absolute injunction to have to
   link up'.
27 The French signifier for 'knotting' or 'tying' (*nouage*) takes on particular significance, for it is the lack of any untying, unentangling, or end of tying – the lack of
   any *dénouement* – that disentangles this notion of practice from the subjective and
   objective teleological dimensions of the traditional models of the political between
   which it is liminally situated.
28 The two interruptions undertaken in the books on *Freedom* and *Community* – the
   interruption of freedom as necessary possibility and of community as necessary
   reality – are linked together in the notion of practice of (un)linkage as formulated
   in *Le sens du monde*. To link is to move out of a community (i.e. out of whatever
   unity one is in the act of representing) to act as a free subject in order to offer up
   one's subjectivity in turn to a new formation of that subjectivity, a new commu-
   nalizing objectification. The politics of (un)linkage would occur as the interplay, a
   necessary interplay, although neither possible nor real, between figures of depen-
   dency within freedom and independence within community, between figures of a
   receptive freedom and a spontaneity of belonging.
29 'Decision *is* existing as such, and existing, inasmuch as it does not take place for

one alone nor for two but for many, decides itself as a certain *in* of the in-common . . . decision consists precisely in this, that *we* have to decide about it, in and for our world, and thus first of all to decide about "us," about who "we" is, about how *we* can say "we" and say *we* to us' (p. 147; my translations of *Le sens du monde* here and elsewhere).

30 'Politics is the place of the in-common as such. Or again, the place of being-together' (p. 139).

31 There 'is no tie except taken up again, projected anew, knotted again without end, nowhere purely tied nor untied' (p. 175).

32 'Politics of knots, of singular knottings, of each *one* as a knotting, as a relay and reprojection of knotting, and of each knot as *one* (people, country, person, etc.), but which is not *one* except in accordance with the enchaining: neither the "one" of a substance nor the "one" of a pure distributive accounting' (p. 176).

33 The politics of linkage 'is the one that will have been sought for, obscurely, from Rousseau to Marx and from barricades to councils, in the diverse figures of the "left", always obscurely mixed with the scheme of self-sufficiency . . . never sufficiently disengaged from . . . the theopolitical' (p. 177). And of the politics of self-sufficiency Nancy says elsewhere: '*the political* as such seems to find therein its very Idea, and . . . in particular this "very Idea" does not permit any distinction between a "left" and "right" politics. There are left and right versions of this Idea. "Left" and "right" – this singular empirico-transcendental orientation ought to mean something else. Its meaning is missing still' (p. 172).

34 On the sense in which the politics of (un)linkage is something like a duty, a necessity in the sense of imposed limitation, but also an impossible necessity, the fulfilment of which is also its non-fulfilment: 'This politics . . . necessitates [*exige*]: it does infinitely more, or something other, than demand, call upon, desire, it is a summons, it has all the invasive violence of each *one* as such. Each *one* as such subverts the virtual closure or totalization of the network. . . . Each *one* displaces or disturbs the sovereignty and the community' (p. 178). And just a bit further on, this excessive obligation takes on the form of a right: 'That all that can constitute a *one* should have the actual power to do so, to link up: *human rights*, yes, of course, but first of all as the *right of a human to tie up some sense*' (p. 178). Cf. Nancy's sketchy but suggestive remarks on the Marxist notion of 'work' between necessity, or necessary reality and freedom, or necessary possibility (pp. 149–63).

35 *Le partage des voix* (Paris: Galilée, 1982). I cite here the published English translation, but alter it where it is inaccurate: 'Sharing voices', trans. Gayle L. Ormiston, in Gayle L. Ormiston and Alan D. Schrift, *Transforming the Hermeneutic Context: From Nietzsche to Nancy* (Albany: SUNY Press, 1990), pp. 211-60.

36 I omit here as not 'necessary' to the present context the entire ensuing discussion of Plato's dialogue, *Ion*, where Nancy attempts to show that the rhapsode is not at all merely an abject figure of non-knowledge as opposed to Socratic philosophical mastery, but a figure of the power of powerlessness, of the performative power of textual repetition that is characteristic of interpretation as announcement, and thus

that Ion exemplifies Heidegger's hermeneutics of announcement, as Heidegger himself had obliquely pointed out in *Aus einem Gespräch von der Sprache*.

37 'In its act of being born, modern hermeneutics is the operation – mediated by a history and as history – of the recovery or the reappropriation of a subject, of a subject of meaning and of the meaning of a subject . . . its fundamental rule is thus that meaning should be given in advance to the interpreter. . . . the most general condition of hermeneutics . . . is the circular condition of a *pre-comprehension* (pp. 214–15).

38 My concern here is not with whether or not Nancy's reading of Ricoeur does justice to Ricoeur's text: what is important is Nancy's account of a general model of hermeneutics as the recovery of meaning.

39 'Thus the hermeneutic circle has the nature and the function of a double substitution: the anticipated belief itself is substituted already for the lost, former belief (for a primitive adherence to meaning, or for a primitive adherence of meaning), and the belief mediated by the critical interpretation substitutes itself in the end for both this lost belief and the anticipated belief. In sum, this last substitution bears the traits of a dialectical sublation [*relève*]: the immediacy of the participation in meaning is suppressed and conserved in the final product of the hermeneutic process' (p. 213).

40 The language of modality I use here enters explicitly into Nancy's treatment at various moments (e.g. with respect to the continuous passage from the lost origin to its recovery by way of interpretation); Nancy writes: 'This possibility – experienced as a necessity – haunted the romantic idealism in which modern philosophy was born; perhaps it even constituted this idealism as such' (p. 214). Further, the hermeneutic circle itself is treated as the *necessity* of understanding, and thus Nancy speaks of 'the necessity of the circle' (p. 216).

41 For an extended discussion of historicism, see Nancy's essay on 'Finite history', in *The Birth to Presence* (pp. 143–66), and for his liminal deconstruction of formalism in aesthethics see his 'The sublime offering', in *Of the Sublime: Presence in Question*, trans. with Afterword by Jeffrey S. Librett (Albany: SUNY Press, 1993), pp. 25–54.

42 *Sein und Zeit* (Tübingen: Max Niemeyer, 1979). The English translation cited here: *Being and Time*, trans. John Macquarrie and Edward Robinson (Oxford: Basil Blackwell, 1962).

43 At the very conclusion of section 32 on 'Verstehen und Auslegung' Heidegger writes: 'An entity for which, as Being-in-the-world, its Being is itself an issue, has, ontologically, a circular structure. If, however, we note that "circularity" belongs ontologically to a kind of Being which is present-at-hand (namely, to subsistance [*Bestand*], we must altogether avoid using this phenomenon to characterize anything like *Dasein* ontologically' (p. 195).

44 Cf. Section 31 of *Being and Time* (p. 183) for the difference between possibility in Heidegger and in the tradition prior to *Being and Time*.

45 Cf. Martin Heidegger, 'Moira (Parmenides, Fragment VIII, 34–41)', in *Vorträge und Aufsätze* (Pfullingen: Neske, 1954). Heidegger reads (pp. 243–8) this pre-Socratic

figure of necessity as the *Schickung* (destiny, fate) and *Zuteilung* (distribution) of the *Zwiefalt* (the twofold) of beings and being. This destiny is situated between the *Denken* (thinking) of being (as possibility) and the *Sein* (being) of thinking (as the reality or material multiplicity of beings), at the point of their undecidable decision.

46 'It is a question here of neither discontinuity nor continuity, but of the beating – eclipse and explosion all at once, *syncopation* of the passing out [*partition*] of meaning – where meaning opens itself up. An opening – in the active sense of the term – is neither interrupted nor uninterrupted: it opens, it opens itself. The *history* which the *hermeneuein* engages, or in which it is engaged, is hence quite different from the historical process of hermeneutics. The *hermeneuein* belongs to time as opening, beginning, sending – not to History as the dialectical or asymptotic completion of time' (p. 223). For Nancy's other recent remarks on history and necessity, see his discussion of the 'nécessité de l'époque' (in *Le sens du monde*, p. 72, and in 'Manque de rien', in *Lacan avec les philosophes* (Paris: Albin Michel, 1991), pp. 201–7, especially p. 202).

9

Alongside the horizon

Rodolphe Gasché

In 'Euryopa: le regard au loin', a short and dense text written in 1994, Jean-Luc Nancy approaches the philosophical question of Europe by way of an investigation of Europe's vision, look, glance, seeing (*regard*).[1] Europe, Nancy writes, 'is the particular way of looking whose singular sighting [*visée*] is the universal as such' (EU, 8). His concern, throughout the essay, is with Europe as 'an idea of a vision': with the particular way of looking that this idea implies, with this vision's limits, as well as with the limits of vision itself.

Nancy's starting point is the admittedly questionable etymological meaning of Europe, *Euryopa* – originally an epithet of Zeus, meaning, according to Liddell and Scott, either *wide-eyed*, or *far-sounding* (i.e. *thundering*). *Der Kleine Pauly* renders it as 'far-sounding and looking far into the distance' and goes on to mention another possible but equally questionable etymology, to which Nancy also has recourse, namely the semitic pre-Greek *ereb*, obscurity.[2] According to this origin, the name 'Europe', to cite Nancy, 'would mean: the one who looks in the distance (or, as well, the one whose voice is far-sounding)'. But Nancy brings to bear the other possible etymology of the word, thus determining *Euryopa*'s glance as a 'look far into the obscurity, into its own obscurity'. Whether or not these etymologies are correct is of no concern here. Indeed, Nancy does not use them in an etymological sense to prove authoritatively or make a point by explaining the concept and the 'thing' called 'Europe' according to its roots. Rather, he means these derivations to incite thought and response to what they could possibly indicate about the direction that a renewed assessment of the idea of Europe could take, as well as reponse to the tension that exists between both etymological derivations. Indeed, independently of what the word *Euryopa* suggests, would anyone wish to contest that Europe looks into the distance, far ahead of itself? 'It belongs to the essence, or idea of Europe that it faces the distant, that it is this headland of the continent that advances towards the remaining world, and from which the conquest, the invasion of the world, or the making of the world world-wide has started' (EU, 5), Nancy writes. And in his essay, he focuses on this way of looking, on this very idea of looking, as well as on its continuing realization; and on whether it is possible for Europe to look further than that glance, further than the distant horizon of universality within which it unfolds and at which it aims.

Undoubtedly, Europe's characterization as a look into the distance has become a historical reality in the form of the world market and the inter-nationalization of the global community. But what makes Europe's identity as a look into the distance distinct from the pure and simple sighting of the 'universal market', and hence what makes it truly an idea, is that it points at the universal as such, which, Nancy holds, is 'evidently, the focus point, the aim, and the theme of the look of *Euryopa*'. Thus understood, Europe is in essence a look at, and a conception of, the world, 'the world' as such: Europe, has the universal in view, it has the world in view as universal' (EU, 6). But, Nancy will ask, given that there is no other idea than Europe, no other idea of Europe, can an idea be the idea of a world to begin with? Can a world be the object of a vision, a sighting, at all; something, in other words, that one takes aim at? To answer these questions one must look more deeply into the distance, into the ideal vision of universality that characterizes Europe. This deeper look, of course, is that of *Euryopa*'s look into its own obscurity.

Still, one must continue to wonder whether it is at all possible to ask further questions about the look in the distance, questions that would go beyond an inquiry into the stakes of universal vision, the idea, or philosophy. And whose response would not be determined by the horizon of the universality into which they are to take a deeper look? What would it mean to look further ahead into the distance than the distant, further than, and beyond, universality? Would such a look into the distance still be a look, a vision, a sighting? In any event, before envisioning a response to these questions, one must first take a good look, an analytical look, at looking itself: that is, at the look into the distance, the look at what is universal.

As Nancy points out, Europe is the idea not only of a vision, but of a vision characterized by a special way of looking. It has a form of its own, and it targets one and only one 'object' – the universal. 'Europe is thus inevitably the idea of an idea – form and vision, in the language of Plato', Nancy adds. Moreover, this idea of a look, and of an ideal form of that look itself, is the idea of a look that exposes and unfolds itself in accordance with a mode of exposition, or a language, of its own. *Logos* designates the language of the idea. The resulting implications for the idea of European vision, if it must expose itself in the medium of *logos*, Nancy explains as follows:

> The idea expresses, formulates, and exposes itself according to the *logos*: this is to say, according to the law of autonomy, the law of what grounds itself upon itself, of what develops and verifies itself through itself, and what returns to itself, in and for itself. *Logos* is the language of the idea insofar as it is its 'reason'. The principal 'reason' of the idea is to be the essential form, essential to the extent that it forms itself, and thus *sees itself* in everything that it makes visible and intelligible.
>
> (EU, 8–9)

Consequently, since Europe as the idea of a look includes this idea of a special form in which that look is realized and exposes itself, it is a look that sees itself seeing and that thereby sees what it sees. 'The idea is the "seeing-oneself-seeing" of vision and what it aims at', Nancy writes (EU, 9). The way the look into the distance (the look at what is universal) is modelled, as a look shaped in such a way that it is able to return to and into itself and thus to become its own ground, makes this look a look that owns itself, that is its ownmost self. At the same time, thus shaped, the vision at the heart of Europe – a vision that sets it apart – gathers its difference into itself, into a self properly closed upon itself.

Nancy draws several consequences for the idea of Europe from this form of '"seeing-oneself-seeing"' that Europe's vision espouses in so far as the *logos* is the medium of its exposition. One of these consequences in particular requires our attention here, and that is that owing to the formal 'reasons' of the idea in question, the look into the distance – the look at universality and the look that sees its own vision – is also a look that leaves itself behind. It leaves itself behind in dissolving and sublating itself. This means that as many times as 'Europe' will have taken place,

> as many times it will have figured, configured, and represented itself as the privileged identity of the vision of the universal until Europe sees itself outside itself as a new subject, until it reengenders itself as 'Occident', as 'occidental civilization' – as a result of which, curiously, it exits itself, goes further than itself all the way to the end of the world and, at the same time,

it sees itself as an other, an other than itself insofar as it is not the *orient*, not the birth of a world, but rather is the world occupied in totality, shaped in totality, and which comes back to itself as its *end*.

(EU, 9)

The moment Europe shapes itself as the figure of the 'Occident' – which means as the figure of the totalization of the world, pursuing that totalization as purpose until its end, until the world as purpose (*Zweck*) has become this end (*Ende*) – then it leaves itself behind in the figure of a fulfilment that is not only a figure of exhaustion, but is also one that, in its distinction from the 'orient', is necessarily a limited figure of its own self. Demarcating itself from itself, Europe, at this point, becomes the look at its own dissolution and disappearance. 'The Occident – or the Erebus – is essentially and structurally a self-dissolving and self-alienating notion: it is the day that sees itself ending' (EU, 9). In this figure of itself, Europe, the look into the distance, the look at universality, leaves itself behind. Yet, seeing itself leaving itself behind, its demarcation from self is also its self-demarcation. In other words, the disappearance is a loss in which losing is not lost; on the contrary, by this loss the look returns into itself. It does so, at the end of the look, and by thematizing its end, precisely by reappropriating that end as the dark spot which is necessarily presupposed by the look itself. Nancy concludes his discussion of this self-overcoming of the glance of universality as follows: 'In this way, the universal that is the theme of its vision . . . returns to itself as the blind spot of its eye' (EU, 10).

Inevitably, then, any attempt to demarcate oneself from the look into the distance which is a look at the universal is already a prescribed movement, and one that will be reinscribed in that look itself. To set oneself apart from the universal, and from the world shaped in accordance with it, is to obey the very logic of the look itself. It is to execute this look's *own* execution by which it transforms its end into a constituting limit of itself. As a result, one faces the question whether it is possible at all to keep one's distance from a universal vision such as the one named 'Europe'. Is each effort to distance oneself from the look into the distance inevitably bound to produce just 'one more turn of this return into self, in a turn each time more *archeo-logical*, which would only make us come back to the principle of Europe in order to better confirm the night of the universal into which this principle makes us enter' (EU, 10), Nancy asks? However, this is also the moment in which Nancy suggests that at the same point where universal vision has achieved its most extreme degree of self-inflection, one might perhaps touch upon – and it will, indeed, be a question of touch – something that leads to this vision's outside, an exiting in which vision would have no longer any part, and that, hence, would no longer be on the part of vision 'itself'. And, Nancy writes: 'It is not one more dialectical turn, not one more *Aufhebung*. Rather it is of the order of an additional affirmation, one more step forward. Instead of taking the form of a return, it is to go further in front of us. Further, that is, deeper into the night, deeper into the blind spot. Deeper into the look of *Euryopa*' (EU, 10). But what is it that remains to be 'seen' in this step that affirms the look of *Euryopa*, the look in the distance, by going further into its look? It is, I recall, to be a look into that end or dusk of universal vision, when the *telos* of this vision has been realized by Europe's worldwide expansion, and when this vision returns to, and reappropriates, 'the blindspot of its eye'. Advancing deeper into the blindspot of universal vision, the look that goes further into this blindspot, while not distinguishing anything in particular, not even itself ('the subject of the look itself') in the darkness, sees the night itself, Nancy claims. The eye that thus advances into the night of the blindspot at the heart of vision, and that sees itself not seeing, achieves a strange proximity to itself. 'It is closest to itself' at the very limit of itself, not yet seeing, but merely a seeing that it does not see. It is not even a seeing that could already see *itself* as *not yet* seeing; no self-objectivation occurs here, nor does its non-seeing become thematic to any seeing. It is a seeing that before having the power of sight 'sees' seeing nothing. It is seeing affected by itself in advance of all 'itself', and hence before all seeing that sees something particular.

Nancy writes of this eye that 'it sees *at itself* (*à même soi*) and not in itself' (EU, 10). Against the possible objection that such a determination of the eye that sees itself not seeing is an identifying determination, one by which even this seeing-not-seeing becomes reappropriated and launched back as the ultimately first moment on to the dialectical circumference, Nancy draws on his analysis, in *La Remarque Speculative*, of Hegel's use of the expression *an sich – à même soi*, at itself – in which text he argued that '"at itself" are in Hegel the only undialectical words'.[3] Thus, in keeping with this earlier analysis, everything hinges on the mode in which the nearness to itself of the eye that sees itself not seeing is thought. This eye, rather than looking outside or inside, looks 'at (*à même*) the limit of thinking', Nancy proposes. In other words, it does not thematize the limit of seeing. The eye that ventures a step further into the constitutive blindspot of universal vision is not a seeing that sees a more essential condition, an even blinder spot of vision which becomes meaningful in view of what it makes possible. Rather, it is a seeing that, without seeing anything, is just seeing: a seeing without a subject, without a vision, without a horizon – absolutely finite seeing. It is therefore, rigorously speaking, not a seeing anymore, but a singular 'awareness' at the border, or on the limit, of the dialectic of the particular and the universal. This 'awareness' of seeing at itself, is, however, not *of* the limit, in so far as the limit would be that of universal vision. It is the awareness of seeing prior to seeing *itself*. It is, says Nancy, a touch. 'One ought to say that it [the eye] *touches* rather than that it sees' (EU, 10). Yet, what is it that is touched by the eye?

> It touches at itself as at the infinite of its vision. It is touched by itself, affected by itself as the infinite of vision. What is nearest is the most distant; in truth, there is no 'near' nor 'distant' anymore: there is a 'self-touching' that is the absolute distance at the heart of the abolishment of distance, comparable to the touching of the eye by the eyelid that closes upon it. There is a finite touching of the infinite – or, more exactly: this touching is the infinite of finitude.
>
> (EU, 11)

Nancy himself admits that this passage, which concludes his analysis of the step further into the blindspot of universal vision and hence into a trait of seeing that is not shaped into a condition of possibility of the horizon of universality, would require lengthy elaborations on an ontological plane. But this, at least, can be said: next to the eye, on the bare surface of it, a seeing takes place, which is non-mediated, but which is not, for that matter, immediate. It consists of the singular touch by the eye at itself. What is touched in this singular look of bare seeing is the infinity of vision; in turn, the infinite of vision touches it. This moment of intimacy, of self-identity at its most profound, this self-affection of bare seeing by its infinite possibilities, is also the place where seeing is most distant from itself. In its invisibility, it is a seeing from which the polarities of nearness and distance are still absent, and not yet to be anticipated as such. What the singular, that is, finite touch touches, is seeing's openness to determinations to come, to the infinite of its possibilities. As such, this touch is also an infinite touch: the infinite of the singularity of that touch, which proceeds from nothing that it might have given to see.[4]

Setting aside the question about the ontological presuppositions of this touch, or 'nocturnal vision', as it is also termed, 'Euryopa: le regard au loin' limits itself to exploring the touch's ethical implications. If, indeed, 'Europe conceived of and presented itself above all as an ethics' (EU, 11), then a touch that touches seeing, and that occurs in the reappropriated blind spot of universal vision, must have a necessary bearing on Europe's self-understanding; and this means also on the accompanying conceptions of world, and of the way in which to inhabit it. As Nancy remarks, the values of universality, and of a world shaped accordingly, have become obscure as a result of the historical process in which the universal has turned into 'the world launched into the space of the universe'. These values are not worth anything anymore. This obscurity and loss of value, which follows precisely from Europe's successful expansion into the world, is the context for Nancy's statement that 'the entire world has become alienated by (aliéné à) the value of the universal and the universal of value' (EU, 11). In becoming worldwide, extending as far as the world goes, and stopping only at the limits of the universe itself, the world linked to the universal – hence the world *of* the universal – has become entirely suspended from the universal. In this suspension, it has given up something of itself, and has become estranged from itself; it has been made other than and foreign to itself by the universal. 'Alienation' is an imminently dialectical term, and suggests initially that the effects of the ideality-constituting-difference of Europe on the world can, and even should be, undone. But by framing Europe's difference from and to itself in terms of alienation, Nancy clearly gestures not only towards a concern eminently his own, which is a concern to think the world on this side of universality, but also beyond the dialectics of the particular and the universal. Nancy's aim is to secure a notion of world prior to the world of universality, one not alienated by the universal, but as the terminology suggests, free from the universal; and this aim shows him to construe the universal as a merely oppressive and repressive gown thrown by a particularity around the world. It is an abstract gown, and since it coincides with ascendancy of one part of the world over the whole world, up to the very limits of the universe, its universality is only disguised particularity. Hence, this gown's intrinsic violence. The difference that it makes is to inhibit the world from being itself. A violent prohibition to be itself, it forces the whole world, Europe included, into being other than itself. Nancy can, therefore, write: 'Europe, or the *Entäusserung* and the *Entfremdung* of self in the other, of self as other' (EU, 11). It would thus seem that Nancy wishes to repudiate the concept of universality (and hence also of Europe) altogether. But what then is this world, which is on this side of universality? Does it still deserve to be called 'world'? Is there nothing universal about it at all, in no possible sense of 'universality'? But a world, by definition, is a world in common! Can this communality of the world not be accounted for at all by means of the category of the universal? Or is the point, perhaps, that the world in question is not the world simply and finally freed from the tenacious grasp of the universal, but rather, in a strange way, one that has never been and will never be under the power of universality? And is it for this reason that this singular world cannot ever, as far as its singularity is concerned, be thought from – whatever the complexity of the renegotiated term might be – a notion such as the universal?

At this point, I wish to recall a statement made by Nancy in *The Inoperative Community*, concerning the declaration by Sartre that communism is contemporary community's unsurpassable horizon. After having argued that communism is no longer that horizon, Nancy remarks that this is 'not because we have passed beyond any horizon. Rather, everything is infected by resignation, as if the new unsurpassable horizon took form around the disappearance, the impossibility, or the condemnation of communism'. Yet, at this precise moment in his argument, Nancy adds: 'It is the *horizons* themselves that must be challenged. The ultimate limit of community, or the limit that is formed by community, as such, traces an entirely different line'. Even though I cannot, in the present context, discuss Nancy's thoughts on community, and on the limit which is entirely distinct from a horizon that characterizes the community, I wish to bring this demand to 'go farther than all possible horizons' to bear on the issue of a world severed from universality.[5] Understood from the Greek verb *horizein* (to divide or separate from, or, as with a border, to mark out by boundaries, to delimit, to determine, to define), the universal – or Europe, for that matter – is a horizon, and more precisely, is the horizon of the world. I do not need to recall this notion's origin in elementary optics and astronomy, nor its venerable philosophical history from neoplatonism to phenomenology as a whole. In the interest of brevity and focus, I shall limit myself to an extremely succinct exposition of the Husserlian phenomenological conception of the horizon. If I single out the Husserlian conception of horizon, it is, first of all, because in Husserl's theory of perception, world and universal horizon are so intimately interconnected that a world without horizon appears as a sheer inconceivability. By contrast, Nancy's proposition to challenge the horizons themselves is exactly what it claims to be: an attempt to think a world not enclosed within a horizon.

The Husserlian conception of the horizon emerges in the process of constitutional analyses, which is to say, of analyses that seek to determine being of all kinds through the accomplishments of transcendental consciousness. Rather than being a geocentric spatial framework for ordinary perception, horizon, in Husserl, is 'a title for what is phenomenologically exhibited in pure consciousness'.[6] To uncover transcendental subjectivity and to reach the field of transcendental experience, a phenomenological reduction is required, in which everything that does not properly belong to the acts *qua* acts is 'bracketed'. Such a reduction starts out from the fact, established in a preliminary description, that every individual act of experience, whether it is one of perceiving worldly objects or ideal possibilities, already implies a consciousness of the world – a consciousness of horizons. Each single act, with its particular horizon, always has *the* world for its *universal basis*. But in the natural attitude, the world presupposed by all positing acts is a world that is presupposed to exist: it is the all-embracing doxic basis of all individual acts. Therefore, in order to reach the transcendental field of experience, and hence the phenomenal concept of the horizon, it is necessary not only to depart from the individual acts, and from the doxic belief in the being of objects, but also to overthrow the doxic positing of being that affects the consciousness of the world present in any single act of perception. In setting all presupposed objectivity out of action, both for the correlate of the individual acts and for the correlate 'world' or 'horizon' as well, phenomenological reduction shows all acts of consciousness not only to include their objects *qua* meant objects, but furthermore to be founded on a 'consciousness of horizons . . . a consciousness which is ultimately consciousness of the world as the total horizon'.[7] It is the consciousness of the world as ultimate horizon, rather than a world behind the world in its factual existence for us, that sustains the ways in which we always already experience the world, and that makes a real understanding of the world possible; that is, makes possible an understanding of the (doxic) way in which the world is and will always be given for man as man. The constitutionally clarified world, the world as total horizon, thus names the trans-subjective understanding of 'world', of what is always 'meant' by 'world' whether it is our own or an alien world.

For Husserl, then, the world has a horizonal structure. Although the horizon is rarely thematized as such, to live in a world is to live within its particular horizon, and ultimately, within the total horizon. World and horizon are inseparable. As Landgrebe notes: 'It is essentially impossible to find men in any "pre-worldly" state, because to be human, to be aware of oneself as a man and to exist as a human person, is precisely to live on the basis of a world'.[8] Undoubtedly, this statement would require a detailed commentary, especially regarding the 'humanist' underpinnings of the concepts of world and horizon. These underpinnings are thrown into even stronger relief in the following statement by Cornelius A. Van Peursen: 'The world without a horizon is unimaginable. The world would lose its framework, along with the horizon, thereby making it entirely different. The world, as a human world, is even impossible without the horizon. . . . To eliminate the horizon is to remove man'.[9] If I stress the inextricable interconnectedness of Husserlian world and horizon, it is precisely because of Nancy's call for engaging the horizons. The stakes are high, given that to attack the horizon is to attack the world. What can it mean, therefore, indeed if it means anything at all, to contend against the horizons, particularly if a world without horizons, and without a universal horizon, seems to be unthinkable? Unthinkable, also, because it would seem to mean the destruction of the scope of human space. Should it thus only be a question of forcing existing horizons to recede, and of forcing them to open up to the 'horizon of the horizon'? Since a horizon, even a limited one, is an openness – and in the case of a limited horizon, is a finite openness – does Nancy wish only to argue for a limitlessly open horizon? He would then be saying the same thing that Husserl has already said. For the latter, as Landgrebe puts it, our own world and alien worlds stand

> in a nexus of possible continuous (direct or indirect) experience with our own, in such a manner that all such 'worlds' combine to make up the unity of the all-embracing world. Accordingly, the world cannot have for us the sense of being a self-contained world . . . we must take it to be a world unlimitedly open on all sides. In this openness it provides free space for all the different home-worlds of the most diverse human communities. It becomes the infinitely open universe as the whole of existence, the completely open horizon in which, ideally at least, our experiences can always be extended *ad infinitum*.[10]

But did Nancy not call precisely for a contesting of the horizons themselves, and for going further than all possible horizons, hence also further than a world unlimitedly and infinitely open? Given the way we have seen him to understand universality as the extension of one particular humanity to the outer limit of the entire (real) universe, in other words, as a universality that is not only repressive of particularity, but one whose infinity belongs to what Hegel called 'spurious infinity', it is certainly safe to say that he wishes to go beyond that world's unlimited openness, beyond its total horizon. In what remains of my commentary on 'Euryopa: le regard au loin', I will seek to clarify a little what it could mean to abandon the concept of horizon altogether.

The world of Europe, as we have seen before, is the world within the horizon of universality. Europe has alienated itself into this world, and this has prompted Nancy to speak of it as the name for an essential or structural alienation of self in the other, of self as other. But, he argues, although Europe sees itself thus defined as 'the *Selbstanschauung* of *Selbstentfremdung*', it is as well 'the *Entfremdung* of *Anschauung*'. What does this mean? As a glance into the distance at the universal, Europe looks at itself as other than itself, as alienated from itself. But, as Nancy suggests, this look at itself is a look no less alienated. Europe is alienated from intuition, that is, from all perception that is unmediated by the universal; hence it is alienated from the immediate perception of evident and self-present truth, first and foremost of itself. Europe, consequently, must also be understood to name an alienation of the possibility of intuiting the other as other, and the self in its 'immediacy'. In other words, Europe also stands for an essential structural inhibition of the self against opening itself to the other (itself included) as other, and to a world whose common denominator would be the self and the other's Otherness. This openness, however, preceeds by right the emergence of Europe as the world subjected to universality and horizonality. Nancy acknowledges as much when he writes: 'Europe opens up the world, as its other self, but it carries it away in its alienation' (EU, 11). Europe, in short, opens up the 'world' in the sense just alluded to, namely as a place constituted by an intuiting of self and other that would not be mediated: but it blocks it out at the very moment it launches it on to the road to universality, that is, at the moment it alienates itself in the value of universality. Nevertheless, as it is an eminently dialectical concept,

> alienation always ends up bringing to light that which is inalienable, and which makes alienation itself possible: the alterity that the 'self' is not, and to which it cannot get through, but that it only encounters, that comes towards and against it, and that is the other 'self' – not the 'self' as other, but the other of the self that is 'self', being absolutely and irreducibly other, infinitely resisting the universal reduction of 'self' to 'self'. The inalienable of the other is, henceforth, what Europe finds everywhere, in front of itself and in itself, since the world is, henceforth, at once what Europe has in front of itself and that into which it has alienated itself, alienating the world itself through its universal vision.

> (EU, 11–12)

The inalienable is the other self in so far as it is not a self carried along by the universal Self. The inalienable is the world of these singular 'selves' as well, the world 'before' universal horizonality. But both harbor 'within themselves' the possibility of alienation, in that they are structured so as to be beside-before-beyond-oneself – beside-before-beyond-'self'. Even as 'extroverted' selves, as it were, they inherently carry the possibility of alienation into the universal Self; and they themselves remain irreducible to the universal reduction. They, and their world, remain on, and at, the margin of the alienated world to which they give rise. The world is hence at least double. It is what Europe encounters outside and inside itself as irreducible to itself, but is also that into which it has lost itself, the horizonal world in which the world has been lost. Once the European universal vision experiences the world both as that which it faces, and as the universal world estranged from the world of alterity, 'the universal itself has taken on the strangeness of a dark night', Nancy continues (EU, 12). In other words, the world alienated in universal vision has itself become strange, no longer familiar as before, uncanny like the obscurity of night.

Once the universal is no longer recognizable as that which is most proper to us, the incumbent task is not to seek to reanimate it by calling upon values, but rather 'to look, without looking away, at what thus happens to us'. Nancy writes: 'One must reaffirm again the *ethos* of the look – not by turning one's eyes toward a firmament spangled with values, but by facing straight ahead into the obscurity' (EU, 12). From everything we have seen hitherto, the way this *ethos* is to inhabit the world is different from that of the *ethos* of European universal vision. There can no longer be a question of a look arising from a world that is *its* world, and embracing the horizon as the horizon of horizons. Rather, the look into the darkness of universality is, in Nancy's words, to be 'a finite look into the infinite. As a matter of fact, what we currently see is nothing other than the infinite. It is no longer the universal, as the gathering and the *Anschauung* by a subject of the world, but its [the world's] *ethos* become infinite' (EU, 12). I recall that Nancy has described the probing of the gaze of *Euryopa* as a glancing into its blindspot, into the night at the heart of universal vision. By looking deeper into this night – in which process seeing is shown to touch itself, in a finite touch that is a touching of the infinite – universal vision has itself become as strange, or uncanny, as the night itself. By touching 'itself', seeing opens upon the infinite of seeing, of a seeing no longer dominated by a totalizing horizon: that is, upon a world that is infinite rather than universal. With the nocturnal vision in which seeing 'sees' itself touching at itself, before it sees and even before it sees that it does not see, it 'sees' the infinite of vision. This is the finite touch that Nancy has called, 'the infinite of finitude' (EU, 10). In short, what such a glance into the blindspot of universal vision reveals, if one can still speak of revelation in this case, is the world as an infinite place of dwelling: that is, a place of finites, of singularities. At the extreme border of the horizon, the world appears in its horizonless infinity, a finite world, and hence an infinite one. Needless to say, it would be necessary to ponder here how the infinity of a world is to be thought in view of its lack of horizon, and of everything that horizonality implies. But, for the moment let me continue to follow Nancy's lead concerning what it means for the world's *ethos* to have become infinite.

'The *ethos* (and the *logos*) which are incumbent upon all, and which bring us all together into the world' are 'existence, and truth', Nancy writes. Given that Nancy understands existence as being 'separated (*absolutum*) from all essence and all fulfillment of essence'[11] it follows that existence, not unlike its Heideggerian homologue, is not so much an (untransmutable) value, as it is what is at stake for all finite beings as beings let within an infinite world. 'Existence and truth are *what is at stake (ce qui est en jeu)*, and there is nothing else at stake. . . . One and the other are sighted (*visées*, related to, aimed at) by something that is not exactly a looking, by a mode of sighting that Europe and the West have called "love" – as if to give it the name of the impossible' (EU, 12). If it is love – something that is 'not exactly a looking' – in which existence and truth are being aimed at, and not a look, glance, or vision, it is precisely because both existence and truth are not, to quote Heidegger, 'to be construed in terms of some concrete possible idea of existence'[12] or, to follow Nancy, because existence is not a positively identifiable reality, nor is truth something that could be cognitively reappropriated. If existence is absolutely separated from all essence, and truth is that which eludes the possibility of anamnestic rediscovery but is ultimately at stake, existence and truth are infinite. Nancy writes:

'Existence' and 'truth' mean the infinite. They mean the infinite alterity that are 'existence' and 'truth': one and the other, and both together, are always absolutely and infinitely other. Differently put, it is always existence and truth themselves which are other in the other, and which comes counter to the 'self' from its own infinite alterity.

(EU, 13)

Yet because existence and truth are infinite, only a finite look that touches at them, at their bare surface as it were (*posé sur lui, à même lui*), is appropriate in their case. In other words, they demand an ethical mode of relating, and the ethical is, for Nancy, a relation to the infinite, that is, to a finite that is infinitely finite because it is always exposed to alterity. Love, although otherwise than in the sense of 'the unappeased tension of desire or the communional fusion of Christian love' (EU, 12), is such an ethical 'relation'.

Love faces the infinite: it is a finite look, a look that gazes into the infinite (*en lui*). If this finite look that comes to rest on the alterity of existence and truth does not see any idea, form, or figure with respect to the infinite, it is because this look is not out to render the infinite intelligible. It does not, in an idealizing gesture, duplicate this infinite in an attempt to make it truly itself. Nor can the finite look's intent be to reveal this infinity's idea. (EU, 15) By this look, the infinite is not alienated from itself in an attempt to establish universally its identity. Just in resting its glance on the mere surface of the infinite, the finite look lets it be the infinite; hence it sees at one stroke right to the end, as it were, of the infinite. Nancy writes:

> The finite look is not a look deprived of the infinite, a look that would not go far enough – on the contrary, it is the look that comes to rest on the infinite as such. It does not see anything. It does not behold any Idea, any Form or Figure in need of a presentation or a production. But this look sees at one stroke right to the end (*d'un seul trait jusqu'au bout*), as it were, of the infinite. It sees that it is existence and truth, their common alterity, that are henceforth the infinite stakes of a finite world.
>
> (EU, 13)

But looking at one go right to the end of the infinite also means seeing its limits: in short, seeing that it is the infinity of finitude, of the infinitely finite. Nancy, therefore, continues: 'This world is finite because it is entirely given back, or restored, to itself. This world no longer opens on other worlds, be they new, ancient, celestial, or infernal worlds. It is not topped by values and Ideas that float above it. It is *the world* that is only world' (EU, 13). Clearly, the Idea of the world is, for Nancy, what prevents a world from being a world. He writes: 'The Idea of a world is still beyond all Idea. The Idea of the world has no figure to incarnate it, no project that would contain it, no ideal that would measure up to it, no universal that would constitute its *arche* or its *telos*, no *reason* (in the sense of a *ground*) to account for it' (EU, 14). To say that the world cannot be the object of an ideal sighting implies not only a vision that is specifically Europe's own, and thus cannot be a vision of a world, but also that this world cannot really be visually sighted. 'A world', Nancy contends, 'is a space for the infinite of truth and existence, of all existence – and is not something on which one can properly set one's sights (*cela ne se vise pas proprement*). It is not the *Angeschaute einer Anschauung*' (EU, 14). What Nancy calls world, which is the 'object' of the finite look of something closer to love than to vision, is a world free of a horizon. If it does not open on to other worlds such as new, ancient, celestial or infernal worlds, it neither opens onto *the* world, the 'total-horizon' supposedly shared by all particular worlds. No universal consciousness of the world, no transsubjective understanding of what world qua world means, pervades the finite world immanently. And because no horizon consciousness overhangs or is immanently implied by the finite world, therefore no universal meaning or essence alienates itself into particular worlds, alienating them in turn; and furthermore, no one single world can maintain the pretense of being more than just itself. In the finite world, no glance into the distance, or sighting of universality, permits a particular world to gain ascendency over all others. If the finite world is without a horizon, this is primarily because it does not rest on visual perception, but rather on what Nancy has called the finite look, and which is a look that is not essentially of the order of vision.

For Nancy, the finite world, the world which is infinitely finite, and infinitely exposed to its lack of a total and universal horizon, is *the world* that is merely world; and after having established this, Nancy concludes by way of a return to the question of the way in which *Euryopa* sees. I recall that *Euryopa*'s glance, in addition to being a look into the distance or the universal, is also a glance deep into universal vision's blindspot; a glance, furthermore, which does not *see* so much as it *touches* seeing, as it were, at its bare surface. He thus holds of the finite world that 'it is *the world* that is just world, become world by means of the expansion of the sighting of *Euryopa* out of itself, and its return to itself – which does not find *itself* in this world, but which finds itself carried away, altered in it, beyond itself' (EU, 13). As has been established before, the glance of *Euryopa* is a glance at what infinitely makes the world finite – its lack of an essence, an Idea, a horizon, and so forth. By probing into the darkness of universality, *Euryopa*'s glance touches upon infinity, rather than upon universality. Now the finite world, not unlike the universal world, is constituted by a glance that expands beyond the particular, and that returns to itself. But rather than achieving an identity with itself, this glance that returns to itself returns only to discover the otherness of its own being. The world that emerges by way of *Euryopa*'s glance is a world infinitely exposed to the lack of horizonal meaning, and also to its own otherness. It is thus a world that is no longer *Euryopa*'s own world, but is instead a world in which it itself, and the vision it represents, have become altered, and othered.

Undoubtedly, the finite world upon which *Euryopa*'s glance touches, because it is horizonless, is a world unlike the Idea of the world that Europe has stood for. It is no longer a human world: not inhuman, though, but a-human. Rather than of humans, this world is one made up of beings for whom existence and truth are the stakes. Unlike humans, whose essence is determined by their gaze at a universal idea of what the human being is (and for whom this idea is of a universalized particularity), these beings that make up the finite world are infinitely exposed to existence as a non-essence. They are thus finite beings, or singular beings, who are not, for that matter, non-infinite beings. Rather, these singular beings that make up this finite and horizonless world – a world infinitely finite, hence infinite – these beings are as many finite looks, exposed to the otherness of what is both before them and in themselves. No horizon that would ensure the scope of human space is tied to these looks as their absolute limit. Rather, these looks touch the infinite; and this tangible infinite is the infinite of the finite beings' exposure to the constituting absence, in their existence, of an eventual fulfilment of essence: in short, to the infinity of the world.

Notes

1 Jean-Luc Nancy, 'Euryopa: le regard au loin', in *Contributions*, a prepublication (in French and German) of the proceedings of a conference at the University of Leipzig (11–14 May, 1994) on 'La philosophie européenne de la culture et le projet "logos" de 1910', pp. 5–15 (the essay has also been published in *Terra Lingonna*, Langres: Lycée Diderot, January 1995). Henceforth, EU. This chapter is taken from a book-length study in progress on various current attempts to probe the philosophical resources of the concept of Europe, in the face of what Massimo Cacciari has termed the senile reactivation of the cosmopolitan idea of peaceful coexistence, or, by contrast, the return to isolationist and nationalist values, that have characterized the ongoing debate on Europe.
2 *Der Kleine Pauly. Lexikon der Antike*, ed. K. Ziegler and W. Sonthheimer (Munich: Deutscher Taschenbuch Verlag, 1979) Vol. 2, p. 447.
3 Jean-Luc Nancy, *La Remarque Speculative* (Paris: Galilée, 1973) pp. 110–18.
4 Let me recall here that, for Nancy, finitude is not to be confused with classical 'finity'. Finitude is infinitely in excess of itself. Speaking of human finitude, Nancy writes: '*Finitude* does not mean that we are noninfinite – like small, insignificant beings within a grand, universal, and continuous being – but it means that we are *infinitely* finite, infinitely exposed to our existence as a nonessence, infinitely exposed to the otherness of our own "being" (or that being is in us exposed to its own otherness). We begin and we end without beginning and ending: without having a beginning and an end that is *ours*, but having (or being) them only as others', and

through others', *The Birth to Presence* (Stanford: Stanford University Press, 1993) pp. 155–6.

5 Jean-Luc Nancy, *The Inoperative Community*, trans. P. Connor et al. (Minneapolis: University of Minnesota Press, 1991) pp. 8–9.

6 Elizabeth Ströker, *Husserl's Transcendental Philosophy*, trans. L. Hardy (Stanford: University of Stanford Press, 1993) p. 90.

7 Ludwig Landgrebe, *The Phenomenology of Edmund Husserl. Six Essays* (Ithaca: Cornell University Press, 1981), pp. 93–4.

8 Ibid., p. 140.

9 Cornelius A. Van Peursen, 'The Horizon' in *Husserl: Expositions and Appraisals*, ed. F. Elliston and P. McCormick (Notre Dame: University of Notre Dame Press, 1977) p. 184.

10 Landgrebe, *The Phenomenology of Edmund Husserl* p. 137.

11 Jean-Luc Nancy, 'Our History', *Diacritics* 20, 3 (1990), pp. 103–4.

12 Martin Heidegger, *Being and Time*, trans. J. Macquarrie and E. Robinson (London: Harper & Row, 1962) p. 69.

10

Sacrifice revisited

Miguel de Beistegui

At first glance one might be somewhat surprised to find a text devoted to sacrifice in the trajectory taken by Nancy's thought. What would drive the philosopher to turn his or her attention to this question so resolutely and traditionally anchored in religious, mythic, or ethnic anthropologies? What, in other words, would be philosophy's interest in this motif, and how would philosophical discourse manage to differentiate itself from the other fields and languages under which the tradition has wanted to think sacrifice? At second glance, and in so far as 'The Unsacrificable'[1] consists for the most part in a rigorous reading of those of Bataille's texts devoted to sacrifice, one sees how Nancy's evocation of the status and the place that need to be granted to this question of sacrifice was, in fact, inevitable since his is a reflection which, starting with the *The Inoperative Community*,[2] has situated community and communication at the very heart of its exigency. It is pointless emphasizing, therefore, that, in a certain way, the relation to sacrifice was, in Nancy, programmed from afar and for a long time by the close relation with Bataille (*The Inoperative Community* had already considered the question of sacrifice, in an oblique and transient way, by means of the 'sacred'), and that the confrontation with Bataille could not avoid this prickly question for long. On the other hand, it would be useful to underline two points regarding the nature of this relation. On the one hand, this relation is of a quasi-insurmountable difficulty to define, in so far as, for a very large part of the time, Nancy finds in Bataille the point of anchorage for his thinking and subscribes unreservedly to the project of Bataillean writing, a subscription going, moreover, all the way up to a sort of elective community or literary friendship, while not ceasing, in other respects, to inflect and to redeploy Bataille's analyses in the direction of an

157

existential ontology in such a way that the reader does not always know what is
paraphrase, what is commentary and what is critique (and in order to follow
the strategies of Nancy's reading, one must properly recognize that, generally
speaking, the traditional borders between paraphrase, commentary and critique
are shown to be displaced, blurred, in any case rendered infinitely complex).
On the other hand, and to the best of my knowledge, 'The Unsacrificable' is
perhaps the most radical attempt on Nancy's part to move away from Bataille,
or at least away from some of his theses and from the climate of some of his
texts, and no longer simply to 'communicate' with his 'experience' (see *CD*,
67; 26). Is this attempt any more accomplished for all that? And what is the
meaning of such a demarcation, the import of such a differend? How, in effect,
to interpret this resistance to Bataillean thought when *The Inoperative Community*
seemed to flirt with all the motifs surrounding that of sacrifice (the 'sacred',
'sovereignty', 'ecstasy')? And, beyond the simple relation to Bataille, can
thinking situate itself away from sacrifice, or is it always and despite itself
inexorably leading towards it?

I. Mimesis

Before considering what, of Bataille, seems to haunt every discussion of
sacrifice, and in order to piece together the moves which lead to the opening
declarations of 'The Unsacrificable', I propose to follow Nancy in his outline of
a history of sacrifice. Although brief, even elliptical, Nancy's sketch offers an
original reading of the phenomena, even if it seems to borrow some of its traits
from evolutionist sociological theories which, from Taylor to Girard and from
Hubert and Mauss to Durkheim, aim to kindle a continuity between ancient
ritual sacrifice and Christian moral sacrifice, in such a way that this latter would
appear as the truth of the ritual-religious sacrifice which was none the less its
point of origin. The originality of Nancy's reading lies in the fact that it affirms
– and this affirmation would doubtless encounter very serious reservations on
the part of various specialized disciplines – the West *as* this truth or this
dialectical sublation, a truth or sublation whose completion would be as much
philosophical as Christian, which would be, in other words, onto-theological.
Which means, purely and simply, and in as much as we, inhabitants of the
West, live within the horizon of this sublation, that we can know, or in any case
experience, nothing of the ancient or real sacrifice, and that the access to its
truth is historically, and that is to say metaphysically, forbidden to us, unless
'truth' be understood in the sense of its overcoming or its sublation which,

precisely, defines us in our essence. Still further: in as much as the history of the West, as the unfolding of onto-theology, is today gathered around its end, all thinking of sacrifice must henceforth be riveted to this closure. No doubt one ought to pause here for a moment and ponder the significance of the onto-theological presuppositions of this rapid analysis, the path which they force us to take, and the avenues of thought which they block from us. It would be prudent, also, to ponder the weight that such an analysis gives to the later considerations concerning Bataille and to the framework at the heart of which this thinking of Bataille would be envisaged. But I will leave these questions hanging in order to keep firmly to the text and thus progressively to start upon the path of the relation to Bataille.

How does the double onto-theological truth of sacrifice historically inscribe itself? And according to what logic? Here is the second originality of the analysis, that of detecting a mimetic logic at the heart of the relation of the West to sacrifice. The onto-theological truth of Western sacrifice is embodied in the double figure of Socrates and Christ. These two figures lead back to ancient sacrifice, repeating it, but so as to modify it profoundly and to exceed it, to realize it in completing it. The properly Western sacrifice is *self*-sacrifice, it is *unique*, it is the *truth* or the *essence* of all sacrifices and, for precisely this reason, it is the exceeding of sacrifice, the *last* sacrifice. In sum sacrifice is sublated, since entirely internalized, and is infinitized, since inscribed once and for all: indeed, for the West sacrifice is 'the very institution of the absolute economy of absolute subjectivity' (*PF*, 83) and accomplishes itself in its dialecticization. Not without retaining, however (and this makes all the difference), a fascination by and for the cruel moment of its economy – and, as his witness to this, Nancy takes the warrior-hero of the Hegelian or Jüngerian state, Marx's proletariat, or even certain texts from Nietzsche, who none the less mistrusted all sacrificial morality.

II. Fascination

Everything happens, then, as if, sublimated and exceeded, sacrifice no less continued to exert its power to fascinate, and was never as alive, as when at the threshold of its announced demise, never as flourishing as when at its end. Living-dead, in some way undecided between the life on to which it opens and the death to which, inevitably and despite itself, it inexorably leads, sacrifice suffers from not being fully able to live its own death. Would sacrifice be, in this sense, *the ghostly return* [revenant]?[3] Would it be that which always returns, and yet which is never simply *there*, or which is there only in not being? Would it be this entirely spectral and specular reality in which is reflected the phantasm of a symbolic economy that the West captures under the term 'truth'? To the list of thinkers drawn up by Nancy, would it not be necessary, then, to add the names of Freud, for whom *Kultur* is the fruit of a psychic self-sacrificial economy whose truth lies, precisely, in looking towards the *return* (of the repressed), and of Lacan, for whom separation and lack, constituents of the desiring subject in their very search for pleasure, demand the sacrifice of the pathological object? In the course of this spectral economy of sacrifice, and in a gesture which would perhaps lead one back to a point prior to Nancy's analyses, it is the whole of religious anthropology which would have to be rethought, if it is true that, in ritual sacrifice, the sacrificer sacrifices to the god that which, by rights and right away, is his [*lui re-vient*],[4] and that is to say, that which originarily comes [*vient*] from him and which never truly leaves him. This aside, and returning to Western sacrifice and its end, it would perhaps be essential, in extending Nancy's analyses, but in a sense which would inevitably draw us back to Nietzsche, to ponder Western morality as the *truth* of the Christian self-sacrifice and as the closure of its history – a closure or end which, as Nietzsche had clearly underlined, continues to die from its own sacrifice. Thus, one must say of morality also that it is phantomatic, and that it does not cease to haunt us, above all at its end. In this sense, the end of (the) sacrifice (of history) would mean something wholly different from its cessation or its disappearance (its death), something wholly different, also, from its *telos* or its completion: rather, the revelation and the exposition of its horizon or of its spectral essence which, precisely, defies every logic of the end in delivering itself over to an economy of ghostly return [*de la revenance*]. It would not so much be a matter of noting the disappearance of sacrifice, nor of recognizing that there would no longer be anything in store for sacrifice, that the symbolic order and the history to which it referred are henceforth concealed and inoperative, than of, and despite this, taking the measure of a shadow which continues to take hold and haunt our minds [*les esprits*]. But we will have to come back to this phantom question which operates in the shadow of Nancy's text.

Be that as it may, it is here, at the site of this sacrifice which, despite its end, does not cease to reappear, that the relation to Bataille begins to take shape. For the entire question would, on this basis, be one of knowing whence this fascination comes, whence it happens that this cruel moment never entirely comes to pass and that this *mimesis* persists in reinscribing the moment which it was supposed to have left behind. This could be linked to the spectrality of sacrifice. The question of this origin, which is left hanging by Nancy himself, is, in reality, Bataille's fundamental question, the one through which he perhaps neglects ontological regions in order to explore the enigmatic paths of the psyche. Nancy declares: 'this perhaps inevitable fascination is intolerable' (*PF*, 85). And therein lies the entire difficulty: in the inevitable *and* intolerable character of this fascination. And one ought to ponder each of these terms: By what, by whom is one generally fascinated? What is fascination? What is it which, in sacrifice, can be declared fascinating? From where does this fascination take its inevitable character? From where its intolerable character? From out of what horizon, what region can I declare it as such? The ambiguity here is vast. As are the stakes. If the fascination is declared 'perhaps inevitable', if one cannot avoid being fascinated, and that is to say captured and swept away by sacrifice or, rather, by its phantasm, and this in spite of oneself, it is as though, despite the cruelty that it supposes, it exercises a power of seduction over us. But this 'despite' is too strong, since it is this very cruelty which seduces. That being the case, the fascination by and for sacrifice can be said to be intolerable because of the cruelty that it supposes and sustains. The statement: 'Sacrifice is intolerable' would thus have a performative, even imperative value ('You will not let sacrifice fascinate you') and would, while exposing it, aim to suspend the cruelty of sacrificial operation and of its phantasm. It is in this sense that Nancy can write: 'Is it not time, finally, to take note, and to take note of the end of real sacrifice and of the closure of its phantasm?' (*PF*, 71). If one can actually take note of the end of ritual sacrifice (in the same way that one can take note of the end of some *res*), can one ever note the end of the phantom which survives it? Will the phantom ever allow itself to be enclosed? Will it ever allow itself to be summoned, seen, dispelled or removed? Will one ever be able to beseech it to vanish, to return it forever to the tomb of real sacrifice? And are we actually certain, moreover, that the phantasm of sacrifice is actually that of *real* sacrifice? In other words, does this phantasm 'really' have its point of departure in the sacrificial operation? Much later, and in the light of a relation to Bataille still to be clarified, we will again have to ask what authorizes such a statement on Nancy's part, what, in this statement, refers to a morality, or at least to something prescriptive. For the moment, let us simply note that Nancy confirms his remark in the sense of a certain upheaval or rejection without, however, clarifying its pathological and moral presuppositions:

It is not a matter, this needs to be said, of *sentimentality* [sensiblerie: also, squeamishness – TN]. But, all the same, it is perhaps a matter of knowing what *sensibility* means or, more exactly, of knowing if sensibility can be founded upon thinking itself to be sublimated in sovereign fashion in what devastates it. It is a matter of knowing if horror ought not to be simply – if one can say this – left to horror, which signals that the transgressive appropriation (that of the death of the subject and of the subject of death) is an *inadmissible* delusion.

(PF, 85; my emphasis)

Because sacrifice puts into play nothing less than 'horror', it is a matter of denouncing the fascination it exerts and of resisting its attraction. It is a matter, in other words, of closing one's eyes before the fascinating passing of a shadow.

Nevertheless, is there not another way of understanding the intolerable character of sacrifice: not from out of the horizon of a prescriptive exigency, but from the aesthetic-pathological constitution of the subject? On closer inspection, and reading the inevitable character of the fascination by and for sacrifice *in conjunction with* its intolerable character, it is sacrifice itself that falls under a new light. After all, would not fascination define itself, in a general way, as that which is inevitable *and* intolerable, as that which one would be unable to avoid while equally being unable to face up to it, as that which seduces by its very power of repulsion and fear, a power before which the subject feels itself exceeded, without either force or resort, as if overwhelmed by a force whose extent it cannot master and whose grandeur it cannot measure? And is it not when before the unlimited and fearsome power of this force that the subject comes to be revealed to itself, in its finitude and its relative greatness, certainly, but also in what points in the direction of what Kant called its 'freedom', and which Bataille will prefer to call its 'sovereignty', in such a way that, as Kant writes, 'the humanity in our person remains unhumiliated, even though the individual might have to submit to this domination'?[5] Is it not in this sense that sacrifice would touch, no longer on sublimation, but on the sublime?[6]

III. Supplement

Bataille will have tested this sublime fascination to the limit. Which also means, according to Nancy, that he will have tested the impossible satisfaction of the exigency of sacrifice. For if the spiritual sacrifice leads back to nothing but a

162

simulacrum and a comedy (such as Bataille saw in the work, for example, of Hegel), the non-comedy of bloody horror is, for its part, intolerable to the *spirit* of Western sacrifice. To the West, then, sacrifice remains, in its exigency, as if suspended between the impossibility of its full actuality and the temptation of its pure simulation. This would seem to signify the impasse of Western sacrifice, an impasse with which, essentially, Bataille would have struggled all his life. 'Thus Bataille's thinking was perhaps, at its limit, less a thinking of sacrifice, than a merciless thinking strained and torn by the impossibility of renouncing sacrifice' (*PF*, 86). Strictly speaking, there would be no thinking of sacrifice as such because sacrifice never gives itself to thinking as an object or phenomenon (which does not mean, of course, that there can be no classifications or typologies of sacrifice), but only as exigency or phantasm.

Consequently, it is through art that Bataille will have experienced this impasse or this double impossibility. To state this is to put forward, as Nancy explicitly does, a vision of art as that which 'comes to supplement, relieve or sublate the impasse of sacrifice' (*PF*, 88). Through a sort of simulacrum and well-ordered emotional stimulation, art would only be valid in so far as it would still refer to the sacrifice which it supplements. The role of art (or of literature), analogous to what Derrida has shown to be that of writing in its relation to the voice and to the word, would be to supplement and to refer to what, of itself, cannot be. It is as substitution for sacrifice that art could be grasped. Which would mean that, for Bataille, sacrifice would live on only in being itself displaced and reoriented. But, given this, is it not necessary, then, to conclude that the supplement belongs to sacrificial logic itself and that, still further, sacrifice does not exist outside of the logic of the supplement which refers to it? Or, to use a Lacanian terminology: is it not necessary to recognize that we are here faced with a pure signifier behind which no signified would be hidden? In other words, it is not as if art, in Bataille, could refer to 'the actual *exercise* of an actual cruelty' (*PF*, 89), but it is through art that sacrifice takes place *as* the impossible, as the title of one of Bataille's articles suggests: 'Art, the practice of cruelty'.[7] Sacrifice cannot take place if not as this impossible which takes place in art. It will always have withdrawn, and gives itself to be seen only in the movement of its effacement. Which, once again, seems to lead back to spectrality. The consequences of such an abnegation, which is perhaps more of a displacement, are enormous. (1) It is the logic of mimesis-methexis itself which is thus challenged: art does not mimic shed blood; it is neither repetition nor resumption: art does not refer to a real horror, and the emotion which it produces is not that of a communion with any such horror. (2) It is henceforth only in and through art – or literature – that there can be sacrifice in the West.

IV. Abandonment

But this time in a totally different sense. Not in the sense of a truth, a sublation or a sublimation of a first sacrifice. Not as that sacrifice from which blood must flow, not as that sacrifice which relates itself to death as to its ultimate exigency and its cruel horizon, nor even as that which refers to or supplements such a possibility, but as the principle of *unreserved* expenditure, as *abandonment* and *gift*. It is a matter of knowing, then, what the relation of sacrifice to death actually is, of knowing whether it only 'operates' by making a work of death [*faire oeuvre de mort*] or whether it operates, on the contrary, not by making a work and, above all, not a work of death, but by revealing the existent in its finitude, by revealing death as the proper horizon of all existence.[8] It is around this question that the conflict with Bataille perhaps takes shape; around, in sum, this short phrase, often commented upon, from *The Theory of Religion*: 'to sacrifice is not to kill, but to abandon and to give'.[9] Which is to say what? Must one not recognize in Bataille, and despite the sum of his sociological, historical and religious 'studies', a form of sacrifice absolutely irreducible to all traditional practices and interpretations? A form of sacrifice which, despite the nostalgia which runs throughout his texts, would not lead to a simple, albeit interruptive, mimesis, nor to a *methexis*, whose fundamental principle would be the inauguration of a community (of brothers) through the death of a single person which would be the death of all (this is the often-repeated Freudian model of the primal horde)? Indeed, is it not true, as Blanchot underlines,[10] that if death is indeed present in the Bataillean project, then murder, on the other hand, as Acéphale testified, eludes it, and does so in two ways: first of all, in the sense that the sacrifice of the consenting victim also presupposed the death of the sacrificer; but also, and above all, in the sense that such a sacrifice was literally *impossible* in so far as the communion which it proposed and which supposed the headlong rush of all into the sacrificial nothing ran precisely counter to the first exigency of the group, which was, precisely, to not make a work, albeit the work of death. From this moment on, sacrifice is pushed in a totally different direction and comes to signify no longer the founding murder around which the community would come to rediscover itself and share [*partager*] its essence, but the impossible *as* which it takes place and through which it comes to expose singularities. And this direction perhaps leads to the literal meaning of Acéphale which, in the very movement of its decapitation, would establish community only in immediately handing it over to the convulsive play of its members and of what, in each, could not be placed in common (namely, death). Sacrifice is thus the community experience of what cannot be constituted in community and which is nothing other than the sacrifice of community or the abandonment of community to its own abandonment. Sacrifice makes sense (but this sense is a non-sense or a counter-sense, a sense which absolutely resists sense and its economy, and which, consequently, signifies the very sacrifice of sense) only from the perspective of an aneconomy or a general economy whose principle is that of expenditure, of the gift and of *unreserved* abandonment. As short as it may have been, Acéphale's existence designated the resolutely aneconomic and genuinely unworking experience of a loss 'without thought of return, without calculation and without safeguard',[11] and the experience of the fact that there can be community only in the endlessly repeated movement of its abandonment and of its retreat, its sacrifice. Needless to say, then, that such a community of sacrifice gives itself only in effacing itself, experiences itself only in the very movement of its dissolution. Its presence is always that of an absence, which does not mean that of a failure. The very time of sacrifice is thus the sacrifice of time, time exposed to its own worklessness: that time does not work in sacrifice, but exposes singularities from out of the impassable horizon of their own finitude, is perhaps what marks the limit, even the essence of all community.

Of that which Bataille ceaselessly experienced, and which, at one point, took the form of a sacrificial concern, but which always referred back to sovereignty, it is a matter of recognizing this: that existence constitutes itself only in exceeding itself and in exposing itself (to itself) as the movement of this excess. That, were it not for the ecstasy in which existence comes to experience itself qua limit, existence would not exist. That, without the principle of an unreserved expenditure, without the possibility of abandonment, in which this limit comes to expose itself, existence would forever be chained to the servile order of things, whereas it is, in truth, only a puncturing of the real, an unreality. That which gives itself in the abandonment of sacrifice is precisely NOTHING, namely sovereignty, being-outside-oneself, ecstasy – nothing real, nothing which gives itself or exchanges itself, not even time, at least not this time which is some*thing* (money), but perhaps the other time, the time of death which 'explodes existence and ecstatically frees it from everything in it which would remain *servile*'.[12]

All of which leads us back to Nancy. For if, as far as the experience of

Acéphale and the place of sacrifice within it goes, Nancy's reading differs from the one, inspired by Blanchot, put forward here, in that, according to Nancy, it is a fascination with communal and fusional community that underpins the sacrifice of Acéphale (CD, 46–7; 17), and not the unworking experience of its impossibility, then this distancing vis-à-vis Bataille is almost immediately, and, once again, reduced by the mobilization of a Bataillean vocabulary that comes infinitely close to the sacrificial motif without ever touching it. I will give only two examples, taken from The Inoperative Community, of what relaunches, almost despite itself, the relation to sacrifice:

1 A propos the statement according to which 'sovereignty is NOTHING', Nancy offers the following commentary: '. . . sovereignty is the sovereign exposure to an excess (to a transcendence) that does not present itself, does not allow itself to be appropriated (or stimulated), which does not even give itself – but rather to which being is abandoned' (CD, 49; 18). Does not this abandonment of existence to itself contain in negative the entire logic of sacrifice as we have tried to describe it? Is not this opening of existence to its own dereliction, in which nothing works, the very movement of sacrifice?

2 If 'the unworking of community takes place around what Bataille for a long time called the sacred' (CD, 79; 32), 'and which, fundamentally, is only the unleashing of passions' (OC VII, 371), 'it is insofar as the "unleashing of passions" is not the free movement of a subjectivity . . . but something of the order of what Bataille himself often designated as "contagion", which is another name for "communication". That which communicates itself, that which is contagious and which, in this way – and in this way alone – "unleashes" itself, is the passion of singularity as such' (CD, 81; 32).

Thus, while recognizing that community can be read as the experience of the sacred or of passionate unleashing, Nancy resists the idea of sacrifice, which, in Bataille, is none the less co-extensive with the sacred. What motivates this resistance? Given that in Bataille the sacred does not lead to a transphysical (divine) reality, but to the sole transcendence – to the being-abandoned – of existence, is it possible to think the sacred other than as an existence sacrificed, given and abandoned to nothing nor to anyone if not to its own dereliction? And is it not with existence thus sacrificed that community can experience itself as sharing and as unworking?

V. Finitude

Would it be, in the end, in the name of that which sacrifice was precisely to expose and challenge that Nancy refuses to embrace the possibility of sacrificial experience, namely in the name of existence as the place of the sacred, this time in the sense of the untouchable, the inviolable, whereas, for Bataille, the sacred entailed the sacrifice of that particular sacred, in any case the possibility that such a sacrifice represented? But then: from where would this ultimate impulse come, this impulse which would wrest the sacred from sacrifice in order to render it 'the unsacrificable'? Perhaps from this: that our century has seen the end of sacrifice, and this means its impossibility. This is perhaps basically a historical question, but it seems, for Nancy at least, to open on to a morality, on to an exigency concerning existence in its essence: one *can*-not, one *must* not sacrifice existence, such a sacrifice being the *intolerable* itself. The limit of the thought of sacrifice, its historical limit, upon which it exposes itself and in which it exhausts itself, thereby rendering itself impossible, this limit is the experience of the death camps, which is perhaps the ultimate horizon of the whole of the modern thinking of sacrifice, which does not necessarily mean its truth. There is, in the very existence of the camps, something which escapes sacrifice and which, *de facto*, announces the end of the sacrificial operation as the work of death. With the holocaust, 'sacrifice has lost every right and every dignity' (*PF*, 98) since sacrifice there became indissociable from murder and extermination, 'a parody of immolation and smoke rising toward the heavens, and which no longer even has the right to this name "parody"' (*PF*, 96–7). Moreover, this extermination, the ultimate immolation in which the West will have revealed the full extent of what it is capable of, marks the brutal interruption of every sacrifice.

It is this closure of sacrifice, as well as the fascination for horror from which this closure demands we liberate ourselves, which, when all is said and done, will have remained unfamiliar to Bataille. In other words, Bataille will have remained blind to what will have made it necessary for our century to think 'apart from sacrifice' (*PF*, 100). Moreover, it would today be necessary, after Bataille and against him, 'definitively to acknowledge that the economy of Western sacrifice is closed' (*PF*, 101), which means to denounce the attempt at the trans-appropriation or infinitization of existence by means of the sacrificial operation. It is a matter, when all is said and done, in the horizon of the interpretation of a bloody process of identification, of delivering existence from its spiritual economy and of returning it to its own finitude. Thought in accordance with its essence and in accordance with the mode of appropriation of what is proper to it, existence signifies the impossibility of its sacrifice: 'thought rigorously and in accordance with its *Ereignis*, "finitude" signifies that existence is not sacrificable' (*PF*, 101).

The unsacrificable character of existence having been established, it is at this very moment in the analysis that, as if from itself and from the heart of existence, sacrifice reappears. As if one could never entirely be rid of it. If existence is not sacrificable, then this is indeed because it is already, in and of itself, 'offered to the world'. 'Offered' and not 'sacrificed'. These words strangely resemble each other, Nancy tells us, and yet 'nothing is more dissimilar'. What is it that radically separates offering from sacrifice? This difficult question would presuppose a reading of another of Nancy's texts[13] in which 'the offering' remains haunted by sacrifice, and in a way which perhaps refers again to Bataille.[14] But this question would also, and above all, refer to all Nancy's texts on existence, from *The Experience of Freedom* to *The Sense of the World* and some of the texts from *A Finite Thought* (notably, 'The decision of existence').[15] With the help of such a reading, it would be a matter of knowing just what is played out under the concept of 'world' and, on the basis of this, of understanding what it would mean to be 'offered' to the world. Indeed, and despite everything that such a notion would owe to Heideggerian facticity, the offering suggests that more is played out in the being-in-the-world of existence than *Geworfenheit* alone, more, even, than *Entwurf*, or that existence does not exhaust itself in its throw [*son jet*], unless we see in the twofold throw of existence something like a 'putting forward', but which never settles in presence, an 'abandonment' which would not suppose any change:[16] something like an abundance, perhaps. But in envisaging existence as abandonment and delivery to the world, are we not led back to the Bataillean sacred and to Bataillean sacrifice (certainly not in the sense of an immolation, which we have seen to be essentially impossible in Bataille, but in the sense of the 'unleashing of passions')? And if sacrifice maintains some sort of relation with sovereignty, then is this not in the possibility of giving itself and abandoning itself, and that is to say, in Bataillean terms, of giving itself over to the transgression of the servile order of things in order to open on to the sovereign order of a general economy (what others would call the symbolic order)? It is here that a thinking that links together the world and the order of 'things' imposes itself. For if in Nancy the world retains something of the Heideggerian world, is this not defined, *zumeist und zunächst*, as the world of everydayness, and that is to say as the world of a certain sequence of things and of existences, of contingencies and possibilities? Is not this world basically that of a restricted economy, a world which manages relations, which dictates conducts and desires? Is it not this same world which existence must sacrifice in the affirmation of its sovereignty, and is it not in the tearing of this world that the existent is revealed to itself in its authenticity? Which, in a way, Nancy seems to admit:

> To say that existence is offered is doubtless to use a word from the sacrificial vocabulary (and if we were speaking in German it would be the same word: *Opfer, Ausopferung*). But this is in order to try to mark the fact that, if we must say that existence is sacrificed, it is sacrificed by no one, and is sacrificed to nothing.
>
> (*PF*, 101)

Is this not *exactly* what Bataille wanted to say? 'By no one' and 'to nothing': existence is not even self-sacrifice, but its abandonment to NOTHING. Which, once again, Nancy seems to grant when he writes: '"Existence is offered" means the finitude of existence . . . . Finitude states what Bataille stated in saying that sovereignty is nothing' (*PF*, 101). But it would still be necessary to qualify this remark by what Nancy says on the following page, and which is an attempt to move still more definitively away from all possibilities of sacrifice, possibilities which Nancy still sees at work in Bataille and Heidegger.

> The existent arrives, it takes place, and this is simply a being-thrown into the world. In this being-thrown, it is offered. But it is offered by no one, nor to anyone. Nor is it self-sacrificed if nothing, no being, no subject, precedes its being-thrown. In truth, *it is not even offered or sacrificed to a Nothingness, to a Nothing or to an Other* [here, as elsewhere, un Autre – TN] *in the abyss of which it would still impossibly enjoy its own impossibility of being*: and it is precisely here that Bataille and Heidegger must be relentlessly corrected. Corrected, and that is to say: further withdrawn from the slightest drive toward sacrifice. For the drive toward sacrifice, or through sacrifice, is always linked to a fascination with an ecstasy turned toward an absolute Other or toward an absolute Outside, into which the subject is poured the better to be restored, promising to the subject, through some *mimesis* and through some 'sublation' of mimesis, the *methexis* with the Outside or the Other . . . .
>
> (*PF*, 102–3)

This passage calls for several remarks:

1 Again there is a certain concept of 'world' underpinning Nancy's reflection. If the existent is offered to the *world*, this is in so far as it is not presented to its sole existence, but is also and immediately linked to an order of things and of others which, to a greater or lesser degree, signifies the possibility of its enslavement, of its appropriation, a possibility in which its existence *also* consists.

2 As for the ecstasy and the fascination which it evokes and to which Bataille (I am here leaving Heidegger to one side) will have remained subject: it is true that the experience of sovereignty, in Bataille, entailed a suspension of the servile order, that it presupposed its interruption and its subversion, and that these were to open on to another community, on to another sociality. But was not this other order the one wherein finitude revealed itself, the order wherein the existent came to envisage its own death, to face up to it? Would transgression not then have the effect of leading back to the immanence of the offering and to the affirmation of impassable finitude? Is it not, once again, the sense of the NOTHING to express the impossibility for such a transcendence of making a work and of forming a unitary body (unless this work be of art or of writing), of referring to an economic (mimetic) and communal (methexic) being-common? Thus, if there is an ecstatic and transgressive appropriation, this does not point in the direction of an Outside or of an Other, but in the direction of an immanence or of a self understood as finitude.

3 This last point refers us to that concerning the *mimesis–methexis* dyad, on the subject of which several conclusions have already been advanced. For if, in the final account, there is, for Bataille, only 'literary' (which does not mean *simulated*) sacrifice, such a sacrifice can neither refer to nor supplement any actual sacrifice. Moreover, the *methexis* to which such a sacrifice opens is like that of Acéphale, whose law defies that of *methexis*, which is basically *religio*.

The dividing line between offering and sacrifice is not always clear. Even less clear, one should add, is the fact that both seem to refer back to the Bataillean motif of sovereignty. And to admit that such a motif expresses the essential finitude of existence is to admit that, as if despite itself, this motif replaces the sacrifice at the heart of existence, but this time in the sense of an abandonment and a generosity, an abundance, even, as Nancy himself lets it be heard in 1987 in a text devoted to God:

The gods prevent the supreme indecision of man, they close off his humanity and prevent him from going off the rails, from measuring up to the incommensurable: in the end, God gives the measure. They forbid that man be risked further than man. And most seriously: they take his death from him.

And that is to say, they take his sacrifice from him – this time in the sense of his abandonment. For there is this abandonment which is not a traffic, but which is an offering, an oblation, a libation. There is that, and there is this generosity and this freedom outside of religion – and I do not know, however, whether this abandonment is still to gods, to another god which would be coming, or to 'no god'. But it has death as its generic name, and an infinite number of forms and occasions throughout our lives.[17]

Thus, as if in spite of ourselves, we are led back to sacrifice, which was seen to reinscribe itself at the very heart of existence, and that is to say on the horizon of finitude. From immolation to abandonment, from violence to generosity, sacrifice seems to mark the passing of an ageless patience. But everything happens as if this reinscription could take place only through writing, as if writing itself were sacrificial: violent and generous, appropriating and abandoning. And is it not, in essence, precisely this gesture which is performed by 'The Unsacrificable' in its relation to Bataille and, dare one say, by all Nancy's texts in their relation to tradition? Is there a writing more appropriating, more violent *and* more generous, a writing whose generosity is so indebted to its very violence? Is there a writing whose economy is more welcoming, and whose welcome can so sustain the name of friendship? With Nancy, it is the double play of reading and writing which must henceforth be questioned in the light of sacrifice and of what can only appear as the place of a duplicitous and inevitable economy.

Translated by Simon Sparks

Notes

[Translator's note. All translations from the French are my own. Except where these seem to me to be misleading, I have provided references to published English versions of all the texts under consideration. I am indebted to the author for his corrections to my version of his text.]

1 In Jean-Luc Nancy, *Une pensée finie* (Paris: Galilée, 1990), pp. 65–106. Henceforth PF.

2 Jean-Luc Nancy, *La communauté désoeuvrée* (Paris: Bourgois, 1986). Henceforth CD.

Miguel de Beistegui

[Trans. Peter Connor *et. al.* as *The Inoperative Community* (Minneapolis: University of Minnesota Press, 1991).]

3 [Translator's note. I have tried to preserve the French distinction between *le revenant* (the ghost), *le spectre* (the spectre), *le fantôme* (the phantom) and their cognates (in particular, *le fantasme* which has been rendered here as 'phantasm' rather than the more usual 'fantasy'). This has been done at the occasional expense of a certain violence not always present in the author's French. It should be borne in mind that whereas the French *revenant* in its noun form is the common term for ghost (that which, precisely, returns), it is also the present participle of the verb *revenir*, to return, and hence, literally, that which returns.]

4 [Translator's note. In its pronominal form here, *revenir* suggests, first and foremost, the sense of an ownership, that which is mine because it is owed to me, that which has re-turned to me.]

5 Immanuel Kant, *Critique of Judgement*, trans. J. H. Bernard (New York: Hafner Press, 1951); First Part, First Division, Book II, section 28: 'Of nature regarded as might', p. 101. Translation modified.

6 Is it necessary to recall that Kant himself, while not ceasing, from the perspective of morality, to condemn ritual or religious sacrifices in so far as they are a matter of superstition and not of religion in the strictest sense (see, for example, *Religion Within the Limits of Reason Alone*, Fourth Part, Second Division, section 1: 'The general subjective foundation of religious illusion'), writes, and in terms reminiscent of certain Bataillean analyses, the following words on the subject of war: 'War itself, if it is carried on with order and with a sacred respect for the rights of citizens, has *something sublime in it*, and makes the disposition of the people who carry it on thus only the more sublime, the more numerous are the dangers to which they are exposed and in respect of which they behave with courage. On the other hand, a long peace generally brings about a predominant commercial spirit . . .' (*Critique of Judgement*, p. 102; my emphasis). It would be necessary also to relate this text to what, some years later, Hegel will say about warrior sacrifice (cf., *Über die wissenschaftlichen Behandlungsarten des Naturrechts, seine Stelle in der praktischen Philosophie, und sein Verhältnis zu den positiven Rechtswissenshaften*, SCHELLING – HEGEL, *Kritisches Journal der Philosophie*, ed. H. Buchner (Hildesheim: Georg Olms Verlagsbuchhandlung, 1967), Vol. II, p. 62, and *Elements of the Philosophy of Right*, trans. H. B. Nisbet (Cambridge: Cambridge University Press, 1991), sections 321–9).

7 [Translator's note. 'L'art, exercice de cruauté', in Georges Bataille, *Oeuvres Complètes*, Vol. 11 (Paris: Gallimard, 1988), pp. 480–6. Henceforth *OC* with volume number.]

8 [Translator's note. The formulation *faire oeuvre* . . . and its cognates has been translated throughout as either 'to make a work . . .' or 'to work . . .', depending on the context. Each time the word 'work' is encountered, however, it should be borne in mind that what is being evoked here is the productive (i.e., Bataillean Hegelian) economy of the *oeuvre* or 'Work' in opposition to *désoeuvrement* or 'worklessness'.]

172

9 [Translator's note. Georges Bataille, *La theorie de la religion*, in *OC* V11, p. 310; trans. Robert Hurley as *The Theory of Religion* (New York: Zone Books, 1992), pp. 48–9. Translation modified.]
10 Maurice Blanchot, *La communauté inavouable* (Paris: Mimuit, 1983), p. 32, note 1. [Translated by Pierre Joris as *The Unavowable Community* (New York: Station Hill Press, 1988), p. 58, note 7.]
11 Ibid., p. 30, note 1. [Ibid., pp. 58–9, note 6. Translation modified.]
12 Ibid., p. 33. [Ibid., p. 16.]
13 'L'offrande sublime', in *Une pensée fini*, pp. 147–95. [Trans. Jeffrey S. Librett as 'The sublime offering', in Jean-François Courtine et al., *Of the Sublime: Presence in Question* (Albany: SUNY, 1993), pp. 25–53.]
14 See ibid., in particular, pp. 185–6. [See ibid., pp. 47–8.]
15 [Translator's note. See *L'expérience de la liberté* (Paris: Galilée, 1988); trans. Bridget MacDonald as *The Experience of Freedom* (Stanford: Stanford University Press, 1993); *Le sens du monde* (Paris: Galilée, 1993); and 'La décision d'existence' in *Une pensée fini*, pp. 107–45; trans. by Brian Holmes as 'The decision of existence', in Jean-Luc Nancy, *The Birth to Presence* (Stanford: Stanford University Press, 1993), pp. 83–109.]
16 These are the terms Nancy uses in 'The sublime offering' to designate this latter.
17 Jean-Luc Nancy, *Des lieux divins* (Mauvezin: TER, 1987), p. 32. [Trans. Michael Holland as 'Of divine places', in *The Inoperative Community*, p. 136.]

11

An 'inoperative' global community? Reflections on Nancy

Fred Dallmayr

Le rendez-vous du donner et du recevoir . . .

Léopold-Sédar Senghor

Perspective matters. Seen from a sufficient distance – perhaps that of an orbiting spaceship – our earth appears as a smoothly rounded globe devoid of rugged edges or fissures. On closer inspection, however, this smoothness quickly gives way to a spectacle of stunning diversity: between mountains and plains, forests and deserts, oceans and dry land. Similarly, viewed from the altitude of speculative metaphysics, humankind seems to exhibit a pleasant homogeneity, anchored perhaps in a common 'human nature'; again, however, this pleasantness is disrupted by the stark experiences of conflict and turmoil in human history. Recently, in an essay which aroused considerable controversy, Samuel Huntington alerted readers to a new phase of political conflict now occurring on a grand or global scale: that of an emerging 'clash of civilizations'. The essay was stunning and provocative for a number of reasons, and particularly because of its timing: the aftermath of the Cold War. Just at the time when the dismantling of the Iron Curtain had engendered visions of a global 'world order' (chiefly under the aegis of a new *pax Americana*), Huntington shattered public euphoria by pointing to profound ruptures. According to Huntington, political battle lines have shifted over the centuries. While the beginning of modernity (after the Peace of Westphalia) witnessed rivalry among princely states, the French Revolution inaugurated a new phase of intensified struggle: that between nations or nation-states. Following the Russian Revolution, this phase in turn gave way to a contest between ideologies – chiefly between liberal democracy and communism – a contest which fuelled the Cold War era. What is dawning now with the demise of this era, in Huntington's view, is a new and unprecedented pattern of conflict: one propelled no longer chiefly by ideological or economic, but by cultural or 'civilizational' motives. Although nation-states will still remain powerful actors in world affairs, it is the 'clash of civilizations' that will dominate global politics: 'The fault lines between civilizations will be the battle lines of the future'.[1]

The vision of conflict projected by Huntington was perhaps overdrawn in its sharp accents, and certainly remains questionable in many details. Nevertheless, several features (in my view) deserve close attention. First of all, Huntington deliberately removed the Eurocentric (or Western-centred) blinkers from the study of world politics. Up to the close of the Cold War, he notes, international politics was overshadowed by struggles among Western states, nations, and ideologies; to this extent, international conflicts were chiefly conflicts 'within Western civilization' or, in a sense, 'Western civil wars'. In the present era, by contrast, international politics for the first time moves out of its 'Western phase' and its central focus becomes the 'interaction between the West and non-Western civilizations and among non-Western civilizations'. While in previous periods, non-Western peoples and governments were reduced to the status of 'objects of history' (mainly by being targets of Western colonialism), they now enter the world stage and join the West as 'movers and shapers of history'. Coupled with this feature, and perhaps still more significant, is another transgresison of the traditional paradigm of international politics: namely, the move from the level of states (or other public organizations) as chief actors in the world arena to the level of cultures seen as comprehensive meaning patterns animating the lives of ordinary people (and not only ruling elites) in a given context. Attentive in part to the post-Wittgensteinian turn to language (or to language games as life-forms), Huntington defines civilization as 'the highest cultural grouping of people and the broadest level of cultural identity people have'; its fabric is constituted both by 'common objective elements, such as language, history, religion, customs, institutions', and by 'the subjective self-identification of people'. As he realizes or concedes, civilizations of this kind are not compact or historically invariant entities; in fact, they often blend, overlap, or are transformed. Nevertheless, despite elements of flux, he holds civilizations to be 'meaningful entities' in the global arena, and 'while the lines between them are seldom sharp, they are real'.[2]

In focusing on cultural meaning patterns, Huntington in a way shifts the accent from competing elite structures – the traditional 'anarchy' of states – to the domain of concrete human experience in ordinary life-worlds; in the useful

terminology coined by Hedley Bull, the emphasis is placed on the emerging
'world society' as distinguished from the familiar international 'society of
states'.[3] To be sure, the turn to world society – or what is sometimes called
our 'global village' – cannot be credited to Huntington alone; as I shall indicate
later, the same move was articulated by other writers before him, and sometimes in more cogent and circumspect language. Yet, the issue here is not one
of originality. Whatever its drawbacks, Huntington's essay, I believe, stands out
both because of its dramatic flair and because of the prestigious status of its
author in the international studies profession. Behind his argument, however,
lurks a question which so far has not received much attention in the literature:
the question of the concrete character of the impending world society or global
family of peoples.

To the extent that parallels can be drawn between global and domestic
politics, several prominent alternatives come into view. Is global society, one
may ask, going to be an assortment of autonomous individuals and social
groupings, after the fashion of Toennies' model of '*Gesellschaft*'? Or will it
be a more tightly knit community – a '*Gemeinschaft*' – held together by shared
beliefs and practices? In Western political theory, this contrast has recently been
debated at great length under the labels of 'liberalism' (or liberal universalism)
versus 'communitarianism', perhaps to the point of exhaustion.[4] For present
purposes, I want to concentrate on a different possibility or conception of social
life, one in which 'difference' plays in fact a crucial role: the notion of an
'inoperative community' as formulated by Jean-Luc Nancy. In the following, I
shall first present Nancy's basic line of argument, in an effort to profile it
against competing, more customary, views. Next, I shall draw some infer-
ences for the study of world politics, invoking some prominent recent
initiatives in this field. Finally, I shall point to some normative implications
of an 'inoperative' or non-managerial model for cross-cultural encounters on
a global plane.

I

Jean-Luc Nancy's *La communauté désoeuvrée* was first published in 1986, in an
intellectual climate saturated with the teachings of Heidegger, Derrida,
Foucault, and Bataille (among others). Subtle in its argumentation, Nancy's
work gathered in itself, but also rethought innovatively, all the major themes
animating recent Continental philosophy: the end of traditional metaphysics;
the decentring of subjectivity (or the *cogito*); the turn to language seen as a

reservoir always in excess of particular speech acts; and, above all, the conception of human existence as an 'ek-static' mode of being (or, in Heidegger's terms, as a *Dasein* in the grip of self-transcendence). Politically, the context of Nancy's publication was marked by monumental changes of a global scale: the progressive disintegration of 'official' (or Stalinist) communism; the impending demise of the Cold War; and the worldwide upsurge of a self-confident neo-liberalism bent on submerging public life in market economics and in considerations of private self-interest. Seen against this background, Nancy's book acquired its distinctive, and even boldly provocative, contours – contours manifest already in its title (which resists easy translation). While acknowledging the bankruptcy of official communism (and all forms of regimented communitarianism), Nancy was not ready to endorse a militantly refurbished individualism, which would only restore a defunct metaphysical 'subject'. Taking its cues both from Heidegger and 'poststructuralist' writers, the study reasserted the primacy of 'the political' over economics (and technology), that is, the preeminence of a public place seen as an arena of democratic interactions. To this extent, *La communauté désoeuvrée* reaffirmed a notion of 'community': but a community without substance, without communion or communism, and in this sense an unmanageable, 'unworking' or 'inoperative' community beyond instrumental control.[5]

The backdrop of global transformations is closely and eloquently addressed in the opening chapter of Nancy's book. Referring to the cancerous decay infesting the Soviet empire and its satellites, the chapter ponders the implications of this decay for political theory in general and for the conception of community in particular. The 'gravest and most painful' experience of our era, we read there, is 'the testimony of the dissolution, the dislocation, or the conflagration of community', a dislocation inextricably linked with the demise of communism. In Nancy's portrayal, communism was not simply or in its intent a synonym for corruption; rather, the term signalled the desire, he notes, to rediscover a sense of community 'at once beyond social divisions and beyond subordination to technological dominion', and hence also 'beyond such wasting away of liberty, of speech, or of simple happiness as comes about whenever these are subjugated to the exclusive order of privatization'. Despite some redeeming virtues, however, communism as a political regime was from the beginning afflicted by a fundamental, even metaphysical flaw: its bent on reducing everything to production, management, and effective control. Quite apart from despotic or corrupt leanings of its leaders, Nancy writes, 'it was the very basis of the communist ideal that ended up appearing most problematic': namely, 'human beings defined as producers' and, most importantly, as 'the producers of their own essence in the form of their labor or their work'. Under the aegis of production and operational control, public community was itself conceived as a constructed or operational goal, a goal effected by humans producing 'their own essence as their work, and furthermore producing precisely this essence *as community*'. What this accent on management side-stepped or ignored was the aspect of excess or 'ekstatic' self-transgression – a neglect which accounts in large measure for the 'totalitarian' or confiningly 'immanentist' character of communism:

> It is precisely the immanence of man to man, or it is *man*, taken absolutely, considered as the immanent being par excellence, that constitutes the stumbling block to a thinking of community. . . . Economic ties, techno-logical operations, and political fusion (into a *body* or under a *leader*) represent or rather present, expose, and realize this essence [of commu-nity] in themselves. Thus, essence is set to work in them; through them, it becomes its own work. This is what we have called 'totalitarianism' but it might be better named 'immanentism'.[6]

The flaw intrinsic to communism is equally shared by other, less radical, forms of 'communitarian' politics, including unorthodox, left-Hegelian modes of Marxism – all of which have been wedded to the goal of a totalizing and manageable community; like their Soviet counterpart, these forms too 'have by now run their course'. What has stepped into the void left by communism/communitarianism almost everywhere is neo-liberal individualism, the most time-worn staple of modern Western politics. Nancy is scathing in denouncing this individualist creed. 'Some', he writes, 'see in its invention and in the culture, if not the cult built around the individual Europe's incontrovertible merit of having shown the world the sole path to emancipation from tyranny' as well as 'the norm by which to measure all our collective or communitarian undertakings'. For Nancy, however, the individual is merely the 'residue' or 'left-over' of the dissolved community; in its atomistic 'indivisibility', it shows itself simply as the 'abstract result of a decomposition'. More importantly, like the totalizing community, the individual reveals an 'immanentist' streak: this time the immanentism of the self-contained and 'absolutely detached' subject 'taken as origin and as certainty'. What cannot be derived or extrapolated from atomistic individualism is any notion of a social world: any sense of a '*clinamen*, that is, of a declination or declension of individuals with or towards each other. This inability has been the traditional defect of modern individualist theories, and it persists in more recent existentialist and neo-liberal guises. As Nancy pointedly observes: 'Neither "personalism" nor Sartre ever managed to do anything more than coat the most classical individual-subject with a moral or sociological paste'; although talking profusely about the subject's situatedness, 'they never *inclined* it, outside itself, over that edge that opens up its being-in-common'.[7]

Like every form of immanentism, self-contained individualism is not only stifling but also paradoxical and ultimately self-defeating: for to know oneself as a distinct individual already presupposes one's differentiation from others. 'To be absolutely alone, it is not enough that I be so', Nancy comments; 'I must also be alone being alone – which of course is contradictory'. Thus, the very logic of absolute self-containment violates and undermines this containment, by implicating it in a relation that it refuses and that 'tears it open from within and from without'. Hence, the absolute separateness of individuals is ruptured in favour of a relationship (which itself cannot be absolutized): this relation, we read, is 'nothing other than what undoes in its very principle – and at its closure or its limit – the autarchy of absolute immanence'. In a philosophically path-breaking way, such a (non-absolute and non-dialectical) relation was prefigured in Heidegger's notion of 'being-in-the-world' and also in his delineation of *Dasein's* 'ekstatic' transgression towards 'being' and towards others. As Nancy perceptively notes, being for Heidegger was neither a thing nor a concept nor a totalizing essence, but rather the very emblem of a differential relation rupturing every kind of self-enclosure. Properly understood, he asserts, 'being "itself" comes to be defined as relational, as non-absoluteness, and, if you will (in any case this is what I am trying to argue) *as community*'. As should be clear at this point, community in Nancy's sense is far removed from any compact or totalitarian type of communism/communitarinism; instead, its relational character is predicated on the very rupture or ecstatic transgression of compactness. In his words, ecstasy defines the 'impossibility of absolute immanence' and consequently the 'impossibility either of an individuality in the strict sense of that term, or of a pure collective totality'. The challenge presented by this outlook is the difficult task of seeing community and ecstasy as inseparably bound together – in a manner which disrupts community's 'operational' management. In a shorthand formula, community might here be described as 'the being-ecstatic of being itself'.[8]

As envisaged by Nancy at this point, community is not simply an empirical reality or presence, but rather an advent or a calling or something lying in wait.

179

Above all, it is not the emblem of a primitive past or a golden age to be retrieved – as imagined by communitarian visionaries. Nancy is stern in castigating longings for a lost innocence. In his presentation, one of the most prominent modern spokesmen of such longings was Rousseau who, perhaps more intensely than others, experienced modern society as resulting from 'the loss or degradation of a communitarian (and communicative) intimacy'. Actually, however, retrospective dreams have been part and parcel of Western self-awareness or historical consciousness from the beginning. 'At every moment in its history', we read, 'the Occident has given itself over to the nostalgia for a more archaic community that has disappeared, and to deploring a loss of familiarity, fraternity and conviviality.' Irrespective of the concrete character of the dream or the precise imagery employed (the natural family, the Athenian city, early Christianity, communes, or brotherhoods) always, Nancy notes,

> it is a matter of a lost age in which community was woven of tight, harmonious, and infrangible bonds and in which above all it played back to itself, through its institutions, its rituals, and its symbols, the representation, indeed the living offering, of its own immanent unity, intimacy, and autonomy. Distinct from society (which is a simple association and division of forces and needs) . . . community is not only intimate communication between its members, but also its organic communion with its existence.

Nancy at this point corrects Toennies' evolutionary sequence of community and society (as well as related developmental schemes). 'No *Gesellschaft*', he asserts sharply, 'has come along to help the State, industry, and capital dissolve a prior *Gemeinschaft*.' What accounts, or may account, for developmental schemes of this kind is the (strategic) desire of present generations to impose their own longings on the past (which remains recalcitrant); to this extent, modern communitarianism may well be 'nothing other than a belated invention'. In Nancy's contrary opinion, community, far from being 'what society has crushed or lost', is '*what happens to us . . . in the wake of* society'.[9]

The 'happening' invoked at this point is not akin to an external fate or inexorable destiny; instead it presupposes a proper human responsiveness or responsibility: above all, the readiness to 'rethink' the meaning of community, to remain alert to its 'insistent and possibly still *unheard* demand'. Rethinking here involves moving out into uncharted terrain, by setting aside the familiar formulas of communism/communitarianism and individualism. Of particular urgency is the replacement of self-contained individuality by the notion of 'singularity' or singular human beings. For Nancy, singularity stands in contrast with the structure of individuality: it never occurs 'at the level of atoms, these identifiable if not identical identities'; rather, it is 'linked to ecstasy' and as such takes place 'at the level of the *clinamen*, which is unidentifiable'. Singular beings, in Nancy's account, are finite beings who, in their finitude, are exposed to mortality as well as the transgressive incursion of otherness (and of being in every form). 'What the thematic of individuation lacked', he notes, 'as it passed from a certain Romanticism to Schopenhauer and to Nietzsche, was a consideration of singularity, to which it nevertheless came quite close.' Whereas individuation proceeds by detaching closed-off entities from a form-less ground, singularity 'does not proceed from anything' because it is not 'a work resulting from an operation' (which might be called 'singularization'). In their finitude, singular beings do not emerge against the background of a prior chaos, or against the foil of an original unity, or else against a process of 'becoming' and wilful construction. Rather, singular beings always emerge together from the beginning; their finitude 'co-appears or compears (*com-paraît*)' in a shared space or world. In Nancy's words:

A singular being *appears*, as finitude itself: at the end (or at the beginning) with the contact of the skin (or the heart) of another singular being, at the confines of the *same* singularity that is, as such, always *other*, always shared, always exposed . . ... Community means, consequently, that there is no singular being without a singular being, and that there is, therefore, what might be called, in a rather inappropriate idiom, an originary or ontological 'sociality' that in its principle extends far beyond the simple theme of man as a social being (the *zoon politikon* is secondary to this community).[10]

What is involved in this originary sociality is neither fusion nor exclusion, but a kind of 'communication' that is vastly different from a mere exchange of information or messages. In opposition to technical information theories (and also theories of communicative interaction), Nancy locates communication on a more primary level: that of the 'sharing and com-pearance (*com-parution*) of finitude'; what happens on that level is a dislocation and interpellation that 'reveal themselves to be constitutive of being in-common – precisely inasmuch as being-in-common is not a common being'. Nancy returns at that point to the theme of an 'inoperative' or non-operational community, seeking to clarify further that notion. Seen as a mode of 'compearance' or a shared space, he maintains, community properly understood is not constituted or constructed, nor does it arise from an act of 'intersubjective' bonding (contractual or otherwise): 'It does not set itself up, it does not establish itself, it does not emerge among already given subjects'. Rather, reflecting a mutuality or mutual transgression without fusion, community signals the place of 'the *between* as such', that is, a dash or incision: 'you *and* I (between us) – a formula in which the *and* does not imply juxtaposition, but exposition' or exposure. Recasting the famous Cartesian adage regarding the *cogito*, Nancy substitutes the phrase '*ego sum expositus*', meaning that 'I am first of all exposed to the other, and exposed to the exposure of the other – a phrase signalling the contours of a mutuality 'about which Descartes seems to know so little, or nothing at all'. Located in the interstices of mutual exposure, in the between-space of co-appearance, community is not producible or 'workable', but rather marked by a basic lack or absence: the lack of a substance or stable identity that could be fixated once and for all. What characterizes community, Nancy writes pointedly, is finitude or, more precisely, the 'infinite lack of infinite identity (if we can risk such a formulation)'. Differently put, community is formed by 'the retreat or the subtraction of something': and 'this something, which would be the fulfilled infinite identity of community, is what I call its "work" (or its '*oeuvre*', hence *communauté désoeuvrée*'.[11]

From this inoperative vantage, a new vista is opened up on to political life, or at least on to a public space in which politics and political struggles can occur. Nancy here takes up a distinction which has become current in recent Continental thought: that between 'politics' and 'the political', where the former designates partisan strategies and concrete institutional devices and the latter the arena or '*mise en scène*' presupposed by these strategies. Elaborating on this distinction, Nancy suggests that the term 'the political' may serve to denote 'not the organization of society but the disposition of community as such'; as long as public life is not entirely dissolved into the 'sociotechnical element of forces and needs', the term can stand as a synonym for 'the sharing of community'. Pushing the issue further by invoking the difference between 'working' and 'unworking' (or non-management), the text states:

> 'Political' would mean a community ordering itself to the unworking of its communication, or destined to this unworking: a community consciously undergoing the experience of its sharing. To attain such a signification of the 'political' does not depend, or in any case not simply, on what is called a 'political will'. It implies being already engaged in the community, that is to say, undergoing, in whatever manner, the experience of community as communication.

The accent on sharing or a shared space need not, and in fact should not, imply a neglect of concrete political struggles. Nancy is keenly aware of prevailing power differentials and hegemonic asymmetries on both the domestic and global levels. Although the political cannot be reduced to power (or an instrumental 'will to power'), he notes, one cannot escape the sphere of power relations: for we never stop 'being caught up in it, being implicated in its demands'. To remedy oppressive or exploitative power differentials, counter-energies must be mobilized and, in a sense, put to 'work'. Yet, caution must be taken in the pursuit of strategic aims or counter-aims, lest they become 'totalizing' and hence oppressive in turn. Thus, strategic struggles must remain mindful of a recessed inoperative domain: that of a shared public space which allots to politics its sense and measure.[12]

II

Having retraced the main steps of Nancy's argument, I want to return now to the global context thematized at the beginning, and especially to the 'clash of civilizations' evoked by Huntington. In light of Nancy's notion of an inoperative community, not only the virtues but also the defects of Huntington's essay come more clearly into view. As indicated before, the chief virtue of the essay resides in the shift from international anarchy (of states) to the level of cultural beliefs and practices, that is, from governmental elite structures to the lived world of ordinary people. This shift is closely linked with the attention paid to religious customs and traditions – a move heralding an incipient departure from homogenizing modes of secularism (as well as social-scientific canons of value neutrality). Unfortunately, these initiatives are marred by a number of drawbacks or defects, of which I shall mention mainly two. Huntington basically views civilizations or cultures as power constellations, which, after the demise of the Cold War, now confront each other in the global arena. To this extent, the traditional model of international politics is modified but not radically transformed: the 'clash of civilizations' simply takes the place of the clash of superpowers and the customary conflict between nation-states. Although acknowledging a certain flux or 'fuzziness' of cultural identities, Huntington none the less affirms the relatively compact status of cultures as 'meaningful entities' – a claim which predictably (and quite properly) has exposed him to charges of reification or a reifying 'essentialism' bypassing internal fissures as well as cross-cultural overlaps. In the terminology employed by Nancy, cultures or civilizations are presented as self-enclosed 'individuals' or totalizing entities, at the expense of their flexible 'singularity' as well as their 'compearing' relationships. A close corollary of this individualizing treatment is the reduction of Western civilization to one power constellation (or cultural actor) among others; even where its special role in global politics is recognized, this recognition takes the form of a dichtomizing opposition (under the label 'the West versus the Rest').[13]

In Huntington's portrayal, civilizations are bound to collide in our age – along 'cultural fault lines' – for a host of interrelated reasons, among which the following seem to be most crucial (and indicative of his individualizing bent). First of all, differences between cultures are located on a basic experiential level nourished by history, language, literature, and religion; to this extent, they are 'far more fundamental than differences among political ideologies and political regimes'. Second, our world is becoming a 'smaller place', with interactions between cultures steadily increasing – which, in turn, leads to intensified 'civilization consciousness' or awareness of cultural identity. Next, the weakening of ideological attachments in the wake of the Cold War prompts traditional cultures and religions to move in 'to fill this gap'. Finally, cultural characteristics and differences, in Huntington's view, are 'less mutable' and hence 'less easily compromised and resolved' than political and economic rifts along nation-state or class lines – a fact amply illustrated by the upsurge of ethnic and religious conflicts around the globe. While these and related factors sharpen and deepen intercultural cleavages in our time, the same reasons also foster a rallying movement within a given civilizational sphere, that is, a strengthening of intracultural cohesion. Referring to this rallying movement, Huntington claims that 'civilization commonality' – what others have called the 'kin-country syndrome' – is today in process of 'replacing political ideology and traditional balance of power considerations as the prinicipal basis for cooperation and coalitions'. Occasionally, especially in response to Western ascendancy or supremacy, this rallying process may extend across narrowly civilizational lines, as can be seen especially in the emerging 'Confucian-Islamic connection'. All these developments clearly spell trouble for our global future. As Huntington comments in a sequel to his essay,

History has not ended. The world is not one. Civilizations unite and divide humankind . . .. What ultimately counts for people is not political ideology or economic interest. Faith and family, blood and belief, are what people identify with and what they will fight and die for.[14]

The cleavage of civilizations also embraces Western culture in its relations with the outside world. To be sure, Huntington is by no means unaware of the distinctive, hegemonic status of Western culture, a status accounting for the close entwinement of modernization and Westernization. In discussing the reasons of contemporary conflicts, he refers explicitly to the 'dual role' of the West, namely, its role as hegemonic or master culture and simultaneously as the foil or target of worldwide reactions, strivings, and frustrations. In Huntington's portrayal, however, this duality quickly shades over again into a harsh contrast or totalizing mutual exclusion. Borrowing a phrase from Kishore Mahbubani, his essay pits the West as a global power constellation 'versus the rest' of the world. On the one hand, we read, the West today is at the top of the global pyramid; at the same time, however, and perhaps as a result, a 'return to the roots phenomenon' is occurring among non-Western civilizations. Thus, Western culture 'at the peak of its power' − in fact, at 'an extraordinary peak of power in relation to other civilizations' − today confronts 'non-Wests' that increasingly have 'the desire, the will and the resources to shape the world in non-Western ways'. In unusually blunt language, Huntington's argument pierces the rhetorical veil seeking to cloak Western hegemony in the guise of 'one-world' or 'world order' formulas. The very phrase 'the world community', he writes with stunning candour, has become 'the euphemistic collective noun' employed to give 'global legitimacy to actions reflecting the interests of the United States and other Western powers'. Behind the screen of international agencies, he adds, global political and security issues are 'effectively settled by a directorate of the United States, Britain and France', while world economic issues are jointly managed by the United States, Germany, and Japan. Thus, the West is in effect 'using' international institutions and other resources to 'run the world in ways that will maintain Western predominance, protect Western interests, and promote Western political and economic values'. While much depends here on perspective, and while complaints against global mastery arise mainly from non-Western societies, there is at least 'a significant element of truth in their view'.[15]

Huntington's bluntness extends from power politics to global cultural aspirations, above all the vision of 'cosmopolis' or a universal civilization of humankind. Such a vision is often promoted by champions of Western culture, including middle-class intellectuals and professionals in non-Western countries, who view cosmopolis simply as a globalized extension of Western standards and ways of life. Such a globalizing process is indeed happening in our time; and Huntington readily grants that 'at a superficial level' much of Western culture

185

has infiltrated and permeated the rest of the world. Yet, appearances here are deceptive; for 'at a more basic level', Western standards and concepts are seen to 'differ fundamentally' from those found in other civilizations. The contrast affects and jeopardizes the idea of cosmopolis itself. For, as Huntington states, 'the very notion that there could be a "universal civilization" is a Western idea', one which collides head-on with 'the particularism of most Asian societies' and their emphasis on 'what distinguishes one people from another'. The contrast percolates down to the level of basic political beliefs and practices, a level inhabited by such key tenets of Western culture as individualism, liberalism, human rights, democracy, and the separation of church and state. Finding 'little resonance' often on foreign soil, Western attempts to propagate or impose these beliefs tend to conjure up charges of blatant interference and even of 'human rights imperialism'. The reasons for these charges are not hard to detect, given the long history of Western expansionism. Seeing that modern democratic government originated in the West, Huntington notes, its emergence in non-Western societies has typically been 'the product of Western colonialism or imposition'. Such imposition has not come to an end with the dismantling of colonial empires – which augurs ill for the prospects of globalism. On the whole, Huntington's global analysis remains tied to the West/rest bifurcation. As such it allows only for an 'operative' or managerial type of world community, leaving little or no room for another alternative.[16]

In order to profile more clearly the limitations of Huntington's approach, I want to juxtapose his argument now to that of another renowned expert in international politics: Immanuel Wallerstein, the most prominent spokesman of so-called 'world-system' theory. In opposition to the prevalent model of international anarchy (among states), Wallerstein for some time now has focused attention on the emergence of a 'world-system' or a global civil society cutting across nation-state boundaries; in a string of publications stretching over the past several decades, he and his associates have delineated the features of a capitalist 'world-economy' seen as the driving force behind social and political developments on a global scale. Despite this breakthrough to the societal level, however, it is fair to say that the focus of world-system analysis in the past has been on economic factors, primarily on the structural determinants of capitalist markets and on economic 'center-periphery' relations.[17] More recently, however, the range of concerns has been dramatically expanded beyond the confines of traditional political economy; this change is particularly evident in Wallerstein's ground-breaking study on *Geopolitics and Geoculture*, where global cultural inquiries are placed at least on an equal footing with geopolitical (or rather, geo-economic) considerations. Like Huntington's essay, but a few years earlier, Wallerstein's study alerted readers to the looming 'clash of civilizations', more specifically to the importance of culture(s) seen as the 'intellectual battleground' in the contemporary 'world-system'. Again as in Huntington's case, this cultural confrontation was presented as the latest stage in a long historical sequence of global constellations (a sequence leading here from 'multiple mini-systems' over 'world-empires' to the modern capitalist 'world-economy'). What is innovative and challenging in Wallerstein's approach, however, is his move beyond individualizing or 'essentializing' modes of conceptualization in the direction of a more nuanced and quasi-dialectical account. Viewed from this angle, cultures are fluid, open-ended meaning patterns, while the syndrome 'West versus the Rest' appears as a complex differential entwinement.[18]

One of the central topics of Wallerstein's study is precisely the latter syndrome: more specifically the relation between indigenous (chiefly non-Western) cultures, on the one hand, and the prevalent global order or world economy, on the other. As he notes, the relation is often portrayed as the opposition between universalism and particularism, between global civilization (in the singular) and local civilizations (in the plural), with the evaluative accent squarely resting on the first of the paired terms. Stated in this categorical fashion, the distinction is a bald metaphysical shibboleth, one which Wallerstein is at pains to dislodge and overcome. One reason for its deceptive character is the long-standing collusion of universalism with concrete power constellations – as is evident in France's *'mission civilisatrice'* used as a prop of colonialism. Recalling the legacy of the Enlightenment and the French Revolution, Waller-stein pointedly reminds readers of the linkage between French revolutionary ideas and Napoleon's armies flooding the rest of Europe in a burst of military conquest. On the one hand, these armies were greeted by many Europeans as the carrier of a universal and emancipatory message, that of liberal 'civiliza-tion'; but, on the other, these same Europeans 'soon reacted as local "nation-alists" against French "imperialism"'. To be sure, the lure of this message goes deeper and antedates Napoleon. According to Wallerstein, universalism is 'dear to the Western heart', finding its roots in monotheistic religion and in the modern 'Baconian–Newtonian paradigm' with its attachment to universal laws of behaviour. During the nineteenth century, the lure received powerful new support and impetus from the doctrine of 'progress' and from evolutionary theories of social development. According to one such theory, human life on earth has always exhibited a 'linear tendency toward one world'. While originally the globe may have contained a large number of disparate groups, the movement of history has been such that progressively these groups have merged, so that 'bit by bit, with the aid of science and technology, we are arriving at one world', a unified cosmopolis. In terms of another account (the 'stage theory' of human development) differences between cultures are structural in kind, but they all form part of a patterned sequence. Since all groups here are destined to move through parallel pages (though at a different pace), again 'we end up with a single human society and therefore necessarily with a world culture'.[19]

In terms of political programmes or ideologies, universalism has been the backbone of modern liberalism and its global repercussions: specifically the process of modernization in its close embroilment with Westernization. In Wallerstein's words, the 'liberal dream' – seen as product of the 'self-conscious ideological *Weltanschauung*' of the modern world-economy – has been 'that universalism will triumph over racism and sexism'. This dream or programme, in turn, has been translated into 'two strategic operational imperatives': namely, 'the spread of "science" in the economy, and the spread of "assimilation" in the political arena'. Seen as outgrowth of a specific socio-economic design, these imperatives could easily be criticized or debunked as ideological by oppositional (say Marxist) movements which hold that 'the ruling ideas are the ideas of the ruling class'. Yet, as Wallerstein shows, oppositional or 'antisystemic' movements for a long time remained attached to the very same liberal vision, in a way which coloured their proposed remedies: faced with existing inequalities or social constraints, they demanded the removal of these barriers through reliance on more rather than less 'science' and through an ever more thoroughgoing 'assimilation' of all groups within the prevailing social system. In Wallerstein's telling formulation, which deserves to be quoted at some length,

> In the political arena, the fundamental problem was interpreted to be exclusion . . .. The unpropertied were excluded. Include them! The minorities were excluded. Include them! The women were excluded. Include them! Equals all. The dominant strata had more than others. Even things out! But if we are evening out dominant and dominated, then why not minorities and majorities, women and men! Evening out meant in practice assimilating the weaker to the model of the strong. . . . This search for science and assimilation, what I have called the fulfillment of the liberal dream, was located deep in the consciousness and in the practical

action of the world's antisystemic movements, from their emergence in the mid-nineteenth century until at least the Second World War.[20]

In the meantime, the situation has changed in a way that renders political struggles more complex and multi-dimensional, and hence also less uniformly manageable. During recent decades, Wallerstein notes, several oppositional movements have begun to express doubts about 'the utility, the reasonableness of "science" and "assimilation" as social objectives'. Thus, ecological or 'green' movements have raised questions about the damaging and sometimes counter-productive 'productivism' inherent in the nineteenth-century linkage of science and progress. At the same time, feminist groups and ethnic minorities have 'poured scorn' upon the demand for assimilation, insisting instead on a greater respect for otherness and difference. Yet, as Wallerstein cautions, the issue is not simply a reversal of priorities, that is, an option for particularism over universalism, for (plural) cultures over (world) civilization. No matter how attractive or tempting, the strategy is bound to fail and even to backfire, by ceding the 'cultural high ground' to the defenders of world order or the prevailing world economy. By equating their opponents with a backward-looking parochialism, these defenders can readily present themselves as the 'high priests' of world culture. For Wallerstein, the crucial move today is the attempt to extricate oneself from traditional dichotomies and priority schemes, instead of remaining 'enveloped' in the paired ideologies of universalism and parochialism. In any event, his study strongly counsels against a lapse into a 'mindless cultural pluralism', which would simply substitute the atomism of (incommensurable) cultures for the traditional anarchy of states. As he writes in a sober vein: 'I am skeptical we can find our way via a search for a purified world culture'. But 'I am also skeptical that holding on to national or to ethnic or to any other form of particularistic culture can be anything more than a crutch' – at least as long as particularism denotes self-enclosure.[21]

What these considerations bring into view is the need for a differential strategy beyond global synthesis and its denial: that is, for a kind of double move or double gesture proceeding cautiously in the interstices of affirmation and negation. Approached from this angle, to avoid totalizing enclosure, universalism or world culture can neither be wholly embraced nor wholly rejected. Although, in its linkage with the dominant world economy, universalism can readily be shown to be 'hypocritical', this is only part of the story. In the face of prevailing hegemonic structures and power inequalities, the idea of universalism still continues to matter as a refuge and a corrective. While it may serve, on the one hand, as a mere

189

palliative or 'deception', it also functions, on the other, as 'a political counter-weight which the weak can use and do use against the strong'. The problem, Wallerstein notes, is thus not purely ideological but structural in a global sense. If universalism were merely a cloak or a smokescreen for oppressive designs, 'we would not be discussing it today'. As things stand, however, universalism is 'a "gift" of the powerful to the weak' which confronts the latter with 'a double bind: to refuse the gift is to lose; to accept the gift is to lose'. Hence, the only plausible reaction of the weak (including minorities and Third World cultures) is 'neither to refuse nor to accept, or both to refuse and to accept', that is, to picture a seemingly zigzag course which both preserves cultural and group difference or distinctiveness while allowing it to grow and mature in a broader global context. As Wallerstein writes in a passage which ably captures this complex double move, as well as the 'dialectic of Enlightenment':

> The way to combat the falling away from liberty and equality would be to create and recreate particularistic cultural entities – arts, sciences, iden-tities; always new, often claiming to be old – that would be social (not individual), that would be particularisms whose object (avowed or not) would be the restoration of the universal reality of liberty and equality.[22]

III

Though exceptional in its clarity and conceptual rigour, Wallerstein's approach today is not entirely unique in the study of international or world politics. His nuanced, quasi-dialectical mode of analysis is seconded, and sometimes further radicalized, by a number of practitioners bent on exploring more fully the hermeneutical promises of cross-cultural relations and the political underpin-nings of cultural identity formation; inspired in part by recent 'poststructur-alist' life-structure, these writers tend to centrestage the porousness of cultural boundaries as well as the non-antithetical 'difference' of universalism and localism.[23] Rather than pursuing this line of inquiry, I want to return now to the central theme of these pages: the character of our 'global village' or of the emerging global community – the last term taken in the complex (and non-communitarian) sense articulated by Nancy. What are the implications – above all, the political and moral implications – of an 'inoperative community' in the midst of our 'clashing civilizations'? For clearly, Nancy's work offers not merely a descriptive account. Apart from its ontological resonances (deriving in part from Heidegger), his conception also carries a profound normative significance:

a significance resulting chiefly from his pronounced 'anti-totalizing' or anti-systemic stance. Politics and 'the political' cannot neatly be divorced. The absence of communitarian substance does not mean a lack of bonding, just as the accent on 'in-operation' does not entail a lapse into indifference of apathetic inaction. Precisely the disruption or 'interruption' of total structures carries with it a political and moral momentum. As Nancy writes in his study (in a chapter on 'Myth interrupted'),

> The passion of and for 'community' propagates itself, unworked, appealing, demanding to pass beyond every limit and every fulfillment enclosed in the form of an individual. It is thus not an absence, but a movement, it is unworking in its singular 'activity,' it is the propagation, even the contagion, or again the communication of community itself that propagates itself or communicates its contagion *by its very interruption*.[24]

Being non- or anti-managerial in outlook, Nancy's argument cannot align itself with the defence of prevailing hegemonic power structures (even while recognizing their 'operative' existence). To this extent, his perspective collides with the major thrust of Huntington's essay. As a strategic policy analyst, Huntington views the struggle among civilizations chiefly with an eye to its impact on the foreign policy objectives of the United States (and the West). Regarding policy recommendations, his essay is as blunt as his assessment of global power constellations. In the short run, he argues, it is 'clearly in the interest of the West' to 'promote greater cooperation and unity within its own civilization' and to 'incorporate into the West societies in Eastern Europe and Latin America' whose cultures display features of kinship. Most crucial, however, is the effort

> to limit the expansion of the military strength of Confucian and Islamic states; to moderate the reduction of Western military capabilities and maintain military superiority in East and Southwest Asia; to exploit differences and conflicts among Confucian and Islamic states; to support in other civilizations groups sympathetic to Western values and interests; [and] to strengthen international institutions that reflect and legitimate Western interests and values.

In the long run, the predictable advances of non-Western societies in both economic and military fields dictate a policy of overall containment (not too dissimilar from the earlier containment of communism); for the West obviously needs to maintain 'the economic and military power necessary to protect its

191

interests in relation to those civilizations'. To be sure, Huntington's view of civilizational encounters is not entirely conflictual. As he concedes, the future may also require the West 'to develop a more profound understanding of the basic religious and philosophical assumptions underlying other civilizations and the ways in which people in these civilizations see their interests'. Yet, understanding here seems to serve mainly a strategic goal: that of containing or subduing other cultures more effectively (as Tzvetan Todorov has argued with regard to the European 'conquest of America').[25]

As in the case of global diagnosis, Wallerstein's work again offers an instructive contrast or corrective. Despite his focus on the (macro-) level of 'world-system' or world economy, Wallerstein's normative or policy preferences clearly have an anti-systemic edge. Precisely in view of the consolidation of economic and military hegemony, *Geopolitics and Geoculture* accentuates the role of 'cultural resistance' and anti-systemic movements throughout the world – thus replicating on the cultural level the 'preferential option for the poor' (postulated by liberation theology). As he observes, one of the most 'striking' features of global politics today is the persistence and intensification of resistance movements ready to challenge hegemonic prerogatives (as part of the differential nexus of 'civilization/civilizations'). Yet – and here a crucial distinction comes to the fore – Wallerstein does not confine these challenges to the level of power struggles, especially struggles for global management and control. 'We have had planned social change ad nauseam', he writes, 'from Jeremy Bentham to the Bolsheviks; and the results have been less than happy'. What planned social change has yielded is mostly increased 'rationalization' both in Weber's sense and in Freud's sense – with the outcome pointing to a worst-case scenario: 'The Iron Cage *and* self-deception'. At this point, Wallerstein offers reflections on the future of world politics which in many ways resonate with Nancy's non- or counter-managerial vista. Perhaps, he notes,

> we should deconstruct [systems] without the erection of structures to deconstruct, which turn out to be structures to continue the old in the guise of the new. Perhaps we should have movements that mobilize and experiment but not movements that seek to operate within the power structures of a world-system they are trying to undo. Perhaps we should tiptoe into an uncertain future, trying merely to remember in which direction we are going.

In moving along this path, traditional cultures and civilizations have an important role to play in helping to maintain both global and cross-cultural difference.[26]

In helping to maintain difference, cultural movements also carry a broader political significance: by preventing the monopolization of 'the political' seen as a global public space or arena. This monopolization is clearly one of Nancy's central concerns. In the face of the prevailing economic, military, and technological concentration of power, the chances of political democracy on a global scale are placed in jeopardy. Although progressive in some sense, the one-sided liberalization of markets is not by itself a substitute for political self-determination. As Nancy writes somberly, '"democracy" more and more frequently serves only to assure a play of economic and technical forces that no politics today subjects to any end other than that of its own expansion'; and a good part of humanity is 'paying the price for this'. The notion of an 'inoperative community' is meant to serve as a bulwark both against a totalizing globalism (dominated by hegemonic powers) and against the surrender of politics to the relentless self-interest of atomistic agents (be they states, corporations, or private individuals). Nancy concludes the Preface to his book with these stirring and unsettling words:

> If we do not face up to such questions, the political will soon desert us completely, if it has not already done so. It will abandon us to political and technological economies, if it has not already done so . . . .. Being-in-common will nonetheless never cease to resist, but its resistance will belong decidedly to another world entirely. Our world, as far as politics is concerned, will be a desert, and we will wither away without a tomb – which is to say, without community, deprived of our finite existence.[27]

Notes

1 Samuel P. Huntington, 'The clash of civilizations?', *Foreign Affairs* 72 (Summer 1993), pp. 22–3.
2 'The clash of civilizations?', pp. 23–4. The essay mentions 'seven or eight' major, historically grown civilizations (p. 25): 'These include Western, Confucian, Japanese, Islamic, Hindu, Slavic-Orthodox, Latin American and possibly African civilization'. The Western type is further divided into 'European and North American' variants, and Islam into 'Arab, Turkic and Malay' subdivisions.
3 See Hedley Bull, 'Human rights and world politics', in Ralph Pettman, *Moral Claims in World Affairs* (New York: St Martin's Press, 1979), pp. 79–91; also Hedley Bull and Adam Watson (eds), *The Expansion of International Society* (Oxford: Clarendon Press, 1984).
4 See, for example, Shlomo Avineri and Avner de-Shalit (eds), *Communitarianism and*

Individualism (New York: Oxford University Press, 1992); David Rasmussen (ed), *Universalism vs. Communitarianism* (Cambridge, MA: MIT Press, 1990).

5 Jean-Luc Nancy, *La communauté désoeuvrée* (Paris: Bourgeois, 1986). For the English translation see Nancy, *The Inoperative Community*, ed. Peter Connor, trans. Peter Connor et al. (Minneapolis: University of Minnesota Press, 1991). The difficulty of translating *'désoeuvrée'* is discussed there on p. 156, note 1. The final conception of Nancy's study coincided roughly with the publication of Maurice Blanchot's *La communauté inavouable* (Paris: Minuit, 1983), which has been translated by Pierre Joris as *The Unavowable Community* (Barrytown, NY: Station Hill Press, 1988).

6 Nancy, *The Inoperative Community*, pp. 1–3. A similar analysis is offered by Claude Lefort in *Democracy and Political Theory*, trans. David Macey (Minneapolis: University of Minnesota Press, 1988). Compare also Hannah Arendt, *The Origins of Totalitarianism* (New York: Harcourt, Brace & World, 1951).

7 Nancy, *The Inoperative Community*, pp. 3–4.

8 *The Inoperative Community*, pp. 4–6. Over long stretches the chapter proceeds in the form of a critical commentary on the work of Georges Bataille – whose outlook is shown precisely to be split between the poles of ecstasy and community. As Nancy writes (pp. 20–1), Bataille 'remained suspended, so to speak, between the two poles of ecstasy and community'. While the pole of ecstasy was 'linked to the fascist orgy', the pole of community was 'bound up with the idea of communism'. The outcome of this conflict was 'community refusing itself ecstasy, ecstasy withdrawing from community'. In the end, Bataille was able only to oppose 'a *subjective* sovereignty of lovers and of the artist', and also the exception of 'darting "heterogeneous" flashes', to the '"homogeneous" order of society, with which they do not communicate'.

9 *The Inoperative Community*, pp. 9–11. In Nancy's own retrospective view, past societies exhibited a fabric which was much too complex and diverse to be captured by the term *Gemeinschaft*. 'It would undoubtedly be more accurate to say', he writes (p. 11), 'that *Gesellschaft* – "society", the dissociating association of forces, needs, and signs – has taken the place of something for which we have no name or concept, something that issued at once from a much more extensive communication than that of a mere social bond (a communication with the gods, the cosmos, animals, the dead, the unknown) *and* from much more piercing and dispersed segmentation of this same bond, often involving much harsher effects . . . than what we expect from a communitarian minimum in the social bond. *Society* was not built on the ruins of a *community*'.

10 *The Inoperative Community*, pp. 6–7, 22, 27–8.

11 *Ibid.* pp. xxxviii–xxxix, 29–31.

12 *Ibid.* pp. xxxvii, 40–1. I have invoked the distinction between 'politics' and 'the political' in my 'Rethinking the political: some Heideggerian contributions' and 'Post-metaphysical politics: Heidegger and democracy?', in *The Other Heidegger* (Ithaca NY: Cornell University Press, 1993), pp. 50–1, 87–8. The phrase *'mise en scène'* is borrowed from Lefort, *Democracy and Political Theory*, pp. 10–11.

13 The charge of a fixating essentialism was advanced chiefly by Fouad Ajami in his response titled 'The summoning', *Foreign Affairs* 72 (September/October 1993), pp. 2–9. Unfortunately, his and related rejoinders are marred by drawbacks of their own, namely, either a return to the anarchy of states or else by the flip-side of essentialism: the endorsement of assimilationism or a 'melting-pot' ideology of globalism (under Western auspices). In his subsequent reply, Huntington correctly labelled these two options respectively as a 'pseudo-alternative' (the statist paradigm) and an 'unreal alternative' (the one-world paradigm). See 'Response: if not civilizations, what?, *Foreign Affairs* 72 (November/December 1993), p. 191.

14 See Huntington, 'The clash of civilizations?, pp. 25–7, 35, 45; 'Response: if not civilizations, what?', p. 194. The last passage contains a veiled (critical) reference to Francis Fukuyama, *The End of History and the Last Man* (New York: Free Press, 1992).

15 Huntington, 'The clash of civilizations?,' pp. 26, 39–40. Compare also Kishore Mahbubani, 'The West and the Rest', *The National Interest* 28 (Summer 1992), pp. 3–13; and his 'The dangers of decadence: what the Rest can teach the West', *Foreign Affairs* 72 (September/October 1993), pp. 10–14.

16 Huntington, 'The clash of civilizations?', pp. 40–1. Despite his accent on radical cleavage, Huntington delineates three possible responses of non-Western civilizations to Western power and values (p. 41): a strategy of isolation from the West; a 'band-wagon' strategy of rapid Westernization; and finally a critical middle path attempting 'to "balance" the West by developing economic and military power and cooperating with other non-Western societies against the West, while preserving indigenous values and institutions, in short, to modernize but not to Westernize'.

17 While cultural aspects were not entirely ignored, they were strongly subordinated to economic analysis (along quasi-Marxist lines). As Wallerstein and Terence Hopkins noted in 1982, there is a 'broadly "cultural" aspect which needs to be mentioned' alongside the specifically economic and political dimensions (dealing respectively with division of labour and formation of states). But 'little is systematically known about it as an integral aspect of world-historical development'; hence 'we do not focus' on it because 'so much preliminary conceptual work needs to be done first'. See 'Patterns of development of the modern world-system', in Terence K. Hopkins and Immanuel Wallerstein, *World-System Analysis: Theory and Methodology* (Beverly Hills: Sage Publications, 1982), p. 43.

18 See Wallerstein, *Geopolitics and Geoculture: Essays on the Changing World-System* (Cambridge: Cambridge University Press, 1991). One of the chapters (pp. 158–83) is titled 'Culture as the ideological battleground of the modern world-system'; but the running banner line reads 'Culture as the intellectual battleground'. For the historical evolution of world politics see the chapter on 'The modern world-system as a civilization', especially pp. 222–3.

19 *Geopolitics and Geoculture*, pp. 186–7, 217, 233.

20 *Ibid.* pp. 181–2.

21 *Ibid.* pp. 182, 198, 235. In Wallerstein's view (p. 233), universalism today is challenged not only by antisystemic movements but 'from *within* science, and on

scientific grounds'. For while classical dynamics was predicated on the calculation of 'linear trajectories' which were said to be 'lawful, determined and reversible', contemporary science has discovered 'intrinisic randomness and intrinsic irreversibility' as the 'basis of physical order'.

22 *Geopolitics and Geoculture*, pp. 171, 199, 217.
23 Compare, for example, James Der Derian and Michael J. Shapiro (eds), *International/Intertextual Relations: Postmodern Readings of World Politics* (Lexington, KY: Lexington Books, 1989); also the chapter on 'Global political discourse', in William E. Connolly, *Identify/Difference: Democratic Negotiations of Political Paradox* (Ithaca, NY: Cornell University Press, 1991), pp. 36–63.
24 Nancy, *The Inoperative Community*, p. 60.
25 Huntington, 'The clash of civilizations?', pp. 48–9. See also Tzvetan Todorov, *The Conquest of America: The Question of the Other* (New York: Harper, 1984), especially pp. 247–8.
26 Wallerstein, *Geopolitics and Geoculture*, pp. 199, 229–30, 234. As Wallerstein adds (p. 230), non-Western cultures or civilizations are 'indeed the foci of important antisystemic movements. We may deconstruct more rapidly in their wake than without them. Indeed, can we deconstruct without them? I doubt it'.
27 Nancy, *The Inoperative Community*, pp. xxxvii, xli.

12

Anger

Alphonso Lingis

It is in our distress, Jean-Luc Nancy says, that we know our coexistence. He identifies the dimensions of our distress: the exterminations, the expropriations, the technicizations, and the simulations that darken the present and the future of our coexistence.[1] How are the exterminations wrought upon peoples in Haiti, Africa or Central and Eastern Europe, the expropriations suffered by tribal peoples and peasants by loggers and landowners and by the depreciation of the market for the products of the land – and also the culture of technicization and simulation that reigns in the richest urban technopoles *our* distress?

Has not the new organization of political economies into the transnational acrhipelago of urban technopoles made expropriation and extermination no longer possible among them? Is not the culture of technicization and simulation felt as a distress only within them, while the outer zone is a theatre of realpolitik and exclusion from skilled labour and high-tech industries?

Is not the separation today of those who live in the archipelago of the urban technopoles and those who subsist and multiply in the outer zones more radical than the organization of human communities into nation-states that made for the inhabitants of a nation-state the inhabitants of the other foreigners and aliens? Is it not more radical than the politico-economic and ideological division that split the world into two blocks during the forty-five years of the Cold War?

The archipelago

In recent decades some twenty regions – for example, Houston, Silicon Valley, the Ruhr, Lyon, Milan, Tokyo-Osaka, Taipei, Seoul, Mexico City, Sao Paulo – have come to form a technocratic-commercial archipelago of urban technopoles. Their dynamism does not come from industrial production, nor from possession of the sources of raw materials, but from the production and control of information. High-tech industries reduce ever more the quantity and even the quality of raw materials used. Researchers find ways to produce using alternative, recycled, ever cheaper raw materials, and to miniaturize the products. Less and less unskilled and even skilled manpower is employed in them. Manufacture is robotized. The communications industries, and the banking and stock exchange giants are consolidated in these urban technopoles.

The capital from landed wealth, from older industrial monopolies, from mining and petrodollars and the heroin and cocaine Mafia are invested in the high-tech industries and real estate of the archipelago. The most gifted scientific researchers, programmers, engineers, financiers, economists, social technocrats are not sent from developed to underdeveloped nations, but to the technopoles and from one technopole to another.

The traditional organization of human societies into nation-states with independent administrative bodies and national industries and local markets is rapidly being displaced by the new archipelago of technopoles. The fifteen largest transnational corporations have net incomes greater than 120 countries and the hundred largest ones control more wealth than half the member states of the United Nations. The capital, the researchers, the investments, the labour force, the markets of the high-tech industries, banking, and commerce are not Japanese, American, or German any more, but transnational. Today the advanced industrial nations have accepted the New World Order of NAFTA, the European Union, GATT, The Pacific Rim and the Southeast Asia Free-Trade zones, and the WTO. The Parliamentary committees of governments, which up until recently were representatives of powerful industries and businesses in their districts, now find that protectionist measures for local industries only reduce their competitiveness before the transnational corporations.

The rise and fall of industries, the development of regions and the abandon of others are determined in the corporate boardrooms of IBM, Sony, Siemens, Philips. They control the extraction of raw materials from underdeveloped regions to industrial regions; they control the investments for industrialization. They determine which regions will be equipped and which will be consigned to assembly plants.

The functions of regulation and reproduction are less and less in the hands of decision-makers and more and more in the circuitry of electronic automation. The management of development and expansion is determined by experts who can access the relevant information. The experts, drawn from everywhere, are trained and equipped by the transnational giants of the technopoles themselves. They are elements within a feedback automatism.

The inhabitants of the urban technopoles are not engaged in industrial production. They are engaged in the programming and management of industry and commerce. They are employed in the production and control of information. And they are engaged in the entertainment and leisure industry – in the production, programming, and marketing of television and cinema, spectator sports, videogames, fashion, and mass and international tourism and vacation resorts.

The urban technopoles require a population of exceptionally intelligent, highly trained, and continually retrained minds. In the archipelago of urban technopoles, great sums of money are poured into training and research institutes, for the most fully equipped laboratories, the most advanced supercomputers, the most bold projects. The intellectually most gifted and motivated are rigorously selected, and trained in the most advanced disciplines, with the most advanced electronic teaching equipment. Facilities for the recycling of brainpower as skills needed and professions change guarantees their employment. Educational institutions must determine the needs of the urban technopoles, and select and train for them. There is no place for those whose IQ tests are low, for the intellectually unmotivated or poorly schooled.

In the archipelago, communication and transportation systems are maintained at the state of the art. Databanks and financial transactions between the urban technopoles are satellite-transmitted. Air travel is no longer from one urban concentration to the next, but to and from the great hubs of Houston, Lyon, Tokyo, Sao Paulo where great airports are built and continually upgraded. High-speed monorail trains connect the technopoles across continents, and rapid transportation systems and highways circulate traffic within the urban complexes.

In the zoned cantonments of the archipelago highly trained researchers, experts, programmers, financiers live in spacious housing complexes with conditioned air, perfect water and sanitation systems, and home entertainment systems. Outside, air and noise pollution is being brought down to zero, streets are spacious, there are splendid parks. Electronic surveillance systems and private police companies ensure security.

The food requirements, whether basic or luxury, of the archipelago of urban technopoles is produced by high-tech agribusiness. In the United States less than one per cent of the population is engaged in agriculture, and even that one per cent produces surpluses dumped on the outside world and the producers compensated with federal subsidies.

Medical research institutions are maintained at the state of the art. The finest medical specialists and high-tech hospitals are located in the archipelago.

The shopping malls of the archipelago spread before its inhabitants staggering quantities of consumer goods. Every commodity comes in an array of different styles. Commodities purchased are replaced as compatibilities are updated and as styles and fashions are changed. Inhabitants of Silicon Valley, Houston, the Ruhr, Tokyo, or Singapore consume annually two hundred times each what inhabitants of Bolivia, Chad, or Nigeria consume. The inhabitants of the archipelago define their individuality, personality, and freedom by taking personal responsibility for the choices they make among innumerable objects offered for their pleasure.

In the technocratic-commercial archipelago of urban technopoles now live about one-seventh of the plant's 5.7 billion people. They are situated in industrialized nations which have already reached, or are tending towards, zero population growth. Germany has been in a minus-zero population growth situation for almost ten years. The population of the archipelago itself will grow in the future. The total population of the planet, now 5.7 billion people, will grow to 11.5 billion in the next fifty years. But since almost all of the population increase of the planet will occur outside of it, the population of the archipelago will represent a declining percentage of the total human population.

The archipelago is defended from the outside by smart weaponry built for Star Wars and tested in the Gulf War waged for the control of cheap petroleum sources. It is protected within by electronic surveillance systems and highly trained police with high-tech laboratories.

The outer zone

Outside of the technocratic-commercial archipelago of urban technopoles, the rest of the planet – and the other six-sevenths of humanity.

Only mass industrial production in these regions is said to be able to supply the needs of a human population which will double in the next fifty years. But the industrialization of the outer zone cannot follow the process by which England, Germany, the United States and Japan became industrial powers in the eighteenth and nineteenth centuries.

Industrialization requires investment capital. In the outer zone agricultural production, and the extraction of raw materials, timber and mining, for export are traditional sources of surplus wealth. However, the price of agricultural products and raw materials exported from the outer zone continues to decrease.

Throughout the 1980s the principal export from the destitute and bankrupt South American countries into the United States was capital. The governments of Mexico, Brazil, and Peru exported an enormous portion of their national revenues to banks in the archipelago to service their huge national debts. But in addition, high interest rates in the United States and the economic, and therefore social and political, uncertainties in their own countries made the indigenous capitalists in the outer zone invest in the United States and Europe. The drain of investment capital from private capitalists in South America to the United States was twice the capital drain from their governments servicing the national debts of those countries.

Unable to accumulate enough capital fom local sources for industrialization, the countries in the outer zone seek to attract foreign capital investment. The Japanese and the Saudis do not invest in the poorest and least industrialized countries – Nicaragua and Haiti and Bangladesh; they instead invest in MGM, the Rockefeller Center, US television networks, and Vancouver real estate. Mexico, Russia, Kenya, Vietnam, Haiti, and Cuba attract capital by offering foreign investors tax-free facilities and the reimportation of their profits. The agricultural and timber and mining industries in the outer zone are purchased by transnational corporations in the archipelago, which provide processing plants, transportation and shipping, and distribution systems. The profits are exported to the archipelago.

In every sector, the transnational corporation with the greatest research and marketing resources drives out the local industries in the outer zone. The processing, distribution, and marketing resources of Delmonte, Gerber, and Procter & Gamble drive out of operation local basic industries. The vast resources of pharmaceutical companies and heavy industries flood the outer zone with foreign-made products sold more cheaply and distributed more widely than local industries can. The subsidized overproduction of agribusiness in the rich nations permits them to dump their rice, wheat, and beef in the outer zone, cutting ever lower the prices of locally produced agricultural products.

As an industry gets bigger, the costs of research and marketing continue to increase as it grows, and the labour costs must be cut by mechanization and robotization. Modern manufacturing industries in the outer zone, whether local or transnational, increase productivity and decrease the number of men and women they employ. In Mexico, Argentina, and Brazil, during the past three years, the growth of locally owned industry has been the growth of big industries, and resulted in a net increase of unemployment.

The vast unemployed population in the outer zone is a source of cheap labour. The great transnational corporations transfer their assembly plants to the outer zone. The heavy industry of Japan was transplanted to Thailand, the Philippines, Indonesia. As wages rise in Thailand, Thai plants will be relocated in Laos, Vietnam, and Africa. The heavy industry of Western Europe is transplanted to the former socialist states of Eastern Europe, most of whose non-competitive industries have been dismantled. The manufacturing industry of the United States is transplanted to the Caribbean, Mexico, and now downward into South America. In Haiti, the poorest nation in the American hemisphere, where the average income of the population is $125 a year, more than three hundred US corporations installed assembly plants. The US giant Sears paid its Haitian workers 13 cents an hour, with no job security or health benefits or pensions, and reimported to the United States $67 million of clothing, sports equipment, and toys a year. The textiles and shoes assembled in Jamaica, high-tech equipment assembled in the Dominican Republic, the production of heavy industry in Mexico is exported to the United States. Throughout Central America, the fertile plains and the deforested hills have been taken over by ranchers exporting cheap grass-fed Zebu beef for the US hamburger industry, while the small farmers have been displaced and pushed into subsistence farming on stony plots higher up the mountains.

Throughout the outer zone topsoil is losing its fertility to overfarming and erosion, rivers are being diverted to supply water to great urban centres, marginal lands are being ploughed. Each year more than 6 million hectares of fertile land are turning into desert; tropical forests are being destroyed at the rate of 11 million hectares a year. The food available to the average African has diminished every year for fifteen successive years. The transfer of heavy industry and assembly plants to the outer zone, the dumping of toxins, and the distribution of mass-produced consumer commodities spread ever further environmental destruction. Today penguins are dying from poisoned fish in Antarctic waters and sheep being blinded in New Zealand and Patagonia from the gaping ozone shield hole over Antarctica.

Throughout the outer zone, transportation systems are crumbling. Education is deteriorating because of cuts in funding and the evident uselessness of

202

schooling for finding better work. What health facilities exist are concentrated in the cities.

What were once cities are becoming swollen concentrations of mass poverty and social collapse. Sao Paulo will have 22.6 million people by the year 2000, Bombay 18.1 million, Shanghai 17.4 million, Mexico City 16.2 million, Calcutta 12.7 million. There are 143,000 people per square mile in Lagos and 130,000 in Jakarta, as compared with 23,700 per square mile in the five boroughs of New York. Public safety is giving way to urban violence. These people know ever deteriorating nutrition, urban sanitation, live in toxic levels of air pollution and lead poisoning. Last year Mexico City had but fifty-three days of air at a tolerable level of pollution. Public sanitation is retrogressing. Only 40 per cent of the population of Lima has even access to purified water.

Eight million children die annually due to diseases preventable with a good infrastructure of running water. As many women die in childbearing in India each month as in North America, Europe, Japan, and Australia combined. The concentration of exhausted masses of people leads to outbreaks of plague – AIDS infecting 30 per cent of the population of Central Africa, new strains of malaria in India, Sumatran cholera which broke out in Lima to spread into the Amazon decimating tribal peoples, and then throughout South and Central America. The last time I was in Central America, World Health officials had published the predications for the susceptibility to cholera in the region; the government of Honduras responded by bulldozing mass graves outside of the cemeteries of Tegucigalpa.

The old notion of a developed *country* no longer has validity. The populations of the industrial nation-states, rebuilding after the Second World War, had come to demand of their governments the management of the national economy for the economic welfare of their nations. But today, within the so-called developed countries, there are the urban technopoles, and the outer zones where what had been developed is deteriorating.

In the United States in the 1980s there was a massive transfer of wealth; today 20 per cent of the population enjoy 48 per cent of the wealth. The working population employed in manufacture in the United States dropped from 36 per cent to 17 per cent in the last ten years; formerly well-paid skilled labourers are reassigned to service jobs, cooking hamburgers at minimum wage. The poorest 20 per cent make do with 3.2 per cent of the national income. Fully one-sixth of American children are growing up in chronic malnutrition and irreversible brain damage. Los Angeles is already a Third World city, both ethnically and in economic and social deterioration. California has just passed a referendum denying access to state-supported hospitals and clinics to undocumented immigrants and their children; 70 per cent of them of Hispanic origin are infected with latent tuberculosis. Unemployment for Black young men is 40 per cent; there are more Black men between the ages of 18 and 22 in prison than in college.

Western Europe has had, for ten years now, 11 per cent unemployment, and slums are now cancerously fixed on to Paris, Milan, and Rome. Japan too is now abandoning the social programme of full employment. Its foreign workers imported as maids and construction workers live no better than Turks in Berlin, Filipinos in Kuwait. In Russia, 80 per cent of the money is concentrated in Moscow, whereas the minimum wage for Russian workers is $14 a month. In China wealth is concentrated on the coast, in Shanghai and Guangjo; the whole of the interior is a rapidly deteriorating outer zone. In Mexico, 10 per cent of the population had controlled 36 per cent of wealth just six years ago; today they control 60 per cent.

In the United States, in Great Britain, in France, state universities are no longer funded to provide a general education for the whole population. The very idea of higher education being open to every intellectually capable citizen who can pay for it is being discarded – by no less than William Bennett, the former US Secretary of Education. The Jeffersonian idea of higher education being necessary for participation in a democracy has been replaced by CNN infotainment and public opinion polls.

Export from the archipelago to the outer zone

Industrial production is not located in the archipelago but in the outer zone. These industries provide the consumer commodities distributed in the archipelago and the mass-produced commodities sold in the outer zone.

There remain four kinds of industries located in the archipelago itself. One of these industries sells its production within the archipelago. The other three export their production to the outer zone.

The production and processing of information are located in the archipelago. The research institutes, equipped with the most advanced high-tech equipment, produce the technological knowledge that enable industrial production to reduce the costs of raw materials, to produce new kinds of raw materials, to recycle industrial waste, to miniaturize products. This knowledge, protected as intellectual property, remains in the possession of the transnational corporations located in the archipelago. Genetic researchers collect biological samples from the rainforests in the outer zone, and produce hybridized crop plants, patented bacteria, plants, and animals which can be marketed worldwide, including back to the tropical countries from which the genetic sources came. Pharmaceutical researchers collect the knowledge of traditional healers, and test and synthesize pharmaceuticals that will be marketed worldwide.

Useable information, controlled by the archipelago, circulates within the urban technopoles of the archipelago. The archipelago also produces futile information, distributed as entertainment to the outer zone. Media news, cropped, edited, recomposed, narrated as instant drama, for thrills, for excitement, for entertainment. The strongest export sector of the US economy is Hollywood and pop music. Videogames. Spectator sports. Sylvester Stallone, Arnold Schwartznegger, Michael Jackson, and Madonna have annual incomes superior to the governments of half of the nations represented in the UN.

It is condescendingly repeated that the masses of people living in the hopeless economic conditions and cultural collapse of the outer zone crave the escapist dreams of Hollywood. Can one really believe that Mexicans and Peruvians really crave to hear the news on television read by blonde women, that Brazilian youth really want to dance only to New York heavy metal disco music? That is to ignore the high-tech marketing resources of the entertainment industry of the archipelago. Hollywood has not only the $60 million and the high-tech resources to make superproductions that Brazil or Vietnam do not have; it also has the marketing resources to distribute them worldwide, to fund advertising campaigns in the media and in entertainment magazines wordwide. Hollywood spends an average of $14 million to advertise each of its films. In the 1960s Brazil had one of the most innovative film industries in the world, consistently winning international awards in Cannes, Berlin, and Havana. The CIA-assisted military takeover of Brazil put it under strict censorship; only propaganda and entertainment films could be made. Four years ago, the civilian government of Fernando Collor accepted the neo-liberal decrees of the World Bank and IMF; all subsidies to the film industry were gutted. Last year only three films were made in Brazil.

The third largest industry in the archipelago is the drugs industry, worth $400 billion annually. From hashish and marijuana for the White middle-class youth, it has found in the unemployed urban ghettos markets for heroin and crack, in the upwardly mobile suburbs markets for designer drugs. The official propaganda blames foreign drug warlords in the Golden Triangle and in Columbia. But the enormous profits of the Medellín and Cali cartels in Columbia come from barely 5 per cent of the street prices of the drugs imported in the United States. It is once the cocaine and opiates are in the hands of the US importers that their price increases twentyfold. These profits stay in the United States, are laundered and reinvested in the archipelago. By ensuring that these imports remain illegal, the US importers guarantee their prices increase and their own profits increase. While cigarette smoking has dramatically declined in the United States, the cigarette manufacturers are enjoying larger profits than ever. The growth of their profits come from marketing their carcinogenics in the outer zone.

The one heavy industry that remains within the archipelago is the weapons industry. The economies of the technopoles within the archipelago are too closely intertwined for wars between them to be more than economic wars. The armaments industries produce for export to the outer zone.

Today, the economic collapse brought about in Africa and Latin America and stagnation in the Asian subcontinent has led the World Bank and IMF officials or local oligarchies to impose neo-liberal regimes on those countries. These economies are forced to reorient for export production to the archipelago, and drastically to cut social welfare programmes and safety nets for their own ever increasing and ever more impoverished masses. The social unrest predicted in those countries justifies the import of police and military experts from the archipelago, and ever-upgraded weapons imports. World military spending in 1992 was $815 billion, equivalent to the combined income of the poorest 49 per cent of the world's population. India, where the average annual per capita income is $290, is the world's biggest importer of arms – purchased for $12.2 billion in four years from 1988–1992. These arsenals in no way threaten the archipelago; of the forty-eight armed conflicts in the world today, all are fratricidal conflicts stirred up by religious fundamentalist or ethnic demagogues, losers fighting losers.

The five nations of the UN Security Council are the world's principal weapons exporters, producing 86 per cent of all weapons sold in the world. The high-tech smart weaponry made it possible for the Americans to massacre 250,000 Iraqis in the sands with a loss of some 200 men, half of whom died by friendly fire. This spectacular satellite-broadcast high-tech weapons show drove into bankruptcy whole armaments industries in Brazil, China, and Russia. The share of the US weapons industry in the world export arms market has jumped from 13 per cent in 1986 to an overwhelming 70 per cent today. The United States sells weapons to 146 of the world's 190 nations. It also dumps, free of charge, more than $2 billion worth of the older but still lethal weapons of its own arsenal annually to fifty countries. Both Israel and Egypt received last year free tanks, fighter plane and helicopters; both Greece and Turkey received free warplanes, tanks, guided-missile destroyers and self-propelled howitzers. The Clinton administration has recently introduced $1 billion of federal subsidies to the weapons-export industry.

The Contract for America of the Republican Party, victorious in the last elections, calls for an ever greater investment in the defence industry, a restarting of Star Wars: not because the United States, the world's sole superpower, can be threatened by some hostile armed power somewhere on the planet; but because the US weapons industry is the most thriving sector of the national economy.

The pressure of population increase

It is in the outer zone, where everywhere social welfare investments are being eliminated, where basic services, transportation, schooling, and health have drastically deteriorated, that the population will double in the next fifty years. The children born there are to an ever greater percentage suffering irreversible brain damage due to child malnutrition. The deteriorated schools prepare them less and less for posts in the high-tech economy. The deterioration of trans-portation networks makes their export industries less and less competitive, their costs greater for export products – raw materials, exotic foodstuffs – that command ever poorer prices. The deterioration of sanitation in the vast shantytowns and the deterioration of health facilities lays them open to out-breaks of previously localized viruses.

This destitute population in the outer zone is filtering across the Rio Grande, through the Coast Guard Maginot Line spread across the Caribbean, across Gibraltar, into the countries where the archipelago has its urban technopoles. Seventy-five million people leave their countries annually as refugees, displaced people or emigrant workers. In February of 1992, a rusty freighter left Bangkok with ninety Chinese refugees, sailed westward to elude suspicion around the Cape of Good Hope for America. Four million chicanos from Central and South America have slipped clandestinely into the United States. A Berlin Wall is now in the process of being built from the Pacific the length of the Rio Grande to the Gulf of Mexico. More and more Draconian legislation has been passed to identify and deport undocumented chicano, Haitian, and Chinese immigrants. California passed a referendum, with overwhelming voters' support, to deny medical attention and schooling to their children, who, born in the United States, are Americans. The new Republican Contract for America will introduce legislation to extend the California law throughout the nation. France has already legislated a zero-immigration policy. Europe and North America, which contained more than 22 per cent of the world's population in 1950, will contain less than 10 per cent by 2025. The archipelago will be using more and more of its research institutes, its think tanks, its high-tech police to build new Berlin walls.

Their distress and ours

Transnational markets for commodities and satellite-relayed information technology have produced for us the image of the global village. However oceans, languages, traditions, beliefs had separated peoples and continues to separate them, a community of euphoria would be bringing them together – the material euphoria of mass-produced consumer products, the immaterial euphoria of information not generating convictions, integrity, and resolve, but marketed as infotainment. To represent the transnational market of commodities and information as a global village is to invoke the image of a community where each individual found his or her own personal identity in and through his or her identification with the corporate body of the community. A coming community of euphoria is represented in the nostalgic image of a community that never existed.

Under the image of the future and past community of euphoria, we know our present coexistence in distress across new kinds of separation and exclusion. It is through expropriations and exterminations that the people in the outer zone are present to those in the archipelago; those in the archipelago are present to one another alienated in technicizations and simulacra.

It is as human resources that the outer zone is present to those in the archipelago; it is as resources exploited that humans in the outer zone are present to them. The destruction of the environment, the constant depreciation of the export prices of agricultural products and raw materials, and the destruction of local industries through the marketing of the products of transnational corporations have all produced massive agglomerations of cheap labour. Their lives are without hope of advance, prey to insecurity and hunger, prey to industrial accidents and epidemics. NAFTA sets up Mexico as the open zone for installation of US assembly plants. When the collapse of the peso threatens the collapse of foreign investments, the US intervenes to support Mexican fiscal stability, at the cost of a freeze of Mexican salaries, whose real value has not ceased to diminish for ten straight years and now diminish another

40 per cent. Mexicans are imported massively to work the Southwest harvests, unskilled factory, and menial service jobs, under legislation that denies them legality and rights to job security, pensions, education, and hospitalization. Fleeing Haitians are turned back on high seas, camped at Guantánamo; a massive military operation on their island restores law and order forcibly to repatriate the refugees and a government invested to secure the installations of US assembly plants.

> In the meantime, there are five billion human bodies. Soon, there will be eight billion. . . . Humanity is becoming *tangible*, and also tangible in its inhumanity. What is the space opened between eight billion bodies? What is the space in which they touch or draw apart, without any of them or their totality being reabsorbed into a pure and nil sign of itself? Sixteen billion eyes, eighty billion fingers: to see what, to touch what?[2]

To see, to touch wounds, bodies exposed to us in their wounds, bodies of misery, bodies of starvation, battered bodies, prostituted bodies, mangled bodies, infected bodies, as well as bloated bodies, bodies that are too well nourished, too body-built, too erotic, too orgasmic.[3]

In the exterminations in fratricidal conflicts stirred up by religious fundamentalist or ethnic demagogues, exterminations of refugees, exterminations through hunger and disease, those in the archipelago feel relief from the rising pressure of population against their Berlin Walls. It is as bodies that can be starved that the pressure takes the form of humans that are present to them.

Since Vietnam, the archipelago has been unwilling to enlist its men to risk their lives to exterminate rebellions in the outer zone; since Somalia, the United States has seemed unwilling to risk one American life. Starving recalcitrant enclaves into submission is now a policy that, having proved itself in Nicaragua and Peru, is reinforced against Cuba, is applied to nations of Africa, to whole continents.

It is starved, deported, massacred, tortured bodies, exterminated by the millions, piled up in charnel houses that the bodies of people in the outer zone are exposed to be seen and touched, present to us.[4]

Within the archipelago, it is as technicized and alienated in simulacra that people come to be present to one another. In the archipelago, where the action is, action no longer means the constitution of meaning and value for one's individual and collective existence through labour that leaves one's forces, one's skills, one's thought and imagination on the products of one's labour. One is trained for a specific function – computer programmer, administrative consultant, electronics engineer, investment broker, celebrity manager and marketer – rather than with a specific product. The individual finds his or her identity in performance, in being active, in keeping up. The dead times, times of recuperation and leisure, are phases of inanity and meaninglessness.[5]

Technologies multiply and render one another obsolete at an ever faster pace before adjustment to them can integrate one's forces, one's skills, one's thought and imagination into the enjoyment of a singular presence. The technologically equipped performance required for an individual to be active expropriates him or her of his or her force, his or her labour, his or her body, his or her sensibility – the space-time of his or her singularity.[6]

Like synthesizers available to composers twenty years ago and which have produced principally pop music commanding the scene by jumping ahead on to still more technically advanced synthesizers, word-processors and Internet have produced an electronic language without producing any corresponding break-through in literature or psychology, sociology, political science, or philosophy. E-mail has produced a decline in the language and in the time and care devoted to communication with individuals. The 600 million trips on aeroplanes now taken annually by US citizens have in no way made them world citizens or participants in world culture; to the contrary, political isolationism, cultural jingoism, racism, and religious fundamentalism have swept the electorate. Deleuze and Guattari explained how the production of knowledge and infor-mation capital requires a machinery of the production of stupidity that absorbs the surplus knowledge and ensure the integration of groups and individuals.[7]

> It will be seen in particular how it is at the level of the State and the military that the most progressive sectors of scientific or technical knowl-dege combine with those feeble archaisms bearing the greatest burden of current functions. . . . Although [the scientific and technical worker] has mastered a flow of knowledge, information, and training, he is so absorbed in capital that the reflux of organized, axiomatized stupidity coincides with him, so that, when he goes home in the evening, he rediscovers his little-desiring machines by tinkering with a television set.[8]

It is also as consumers that the economy of the archipelago requires its inhabitants – consumers of commodities representing styles, fashions, consu-mers of information and infotainment. It is in the culture of spectacle and simulacra that individuals are called upon to devise the meaning and worth of their individual and collective identities. They are called upon to devise them out of forms, images, games, spectacles, that is, the excess over the necessities of life, and from which the meaning of existence is eclipsed before the instant gratification of the spectacle.

The classical, and Marxist, critique of alienation — alienation from the products of one's labour — is now repudiated with the argument that it presupposed that man originally and fundamentally is a positive force that freely produces his own existence by freely producing the means for his own life and growth. It has been much argued that consumption is itself a production; the modern consumer who wanders the shopping malls wanders as a freedom before quasi-unlimited choices, and exercises his or her responsibility by making a personal selection of commodities to array on his or her body and in his or her house. The technologically equipped active individual enlisted in the frenetic process of information and infotainment production in the archipelago would be invested with an unprecedented freedom actualized in a world given over to consumption.

But it is not the abundance of commodities available for consumption that make free individuals possible; instead, the value assigned to the free individual, as a positive force that freely produces his or her own existence by affirming the sovereignty of his or her desire, produces the contemporary form of consumption. The commodities required must express free individuality, offering immediate pleasure and demanding no effort. Commodities are but the materialization of style or fashion, and as such transitory, made to be discarded when the style or fashion changes. Any loyalty or attachment to them would compromise the sovereign independence of individual freedom. The freedom of the free individualism valued in the culture of the archipelago is a freedom without tasks or commitments, disconnected from history. Wanton consumption reveals a profound indifference to the objects consumed; the insatiable consumer can desire everything because he or she desires nothing in particular.[9] The new form of alienation is not alienation from the products of one's labour, but alienation from the world reduced to consumption — a world consumed in advance.[10]

If feudalism, then colonialism, lasted but a few centuries, neo-colonialism but a half-century, the era of nation-states now coming to an end, the archipelago feels already, on the other side of the Berlin Wall rising ever higher about it, the pressure mounting — pressure of global ecological devastation, of river, ocean, and atmospheric pollution, pressure of six-sevenths, soon 90 per cent of humanity. 'Humanity is becoming *tangible*, and also tangible in its inhumanity.'

The pressure is not that of barbarians — unskilled, uneducated undernourished, ragged, and diseased hordes – infiltrating and invading to lay waste to the urban technopoles. It is the pressure of six-sevenths, soon 90 per cent, of humanity who demand the economic and political conditions for the place which is this earth where the individuals are ensured the resources and the protection that make it possible to them to live and prosper together. These ecological, economic, and political structures will have to be built with the information, the wealth, and the high-tech industries of the archipelago.

These ecological, economic, and political structures will have to be conceived by exceptionally intelligent, highly trained minds in the research institutes of the archipelago and built with the political power of decision-makers who seize the initiative from the electronic circuitry and the experts. They will have to be built by exceptionally intelligent, highly trained minds who see in the bravery, endurance, fidelity, pride, beauty and passion of lives of the disinherited an ethos of character and conviction that contests the ruling hedonist/hedonistic individualism of the archipelago. If now the inhabitants of the archipelago see only the hordes of the filthy, the diseased, the violent on the other side, in the coming confrontation they will learn also the community, the being-in-common elaborated in the outer zone.

These ecological, economic, and political structures will have to be built in contact with a humanity and an inhumanity become tangible.

The wounds, the hunger, and the fear of the outer zone, the activism and the insubstantial and insignificant freedom of the archipelago, become *our* distress – a distress that puts us in the presence of one another – in anger. 'Anger', Jean-Luc Nancy writes,

> is the political sentiment par excellence. Anger concerns the inadmissible, the intolerable, and a refusal, a resistance that casts itself from the first beyond all it can reasonably accomplish – to mark forth the possible ways of a new negotiation with what is reasonable, but also the ways of an untractable vigilance. Without anger, politics is accommodation and influence-peddling, and to write of politics without anger is to traffic with the seductions of writing.[11]

This anger exists today, Nancy writes, as the anger of thousands of intellectuals and millions of humans before the silencing of the ethics of humanity and the political-economics of one world which communism represented, and which we are told by the technocrats of the archipelago and their neo-liberal and free-market theorists was nothing but an error and an illusion that failed of itself. Anger declares inadmissible, intolerable the walls of technicization and simu-

212

lacra that shut off one finite and singular life from the presence of others, and the Berlin Walls everywhere being built to shut off the finite and singular lives of those in the outer zone. It is the force that alone can produce for us a political existence.

The distress before the humanity and inhumanity we touch becomes anger over the inhumanity that subordinates and excludes the animals, the inhuman and the superhuman. It becomes chthonic, oceanic, celestial rage. This anger does not arise in the midst of the shifting, spontaneous, and capricious, instantly gratified, individual freedoms of our fellow-activists in the archipelago. It does not arise in the measure that we see – that the information media allow us alone to see – the brute lives of the exploited and the corpses of the exterminated in the outer zone. It arises when we come into the presence of singular lives in the outer zone, and the significance of their singular and communal forms of life.

Much has been written about the illusions now dissipated of class consciousness and worker solidarity among the disinherited. Sociologists have written much of Blacks plundering Blacks in Soweto and Watts, even Jesse Jackson spoke of relief, upon hearing footsteps behind him in the dark of the night, to see it was not a Black man. Primo Levi, in the last of his efforts, before his suicide, to understand Auschwitz, wrote of the 'grey zone' of that vast, uncircumscribable multitude of the incarcerated who collaborated, in ways cunning or pathetic, with their incarcerators.[12]

In the outer zone, you trust the ones you know. But social skill consists in knowing who is around you. For this reason you may turn to the pimp, drug-dealer, or street gang in times of disaster rather than the forces of law and order. Social existence which does not, cannot, consist in having something in common or building something in common, consists in keeping one's eyes open to the presence of singular ones.

In the denuded and depleted fields of Africa, men and women find in their singular lives a source of bravery, of endurance, of fidelity, and even of pride. In the fetid slums ingenuity and disabused realism blossom periodically into peals of laughter. In the favelas of Rio, the crumbling buildings of Havana, the swampy shantytowns of Jakarta, men and women rejoice at the singular beauty of their faces, the singular passions of their loins. Even in the subjugation to the continuous, linear time of programmed labour in assembly plants or in the bricolage of the 'informal zone', they find stretches of finite here-nows which are not those times of recuperation and leisure subordinated to the process –

213

Alphonso Lingis

finite stretches of the here-now which are meaningful, and whose meaningfulness is given in singular pulses of enjoyment.

Men and women labouring in assembly plants without job security or health
benefits, or in contrived and transitory street occupations, devise ways to get
along with one another and support one another. However destitute and
despised, they find in one another people who show and who share radiant
bravery in the face of sickness and disaster, people who have a talent for
understanding how to survive, how to ward off despair, old people whose
character does not decompose with their ageing bodies, children whose eyes
catch sight of marvels. Anyone who leaves the television set with its images of
consumer euphoria and goes out to visit someone's village in the Isaan, in the
favelas of Rio, the slums of Jakarta, the villages of Africa discovers the
character, the bravery, and the pride of singular people; discovers also the
community of the outer zone addressed in distress and in anger to us.

Notes

1 Jean-Luc Nancy, *Une pensée finie* (Paris: Galilée, 1990), pp. 32ff.
2 Jean-Luc Nancy, 'Corpus', trans. Claudette Sartiliot, in *The Birth to Presence* (Stanford: Stanford University Press, 1995), pp. 196–7.
3 Ibid., p. 195.
4 Ibid.
5 Jean-Luc Nancy, *Une pensée finie*, pp. 38–39.
6 Jean-Luc Nancy, *La communauté désoeuvrée*, 2nd edn (Paris: Christian Bourgois Editeur, 1990), p. 38.
7 Gilles Deleuze and Félix Guattari, *Anti-Oedipus*, trans. M. Seem, R. Hurley, and H. R. Lane (New York: Viking, 1977), pp. 235–6.
8 Ibid., p. 236.
9 Anne Godignon and Jean-Louis Thiriet, 'The end of alienation?', in Mark Lilla (ed.), *New French Thought: Political Philosophy* (Princeton: Princeton University Press, 1994), pp. 221–2.
10 '"Alienation" has been represented as the dispossession of an original authenticity, to be preserved or restored. The critique of this determination of an original property, an authentic plenitude and reserve contributed to a great extent to the extinction of the theme of alienation as the theme of a loss or theft of an original autoproduction of man. In fact, existence is not self-productive, although it is not the product of something else either. . . . Nonetheless, we have seen, an existent can be expropriated of its conditions for existing: its force, its labour, its body, its meanings, and perhaps always of the space-time of its singularity. And this happens continually; it is part of the extermination we described; "capital" or the "world market", until further notice, are ensured and proper only in such a massive

214

expropriation (today, above all of the South by the North — but we know that not only there). There is then no question of renouncing the struggle. . . . Hitherto the struggle has been guided by the regulative idea of the original and final autoproduction of man, and by a general and generic concept of this "man"' Jean-Luc Nancy, *Une pensée finie*, pp. 37–8.

11 Jean-Luc Nancy, 'La comparution', in Jean-Luc Nancy and Jean-Christophe Bailly, *La comparution (politique à venir)*, Paris: Christian Bourgois Editeur, 1991), pp. 58–9.
12 Primo Levi, *The Drowned and the Saved*, trans. Raymond Rosenthal (London: Abacus, 1994), pp. 22–51.

Index

Index

Phenomenology 147f
Photography 36, 84, 85
Plato 8, 25, 44; *Ion* 63, 131, 137 n. 36, 141
Poetry 17, 69, 98
Poiesis 92
Political, the 22, 23, 25, 26, 51, 58, 93, 97, 98, 126, 191
Political Imaginary 96–8
Politics 19, 27, 34, 60, 98, 103, 104, 110, 111, 116, 117, 123f., 132, 191; International 175ff.
Possibility 104ff
Postmodern 16, 99; aesthetics 13, 96
Post-political 91
Power 103, 111, 118, 183
Praxis 53, 57, 109
Progressivism 104, 113
Psychoanalysis xi

Rashomon, the 64ff.
Reality 104ff.
Redemption 21, 22, 122
Revenant le 159, 172 n. 3
Revolution 13, 25
Ricouer, P. 127, 138 n. 38
Rights 111ff. (see also *Duties*)
Rimbaud, A. 13, 14, 17
Romanticism 96, 97 (see also *German Romanticism*)
Rousseau, J-J. 12, 180

Sacred, the 157, 166, 167
Sacrifice 20, 22, 157ff.
Sartre, J-P. 14, 34, 147, 179
Schelling. F. W. J. 45, 92, 97, 98
Sense (*sens*) 13-17, 32, 33, 165; of touch 165
Shakespeare, W. 4
Share/Sharing 21, 22–7, 63, 82, 88, 164, 181–3; shared world 19, 28, 30
Singularity 23, 34, 36, 38, 42, 49, 50, 51, 54, 58, 76, 132, 147, 151, 164, 165, 166, 181, 184, 210, 213
Socrates 159
Sovereignty 13, 97, 98, 124, 158, 162, 165, 168, 169, 170
Spirit 98, 99
St. Just 25
Strauss, L. 134 n. 10
Ströker, E. 156 n. 6
Structuralism 12
Sublation 14, 113, 144, 158, 164
Sublime, the 91, 96, 162
Supplement 162, 163, 164, 170

Technology 27, 36, 99, 100, 193, 197f.; essence of 96
Temporality 94
Time 91; difference in 91; experience of 100; historical 26
Timecapital 100, 101
Todorov, T. 192
Tradition xi, 19, 21, 157
Trakl, G. 91
Translation 77, 80

Undecidability 44, 46, 53, 56, 118, 120, 122
Universality 141f., 187, 188–90

Van Peursen. C 148
Violence 15, 19, 21, 25, 26–30, 73, 171

Wallerstein, I. 186ff., 'Geopolitics and Geoculture'
Will, the 45, 56, 119; metaphysics of 45, 48; ontology of 46
Will to Power, the 44, 183
Wittgenstein, L. 33, 175
World Economy 186ff.
Writing 19, 21, 30, 35, 41, 80, 92, 163, 170, 171